THIEVES,
RASCALS
and SORE LOSERS

THIEVES, RASCALS and SORE LOSERS

THE UNSETTLING HISTORY OF THE DIRTY DEALS THAT HELPED SETTLE NEBRASKA

MARILYN JUNE COFFEY

OMEGA COTTONWOOD PRESS

OMAHA, NEBRASKA

Paperback ISBN: 978-0-9961399-1-5
Kindle ISBN: 978-0-9961399-2-2
EPUB ISBN: 978-0-9961399-3-9

Library of Congress Control Number: 2015904353
Cataloging in Publication Data on file with publisher.

www.MarilynCoffey.net

Omega Cottonwood Press
c/o CMI
13518 L St.
Omaha, NE 68137

Production, Distribution and Marketing: Concierge Marketing Inc.

Printed in the United States
10 9 8 7 6 5 4 3 2 1

No iniquity, no bribery, no ballot-box stuffing
no trick known to the whole catalogue of deceit and villainy
was left out of the raging battles for county seats.

—Addison Erwin Sheldon, *Nebraska: The Land and the People*

To Annie Moncayo,
who saw my story before I did
and challenged me to write it.

CONTENTS

Introduction. 1

Part I—William Parker Carr. 5

1. Hauling Mail on a Mule 7

2. Colonel Manypenny's Gift.............................11

3. Wild Jim Lane...19

4. Rubbing Out Men and Other Critters......................27

5. Wukkin' on the Railroad...............................35

Part II—Victor Vifquain 43

6. *Mal de Mer*...45

7. Doubling Back.. 49

8. His Father's Fortune....................................55

9. 300 Indians & One Fat Ox 59

10. The Three Musketeers 67

11. Oh, Glorious!..73

Part III—Unscrupulous Models 81

12. A Colicky Baby 83

13. Red Blankets...87

14. Slave or Free?.. 99

Part IV—Taming the Wild Tribes. 115

15. The "Fighting Parson" 117

16. Payback for Sand Creek 125

17. Incandescent Glory 131

18. The Black-Bearded Cossack 141

19. Staking the Land 151

Part V—Harlan County's Bitter Birth 161

20. Vifquain's Bunch................................... 163

21. Thomas Harlan's Boys 173

22. Chicanery 101 183

23. The Dirty Deal Election.......................... 197

24. Fireworks on the 4th.............................205

25. Her Buffalo Skull 213

26. Shenanigans Galore 223

27. County Seat on Wheels.........................229

28. The Harlan County Shuffle 237

29. The Floating Courthouse 247

30. A Billion Hoppers & Two Thieves............257

31. Knocking Alma Off Her County Seat 269

32. The Impulsive Election 279

33. The Supreme Court Rules 287

34. Picking at Old Bones 293

Early Settlers in Harlan County **304**

General Vifquain's 1870 Settlement............................. 304

Thomas Harlan's 30 Alma City Settlers, March 1871..... 306

205 Harlan County Settlers, 1871................................. 308

Harlan County Men in 1871 320

Acknowledgments . . . . ·327

Selected Bibliography 329

About the Author. . . . . ·335

Index 339

INTRODUCTION

The dirtiest deal in my home county happened when settlers near the tiny town of Alma snagged the Harlan County seat in the late 1800s. A native of that Nebraska county seat, I didn't find the affair that scuzzy, but descendants of the nearby town of Orleans still do.

Mention the county seat there and faces redden and glower, voices snarl and snap.

Indeed, Orleans's descendants seem to think that locating the county seat in Alma was Harlan County's worst calamity, more unfortunate than the 1935 Republican River flood that killed 110 people, destroyed 11,400 head of cattle, and wiped out trees, houses, barns, bridges, and railroad tracks. "At least," they say, "we recovered from the flood," but not the Harlan County seat fight, still taking its toll in Orleans.

What in the world happened in early Harlan County, I wondered, to create a fury that burned for generations? What took place between 1871 when forty-two settlers voted to make Alma City the county seat and 1884 when the Nebraska Supreme Court settled the inevitable disputes?

A few trips to Alma and Orleans libraries, I felt sure, would satisfy my curiosity.

Was I wrong!

Trying to discover what happened during those thirteen years felt like struggling to solve a huge jigsaw puzzle riddled with missing pieces. No single account described the entire conflict. Speeches, letters, interviews with old timers, and reprints from early newspapers contradicted one another or dealt with isolated aspects of the quarrel. Even legal records, including county commissioners' journals and district court records, were incomplete.

As I searched, I realized that the Harlan County fight was far from unique. All over the Midwest at this time, the creation of counties and the locating of county seats turned into bitter dogfights.

Small wonder at the zeal in these little towns. Securing a county seat brought more than prestige to a community. It brought a government payroll and rapid growth generated by private businesses that sprang up to profit from the traffic created by governmental activities. Speculation alone could generate amazing amounts of money. A railroad might even stop in the lucky community.

The town that lost, by contrast, often died out. In county seat fights, no second-place prize existed. This made many of these contests rancorous, even violent.

I also noticed, as I researched, that the Harlan County contenders had plenty of models of thieves, rascals, and sore losers. Everything Harlan County citizens did—lying, cheating, stealing records, stuffing ballot boxes, building courthouses—also happened in other county fights. Plus the state, the territory, and the national Congress of that time provided Harlan County residents with plenty of examples of dirty deals.

A senator pulls a pistol in Congress to shut up a speaker. An acting governor deals out counties like playing cards. The army sets the partially settled prairie ablaze. Territorial senators stupidly repeal all of Nebraska's laws. Indians kill white folk and white folk massacre Indians. Voters burn a senator in effigy. The United States entertains Indian chiefs in Washington, the better to intimidate them.

These stories seem endless.

Such patterns of behavior must have enabled Harlan County settlers to justify their friction. These familiar tales must have led settlers to believe that, in Nebraska, a person could get away with as much as he dared.

I also discovered, while researching, that little is known about most Harlan County settlers. I have listed the names of the early settlers in a detailed section at the end of the book—not to assign blame but to chronicle once and for all the first players in this ongoing battle, from whom many readers of this book may have descended.

However, a great deal is known (or can be deduced) about two settlers: William Parker Carr who settled near Alma and Victor Vifquain who left Harlan County in disgust.

Of third generation New England stock, Carr, a visionary, laid eyes on the paradise that would become Harlan County while it was still Indian land. What he saw persuaded Thomas Harlan and his settlers from Wyoming to come stake claims in the Alma area.

Vifquain, an immigrant from French-speaking Belgium who became a Civil War hero, led the first settlers—forty men—to what would be Harlan County. They chose claims in today's Orleans area months before Thomas Harlan and his men scouted the land.

In the first two parts of *Thieves, Rascals and Sore Losers,* I introduce you to these two men and explore what drew them to the area that became Harlan County.

The next two parts, Unscrupulous Models and Taming the Wild Tribes, describe the Nebraska worlds these two men found when they arrived. Unscrupulous Models focuses on the national, territorial, and state governments whose actions brought, eventually, Harlan County into being.

The Cheyenne, Arapaho, and Sioux who lived along the Republican River paid an awesome price for trying to stay on their land in the face of the intruding white culture. Taming the Wild Tribes describes those fights, necessary before folks dared settle near the Republican River.

In the last section, Harlan County's Bitter Birth, I tell you—here for the first time—the entire story of what happened between 1871 and 1884 in Harlan County, Nebraska. You'll learn why Tom Harlan stole county minutes, why the Reverend John Whiting hid election returns, how young, strong Joel Piper stole the records back, and what set the county seat on wheels.

From my book, you can understand why these early settlers scrapped so. You may even see why the righteous indignation that trickled down through the years has a certain logic. Won't you journey with me through this strange and often amazing world?

PART
I

William Parker Carr

⌣ CHAPTER ⌣
1

HAULING MAIL ON A MULE

I f it weren't for William Parker Carr, the county I grew
up in wouldn't be named "Harlan." Not that Carr
planned this. No, when he left New England forever and
traveled to the swift Missouri, he just intended to find work.
Plus maybe a girlfriend.

In 1853, he crossed Old Muddy from Kanesville, Iowa
(now Council Bluffs), on Bennett's Ferry, a flat-bottomed
wooden boat that lurched from bank to bank using a wire
cable. Its operator, Gideon Bennett, had run the boat only
four years, but he'd thrived, thanks to hordes of Forty-niners
rushing pell-mell to California. Never mind that the river
banks belonged not to Bennett but to the Otoe-Missouri
tribe, a common dirty deal.

Bennett, twenty-eight, and Carr, twenty-seven, hit it off.
That friendship would profit both, but not right away.

When Carr stumbled from the ferry, he set his boots on
Unorganized Territory. It wasn't Nebraska yet, but it would
be soon. Folks already conjured up dirty deals to get rid of
the inconvenient Otoe-Missourians.

Carr landed six miles south of Table Creek (soon to be Nebraska City) where he found his first job: delivering mail on a mule. If he'd known better, he might have declined. The former mail carrier set out with his load of letters and never came back, perhaps because the mail route crossed the land of the Pawnee, those skilled robbers of horses and mules. But Carr needed a job so he took it.

He rode west from Table Creek 180 miles to Fort Kearny, where he delivered mail and filled his pouch for the return trip. At Fort Kearny, Carr stood 50 miles northeast of the county he would help create, nothing but wilderness then. "Highdy, highdy, haw," he hummed, itching to see that backcountry.

One night, Carr's mule acted queerly.

"What's eatin' him?" Carr wondered. Then an image crossed his mind: a half-naked savage swinging a tomahawk, a ridge of porcupine hair rising from his shaved head.

"Pawnee!" he shrieked, and dug his heels into his startled mule's flanks. They tore along, galumphing over the moonlit path, Carr starting at each night noise.

Was Carr relieved to reach the next station intact?

Certainly.

Did he entertain second thoughts about remaining in such a dangerous profession?

No, he did not.

Instead, he increased his range, delivering mail from Rulo, in the southeast corner of what would be Nebraska, to Hamilton City in today's Nevada, 1,300 miles west. When Carr set out, he hoped to spot a Jeanee with light brown hair; coming back, he'd have settled for a Buffalo Gal with her stockings full of holes. The few girls he noticed paid him no mind.

Back in Table Creek, Carr met an ambitious Virginian, Stephen Friel Nuckolls. He planned to survey Table Creek and turn it into a city. Nuckolls, twenty-eight, already owned a chain of five dry goods stores in Missouri.

At the moment, however, he needed two good bull whackers, or wagon drivers, to join his train and haul freight twice to Fort Kearny and once to Fort Laramie. A team of eight oxen would pull each driver's heavy wagon. The drivers earned their nickname, "bull whackers," from their habit of whacking, or striking, their oxen, or bullocks, to inspire them to move.

So Carr and Gideon Bennett, the river cable operator, teamed up to haul shelled corn to the forts. Off they went, inspiring their oxen teams to move alongside the flat, meandering Platte River. This "highway," the Oregon Trail, ran from the Missouri River to the Rocky Mountains—a route protected by a smattering of forts and stagecoach stations.

By night around the campfire, Carr listened to bull whackers' tales: The one about the guy who drove a flock of turkeys a thousand miles to Utah. Or the chap who hauled frozen oysters to market along the trail. Or the freighter who made a mint selling a load of cats to Denver miners. They used the cats as mousers—or even as companions. At least that's what those bull whackers said.

And by day Carr brandished his long whip until it split the sky with cracks. Highdy, highdy, highdy, haw! He also engaged in the fine art of twisting an ox's tail to get his attention.

CHAPTER
2

COLONEL MANYPENNY'S GIFT

W hen William Parker Carr wasn't slung over a mule or coaxing a team of oxen, he learned Otoe, Missouria, and Iowa languages. That's not so difficult, since the three languages, like their tribes, are interrelated. They all belong to the Siouxan family, so the languages, called Chiwere, differ like dialects of a single tongue.

Carr had an excellent opportunity to learn Chiwere. From Nebraska City, it surrounded him; Otoe land stretched to the horizon in all directions.

Congress also had an eye on Otoe land. Eager to open Unorganized Territory for whites, Congress wanted not only Otoe-Missouria land but also Omaha land, all bordering the Missouri River.

In January 1854, the U.S. Commissioner of Indian Affairs, Colonel George Manypenny, traveled from Washington, D.C., to meet with those Missouri River tribes for a "talk."

They met in Bellevue, Nebraska, population fifty, the only white settlement on the river's west side. Conveniently, Col. Manypenny's local agent, Major James Gatewood,

George Manypenny

headquartered there. Well-known as a gathering spot for native people, traders, and travelers, Bellevue gave the federal government an ideal place to fleece the Missouri River tribes. Already a dirty deal brews, and we're not at the end of the story.

The Missourians and Otoes arrived together for Col. Manypenny's "talk." Then the Omahas, or "those going against the wind," breezed in by the dozens. Their sixty chiefs represented a large, dominant tribe.

Col. Manypenny soon talked the tribes into selling their lands for cash, goods, and a reservation all their own. That settled, he left for Washington to oversee the official treaty signings.

Maj. Gatewood then rushed a delegation of chiefs (seven Omahas and a "small group" of Otoes) to Washington. Or tried to. They refused to leave without a treaty in hand. Maj. Gatewood, uncertain, drew up treaties to the best of his ability. Off he and the chiefs went.

In Washington, Maj. Gatewood's treaties infuriated Col. Manypenny. He and his staff made major reductions in them—above all, in the amount of money. Col. Manypenny's dirtiest deal? Reducing the $1,200,000 promised to the Omahas to $84,000. That came to two cents an acre, for the amount of land purchased remained the same: 4 million acres from the Missouri River to the Sand Hills and from the Niobrara River to the Platte.

On February 15, the Otoe delegates signed their smaller but still dirty deal, a revised treaty handing over 162,000 acres. When the treaty became official June 21, the Otoe-Missouria tribe would move to its reservation.

An Otoe chief returned in March dismayed to find white settlers, those thieves, making themselves comfortable on Otoe-Missouria land months before it became theirs to inhabit. They pounded down stakes, even though Congress, twenty years earlier, forbade unlicensed whites to trespass on Indian Territory. The squatters seemed to flow into Otoe-Missouria land like a river into a lake.

Arkeketah, the Otoe chief, complained to Maj. Gatewood, who couldn't stem this illegal inpouring of squatters. Given the circumstances, the Otoe-Missourians decided to depart early for their reservation.

Maj. Gatewood couldn't stop trespassing whites, but he knew how to move 700 Otoe-Missourians 75 miles to their new reservation. He hired Carr, that capable teamster who spoke Chiwere. Carr agreed and signed a contract to head the move.

Practical Carr invented a strategy for making excellent time with a minimum of fuss when traveling. Maj. Gatewood had supplied Carr with food for the trip—flour, bacon, and sixty head of cattle. Carr then hired fifteen men to guard these rations from theft.

The first day, he distributed five cows plus ample flour and bacon to the 700 travelers. He waited until all had eaten their fill. Then he announced where their next meal would be served. Anticipating food, the Indians sped to the next location.

~

The 250-square-mile Otoe-Missouria reservation straddled Nebraska and Kansas. Twenty percent lay in Kansas, although who knew exactly where. The border had yet to be surveyed.

Drooping willow trees lined the Big Blue River, a clear, fair stream that flowed through the reservation. Timber bordered the river's gentle hills. Rolling prairie surrounded the reserve.

The federal agency chose this reservation hoping its stream-fed land would transform the Otoe-Missouria hunter-gatherers into farmers. Historically, these Indians never sowed. The women, it's true, planted maize, beans, squash, pumpkin, and sunflowers, but they never plowed. They just scouted around the village, looking for soil broken enough to take seed.

The men hunted. Otoe-Missourians, like many plains tribes, hunted on horseback. However, the government, determined to civilize these men, confined them to the reservation and banned buffalo hunting.

Carr stayed to help. The Indian Agency paid him $6 an acre to break a quarter section of prairie sod, but what a chore! Virgin prairie sod had laid unbroken for tens of thousands of years. The soil contained sturdy roots of grass all knitted together, forming a tangled network that stretched for miles.

When early settlers tried to break this matted sod, their wooden plows bounced. Cast iron plows worked better, but soil clung to their blades, forcing farmers to stop and clean them. Soon sod busters for hire used oxen to pull heavy cast iron plows that broke sod with brute force. But sod busters were expensive.

Then in 1837 John Deere invented a self-scouring steel-bladed plow. Sod didn't cling to its polished blade; its plow angled into the earth and turned a decent furrow. And the farmer didn't need oxen to pull it. A team of horses would do. Soon popular, it became the "Plow that Broke the Plains."

Folks called it a singing plow, for sing it did, or ring, or twang, creating gusts of wild music when steel blades upended tangled roots. Carr must have used this plow to crack open 160 acres for the Otoe-Missouria tribe. Seventeen years later, Harlan County settlers may have used this plow to turn their sod. When they weren't wrangling.

Either Carr liked living with the untamed Otoe-Missourians or else he liked the good government money he earned, for he hung around the reservation seven years.

Life there was casual. Men went around stark naked except for a well-positioned breechcloth. In cool weather, braves might toss a blanket or a buffalo robe over their shoulders.

The Indians embraced music, including one type of drum they favored but Carr had never seen. The instrument looked like a stick with a row of notches along one side. A musician played it by scraping a smaller stick across the notches. It looked easy, but the braves laughed at Carr, awkward as a kid, when he tried to play it. And they broke up when he danced and sang "Turkey in the Straw" with a "Hey highdy heydy, and a haw haw haw."

The women chuckled, too, and that pleased Carr. He was drawn to the women, the girls in particular, with their raven hair, sometimes braided, sometimes loose and lustrous. More modest than the braves, the girls wore poncholike blouses and deerskin skirts that clung to their thighs like skin.

Sometimes women invited him to play their games with them, Plum Pit, using pits as dice, or Ring & Pin, a love game during which the girls routinely declined him.

One woman liked to tease him, asking, "You been eating rabbit?" Carr denied it, because he knew she was asking if he, like a rabbit, was timid, easily spooked, and likely to misplace his wits. Even if he were, he'd never admit it.

Carr liked the girls less when they painted their faces for their religious ceremonies. Then garish colors made the girls seem more like Buffalo Gals than women. And nowhere on the reservation lingered a Jeanee with light brown hair.

President Franklin Pierce liked to spend tribal money—for the natives' benefit, of course. For their moral improvement. Like a stubborn schoolmarm, Uncle Sam insisted on creating an educational program and a farm for the Otoe-Missouria.

Indian agents on the reservation spent tribal money as though it were their own. They ordered cattle, medicine, and agricultural implements, the likes of which no self-respecting Otoe or Missouri brave had ever seen. The agents spent tribal money to build a blacksmith shop, a saw and grist mill, and a school. That provided plenty of work—for Carr.

On March 1857, William Wallace Dennison showed up to be the reservation agent. He thought just like the others, Carr noted. He marveled at the way the agent ordered goods: twelve yoke of oxen, one pair of mules, two wagons, and plows, hoes, axes, and scythes.

When the government sent its annual payment to the tribe, Dennison took it—$13,554 in cash—and split. Enraged Otoe-Missourians, including women and children, tracked the agent down and demanded their money. His back against the wall, Dennison gave them $4,000. (What a rascal!)

A drought destroyed the tribe's crops, leaving them devoid of winter rations. That frustrated the Otoe-Missourians so they burned the agency wheat field. But burning the field didn't modify the life that the government had forced on them. It seemed that nothing would.

CHAPTER

3

WILD JIM LANE

When Carr discovered that the reservation dipped down into Kansas Territory, he spent time down that way, talking to the few settlers. What he heard, mostly dirty deals, disturbed him.

In March 1855 at a Kansas election, 6,000 Southerners dropped by from Missouri to stuff ballot boxes. They had no right to vote, but they voted anyway, waving pistols to "prove their rights." Only 2,000 Kansas settlers voted, so the winning legislators lived mostly in Missouri and favored slavery, but President Pierce recognized them.

The stories got worse. Pro-slavery Border Ruffians crossed into Kansas Territory from Missouri to loot stores and houses belonging to antislavery Free Staters. The Ruffians kidnapped Free State men, tarred and feathered them, sometimes killed them.

Such craziness bothered Carr, a typical antislavery Northerner. Born in Antrim, New Hampshire, and raised in that state, what else could he be? Carr's New England folks had never cottoned to slavery, and neither did he.

The young man rode back to the reservation with war stories swirling in his mind: pits dug in the street, each hole occupied by a sharpshooting Free Stater, to protect against marauding Border Ruffians. Towns burned, people hacked to death with broadswords.

"These were times," Carr would say later, "when no man ever opened his door wide until he was sure a friend stood outside."

~

Then Kansas folks got excited about a man known as "Wild Jim" Lane, a Free State leader. Though odd and poorly educated, he had served as an Illinois Senator before he came to Kansas. "His energy was amazing," a biographer wrote, "and his calfskin vest was likely to appear in any part of the wilderness." Which it did, as Carr found out.

When the Topeka legislature of Free Staters elected Wild Jim to the U.S. Senate, he carried a Topeka Constitution with him to Washington, D.C. Before Wild Jim could serve, Congress must accept that constitution instead of the pro-slavery one. But it did not.

Wild Jim couldn't return to Kansas. If he did, federal troops would imprison him for treason. A grand jury had indicted him, plus other antislavery leaders, for resisting territorial laws. So he toured, promoting Kansas Territory. How he could sway an audience! Sometimes his voice wooed like a lullaby, sometimes stirred like a bugle.

~

Hostility about slavery thrived beyond Kansas Territory. In the U.S. Senate, an exceptionally violent disagreement took place May 22, 1856.

Charles Sumner of Massachusetts, an arrogant abolitionist, had ranted about the Kansas crimes for two days. He jawed at Southern Senators for causing the Kansas violence. Border Ruffians, he said, are "hirelings picked from the drunken spew and vomit of an uneasy civilization."

On his second day, Sumner launched a tirade against Senator Andrew Butler of South Carolina, calling him an imbecile who has taken "a mistress who, though ugly to others, is always lovely to him; though polluted in the sight of the world, is chaste in his sight—I mean, the harlot, Slavery."

Two days later, Sumner sat writing letters at his desk in a secluded Senate chamber. He failed to notice Representative Preston Brooks until he spoke.

"Mr. Sumner," Brooks said, "I have read your speech twice over. It libels South Carolina, and my white-haired old relative, Senator Butler, and I've come to punish you for it."

As Sumner started to rise, Brooks attacked, smashing the Senator's skull with a gold-headed cane, knocking him under his desk. As Brooks walloped him, the Senator, quite tall, struggled to rise from under the heavy desk, which was bolted to the floor. Blood gushed down his face. He strained to ward off Brooks's repeated blows.

Several legislators rushed to help Sumner, but a colleague of Brooks blocked them, waving his pistol and shouting, "Let them be!"

SOUTHERN CHIVALRY — ARGUMENT versus CLUB'S.

Brooks wields his cane

Using his thighs as levers, Sumner ripped the desk loose from its bolts, setting himself free. Blinded by his blood, he lurched about the chamber, trying to protect himself by flailing his arms. Brooks followed, delivering a rain of blows that shattered his cane.

Sumner staggered, then buckled and passed out. Brooks continued to pummel the motionless Sumner with pieces of broken cane until legislators restrained him.

Then Brooks left, as others carried away the unconscious Sumner, who was spurting blood. Three years would pass before he could resume his Senate duties.

Dirty deal indeed. Mischief magnified. Villainous violation. Makes the Harlan County rowdies look positively gracious.

While on tour, Wild Jim learned that armed Border
Ruffians had looted his hometown, Lawrence. Some 800
Ruffians demolished two newspaper offices, busted presses
and dumped type in the river. They pitched furnishings
from the hotel window, then tried to blow up the building.
When that failed, they set the hotel on fire.

Wild Jim could no longer justify promoting Bloody
Kansas. Instead, his lectures championed the creation of a
great army, Lane's Army of the North, to fight Border Ruffians.

In Chicago, his speech about this army created
pandemonium. Gamblers threw their pistols on the stage for
Wild Jim to take to Kansas. Staid businessmen, surrounded
by the weeping, singing and shouting audience, tossed in
their wallets. Even newsboys cast up their pennies. Wild Jim
collected thousands of dollars for his fight, and a thousand
men joined his Army of the North.

Wild Jim and his army ferried over the Missouri River
on Gideon Bennett's flat-bottomed ferry boat, then cut
across Nebraska Territory. As they neared Kansas, they
dared not be seen traveling on regular roads, so their fellow
Free Staters marked a trail through the great Kansas sea of
grass. Tall poles on top of ridges and huge piles of stone at
high spots on the prairie showed the way. "The Jim Lane
Trail," they called it.

Wild Jim's soldiers bellowed patriotic songs as they
crossed into Kansas.

When they reached Border Ruffian territory in southeast
Kansas, they walloped some New Georgia Ruffians,
captured fourteen at the Franklin blockhouse, and trounced
eighty at Fort Saunders. Inside the abandoned fort, dinner

steamed on the table. "Don't eat it," Wild Jim said. "Could be poisoned."

Tiny Fort Titus, owned by a thirty-three-year-old braggart, Colonel Henry Titus, held out until soldiers backed a load of hay to the fort and held a torch ready. Then a white flag popped out the porthole.

The tide had turned. The dirty deal fit the other foot, so to speak.

~

In August, still wanted for treason, Wild Jim pulled out of southeast Kansas with 300 followers and moved north. They set up a campsite 40 miles from the Otoe-Missouri reservation.

When Carr found out, he moseyed over. The well-guarded campsite stretched out so far he couldn't see the other side.

Carr greeted the soldier posted near the entrance, but the soldier didn't comment until Carr said, "I've been rooting for Lane and the Army of the North, ever since I heard of them." Then the soldier found his tongue.

"See this Springfield?" he said. "We got them when we whipped Fort Saunders. A thousand of them, still in their boxes."

The soldier spun and glanced behind him. "It's so quiet out here most anything can spook you."

He listened, then shrugged. "And twelve-hundred pounds of bacon at Franklin. But nothing compared to what we got at Fort Titus. I mean besides the usual stuff—horses, wagons, provisions. That Colonel Bag-of-Wind Titus had hoarded up ten-thousand dollars' worth of gold!" He rubbed his thumb over his fingers. "And we got it all!"

The soldier pointed out Wild Jim to Carr. The Free State leader stood above the other men. He wore a fancy jacket that hung open to reveal his trademark calfskin vest. Wild Jim's hair stood up every which way, and his stern mouth slashed across his face. When he spoke, he swore and worse. Laughter rippled his belly. Carr marveled that this man could transform hundreds with his speeches.

A group of fifty armed men stopped Carr when he had ridden about halfway home. South Carolinians, they said they were.

Border Ruffians, Carr thought as they surrounded him.

"You live around here?" the leader asked.

"Not too far."

"Then take us to Jim Lane."

When Carr didn't move, the soldier said, "Go on. If you live around here, you know where he is."

With a pistol cocked alongside him, Carr's breath slowed. He turned his horse and led them to Wild Jim's camp.

The leader sent out two scouts. When they returned, one shook his head and said, "There's hundreds of them. If we go in there, we're dead ducks!"

"Go on!" the leader told Carr. "Get out of here. You never saw us. Remember that."

The fifty South Carolinians whirled and headed away. Soon even their dust vanished.

As time passed, a majority of Free Staters settled in Kansas Territory. The South, then, stopped trying to force Kansas to be a slave state, and on January 29, 1861, President Buchanan signed a free Kansas into the Union. At once, Kansas voters elected Wild Jim Lane, no longer wanted for treason, to the U.S. Senate.

∽ CHAPTER ∽
4

RUBBING OUT MEN AND OTHER CRITTERS

By the time Abraham Lincoln gave his inaugural address in March 1861, the nation had shrunk. Seven Southern states had withdrawn from the Union. About a month later, the Battle of Fort Sumter kicked off the American Civil War.

Following a family tradition of fighting, William Parker Carr enlisted in the Union army with the Second Kansas Cavalry. His unit traveled to Missouri singing, oddly enough, "I Wish I Was in Dixie's Land." Lincoln, by calling "Dixie" his favorite song, made it as popular in the North as in the South.

When Colonel Franz Sigel's troops, including Carr, arrived in Missouri, they intended to keep the border state part of the Union. That proved difficult.

Missouri Governor Claiborne Fox Jackson, like every other Northern governor, had heard from Lincoln asking for troops. Governor Jackson refused to send any.

Instead, he called up the pro-Southern Missouri State Militia and commanded it himself. This made him the first sitting governor to lead troops into battle and the first to lead troops against his own Union.

That July, Carr fought in the Battle of Carthage, the Civil War's first major on-land battle. It would pit 1,100 Union volunteers, armed and well-drilled, against the Confederate force of 6,000 led by a governor with no military authority. Just 4,000 of the governor's men bore arms; the rest were raw recruits, hurriedly gathered, barely trained.

The July 5 fight featured fluttering battle flags, cannons booming, and a bayonet charge. As Union forces retreated, soldiers saw Governor Jackson's 2,000 weaponless recruits, unable to fight, hanging about in the woods, moving like deer among the trees.

Carr heard gunfire, a voice shouted from the woods, "For God's sake, stop! You're shooting your own men!"

Who's to know? Recruits, who had no Confederate uniforms, wore whatever they could.

Union troops fell back, fought house to house. Sun set on a barrage of bullets. Union forces retreated under the cloak of darkness. Both sides claimed victory.

(Armed battles usually result in one dirty deal and one sore loser. Here, with both sides claiming victory, the dirty deals cancel each other, resulting in no sore losers. If anyone can claim a dirty deal here, it would be those raw recruits being shot by their own troops.)

Carr stayed in the army another year. He served as a mounted scout under General Samuel R. Curtis, an outstanding general, but sometime in 1862 the army discharged Carr because of a disability. He returned to Kansas near the Otoe-Missouria reservation. He must have considered that home.

He'd been away from his New Hampshire family for a decade, now, happy not to return and explain to his parents what had happened to his army career. His father had served at Portsmouth, New Hampshire, in the War of 1812, when the British were expected to attack via the harbor. Carr's grandfather, also named William Carr, had fought in the Revolutionary War for seven years.

~

Carr didn't linger near the reservation. By the next year, Benjamin "Ben" Holladay had hired Carr, the teamster. When they met, Holladay, forty-four, retained a Kentucky accent from his childhood. As a lad, he helped his Pap lead wagon trains through the Cumberland Gap, so it's not surprising that he now owned the largest stagecoach line in the world, the Overland Stage Company.

But the Stagecoach King, as some called him, didn't hire Carr as a driver. Instead, Holladay wanted Carr to shoot deer, elk, and buffalo for the stage line that ran from Atchison, Kansas, to San Francisco.

"Locate yourself in the Republican River valley," Holladay said. "It's a world-class place to find game."

So Carr headed west. He stopped on a bluff for his first view of the wide Republican River. A major river, he knew, although not as notorious as the Platte or as huge as the Missouri. Carr watched the water barrel south to Kansas, then he followed the river valley west. He rode for miles. The river seemed to wiggle and jiggle along, but its path, as a whole, ran straight.

As he rode, he moved, without knowing it, closer to the land where he would witness the nasty Harlan County

Holladay's stagecoach line

seat fight. Just riding down the valley took his breath away. When the sun rose high, blue sky matched the gleaming blue water. From time to time, enormous flocks of birds cast shadows on his path.

Then Carr's trail shifted north and west. Riding became rougher. He crossed any number of steep-banked tributary streams, flowing in from the north. He knew he'd found the spot, just as he'd been told, where the river curved up and the creeks streamed down.

Carr rode around, exploring. Each creek wandered back for miles, it seemed, before it reached the high plains, their wild grasses undulating in the wind.

A wide variety of leaf-shedding trees hugged the edges of the river and its creeks. Each type of leaf burst forth in its own shade of green, making a variegated canopy that shimmered in the wind.

When Carr stopped, bird calls crescendoed, chirps and chatter, trills and twitters, warbles, whistles, and hoots. He inhaled gulps of fresh air that the wind brought off the river. He'd never fallen in love with a place before, but then he'd never experienced one so idyllic.

Visiting this area in 1863, Carr arrived at an ideal time. Had he come earlier, he would have trespassed on Pawnee land, which for hundreds of years covered most of Nebraska. However, by 1857, the Pawnee had given it all up to the U.S. except for their reservation on the Loup River. They no longer lived along the Republican in large communal lodges, cultivating corn, beans, and melon or hunting raccoons, quail, skunks, and prairie chickens. And buffalo. Pawnee by the hundreds still left their Loup lodges twice a year to return to the Republican River to hunt buffalo.

Had Carr stopped by this area a year later, he would have risked his life. After 1864 this part of the Republican River valley became a hornet's nest of Indian raiders. War between the Plains Indians and the U.S. Army had become heated. Sioux, Cheyenne, and Arapaho raided overland travelers and Union Pacific construction crews. Then they'd retreat to the shelters in the banks of the river's creeks, making the area dangerous for outsiders. Even military commanders were unwilling to fight at such a disadvantage.

Finding game for Ben Holladay's stagecoach turned out to be easy. The valley proved a marvelous hunting ground, one of the West's great ones, just as Holladay had said. Carr found deer, elk, and buffalo plentiful—above all, the buffalo. Those beasts swarmed as thick as locusts, which made hunting a snap.

Carr could have killed hundreds and still failed to dent the enormous herds. Elk covered more than an acre; scads of black-tailed and white-tailed deer and antelope dotted the plains. But all kinds of game flourished. Wild turkeys and rabbits, grouse and coyote had multiplied so that thinning them out seemed impossible. All these zillions of creatures had been drawn to the valley for the same reason: a profusion of tender grasses and clear spring-fed creeks.

Carr didn't know yet that this lush paradise would become Harlan County.

~

For the next five years, Carr drove a stagecoach for Holladay. Besides passengers, the Overland coaches held U.S. mail, making them an excellent target for robbery. Indians, in particular, liked to hold them up.

Indians robbed Carr just once. In 1864, as he drove on the Little Blue River trail, he had a close call. Two men, a woman, and two guards protecting the U.S. mail rode with Carr.

With no warning, two dozen Indians on swift ponies fired on the coach. Carr lashed his four horses into a dead run as bullets cascaded around him. A fourteen-year-old, one of the guards, leaped on top of the coach and rode there, firing again and again.

One Indian's bullet struck the bridle of Carr's horse and brought it to its knees, but just for a second. Then the horse righted itself and continued to gallop. Another bullet lodged in the seat behind Carr, and still another shattered the lamp beside him.

The Indians chased the stagecoach right up to the next station. When the guards heard fighting, they ran to help. By the time Carr's coach rolled into the station, the Indians had retreated.

(Thieves, would-be thieves, rascals. Certainly Carr saw the bands of Indians that way. And the Indians? I'm sure they thought that the whites had delivered dirty deal after dirty deal. Which they did. As we'll see.)

~ CHAPTER ~
# 5

WUKKIN' ON THE RAILROAD

After voters chose long, lanky Abraham Lincoln to be President, eleven Southern states broke away from the United States. This ignited the Civil War, of course, but it also boosted the transcontinental railroad. Southern legislators, now absent, could no longer insist on a southern route for the train. So July 1, 1862, Lincoln signed the Pacific Railroad Bill, which supported a middle route running from the Missouri River to California.

The war hindered railroad construction, but in July 1865, a few workers laid down Union Pacific track in mud flats near Omaha. By then, U.S. Army surveyors had roughed out a route from Omaha following the Platte River and passing over the Rocky Mountains.

Construction crawled. Surveyors had to mark a route exact enough for workers to create the track's grade. Then other crews spiked cumbersome rails one by one.

At the end of 1865, Union Pacific tracks totaled just 40 miles. But by June 4, 1866, workers hit the 100-mile mark. In July, they passed Grand Island. By October, the rails reached the 100th meridian, 247 miles west of Omaha.

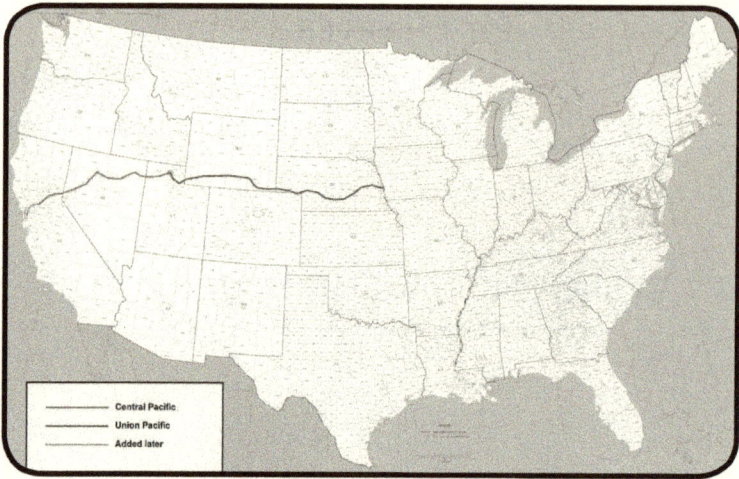

Cross-country route of the transcontinental railroad

Union Pacific celebrated. Two trains chugged down the track to the 100th meridian. Red, white, and blue streamers billowed alongside the cars, and festive antlers perched on top of locomotives. The first train lugged supplies for a party, Western style, including tents, buffalo robes and cases of champagne. The second train brought 140 party goers—the guest list loaded with influential capitalists and Congressional dignitaries. They whooped it up for three days, dancing around a huge bonfire, peering at a prairie dog town, applauding Pawnee war dancers, and eating fresh-killed antelope for dinner.

By now, Ben Holladay had predicted that railroads would halt his vast fleet of stagecoaches, horses, and freight wagons. His losses had become steep; during one year Indian raiders cost him $1,500,000. So Holladay sold his Overland Stage Company to Wells Fargo for $1,500,000 cash and 500,000 shares of stock.

After Holladay sold out, Carr and a friend, Joseph Reed, worked at a Kansas ranch on the Smoky Hill River. There they looked after a stable of stagecoach horses. Carr hired a black American, E'lon, to shod the horses.

Carr liked this job just fine until two dozen whooping Indians galloped up late one afternoon. He knew they hadn't come to hire stagecoach nags. Leaving the Indians to steal whatever they wished, Carr, Reed, and E'lon hightailed it through the barn's back door.

Ahead in the prairie lay a sizable depression. "A buffalo's bathtub," Reed had called it. When it held a couple inches of water, herds of buffalo rolled in it, throwing dirt and water this way and that, then rising up plastered with mud. In this way, they fought flies.

The three men dashed to the now-dry buffalo wallow. It dipped eighteen inches, deep enough for the men to lie down and hide. They didn't remain safe for long. The Indians, intent on mayhem, showed up and put a bullet in E'lon's forehead. Carr and Reed dragged his body in front of them to act as a barrier.

Sundown rescued them.

After the Indians left, Carr and Reed crawled out of the wallow. E'lon, more alive than supposed, stirred. Soon he appeared as alert as they did.

"We thought you were dead," Carr said, "or we never would of used you that way."

But E'lon shrugged it off, saying he didn't mind defending them.

Carr had had his fill of fighting Indians. In spring of 1867, he took a notion to see if he could work for the Union Pacific railroad, now crawling through western Nebraska. He rode from Smoky Hill, Kansas, to Julesburg, Colorado Territory. On the way, he crossed gingerly through the Republican River hunting ground he'd loved so much. Would it be as gorgeous as he remembered?

Yes! Even more stunning! The greenery, the wildlife, the river and its tributaries staggered him. If only he could settle here. Plenty of water, shelter, and game. But those furious Sioux, Arapaho, and Cheyenne controlled it now. He didn't tarry.

From Colorado Territory, Carr pushed on into Dakota Territory (now Wyoming) to catch up with the Union Pacific. It hired him at $6 a day to help build bridges and $18 a day when he worked three teams and three men.

Working on a construction crew educated Carr. He met such a variety of people. They hailed from all over: Vermont and Virginia, New York and Iowa, Michigan and Pennsylvania. Most laborers, though, came from Ireland.

He heard a lot of talk about "Hell on Wheels," a temporary shanty town that popped up at supply bases where the track ended. "Made of tents and shacks and whores, you know," one worker said. "Liquor and gambling dens."

Soon Carr saw for himself. At the track's end, camp followers descended like a dark cloud of bees swarming out of their hives. For shelter, they set up wagons, tents, dugouts, or cabins improvised from railroad ties. Shrill-voiced, painted women beckoned while men cut a deck (favoring poker or three-card Monte), poured a dram or two (for sale), or offered good deals on amethysts, agates,

"Hell on Wheels"

opals, and rubies, so commonplace in the mountains that dealers displayed them in heaps.

Their feverish carnival atmosphere, pitched so high, stunned Carr. He didn't notice the Union Pacific photographer standing beside him until the cameraman said, "You know, I've never seen a harder set of men. Twenty-four killed in the last month. They earn their money like horses and spend it like asses."

～

Carr did work like a horse along Bitter Creek's road in Dakota Territory. That creek, full of alkali, had acrid, almost undrinkable, water.

The creek rushed for 80 miles through the little towns of Rock Springs and Green River City before it dumped into Green River; it ran parallel with the railroad line the entire way. The Great Cut there stretched out longer than most on the road. Workers created that deep, extended cutoff by hacking out rock, dumping it into small square carts, and emptying those loads a cart at a time. Carr oversaw his three drivers and their small big-wheeled carts, each pulled by a single horse.

As 1868 pushed into 1869, survey parties finished with work and disbanded. Carr and others argued about what to do once railroad construction stopped. Carr thought he might settle down. Now thirty-seven, he had to act soon if he wanted a wife and children. Who knew how much longer he had to live? To live to fifty would be to experience a ripe old age. None but a few died older.

Carr thought he might live in Laramie. Kind of pretty, its mountain tops and lots of green pine trees made it more attractive than Bitter Creek's plains and hills all dotted with sagebrush. Carr often remembered the Republican River valley he loved. Cheyenne looked pretty like that. Coming through in spring, he'd seen its wind whipping grass like a green sea. Flowers tinted everything. Delicate white lilies burst up through green shoots. Even the cacti featured red and golden blossoms.

But what was Cheyenne? Just a bunch of tents.

As nights around the campfire passed, Carr and Thomas Harlan talked until the coals burned low. Harlan impressed Carr. A Civil War vet and a personal friend of Abraham Lincoln, he'd been appointed Internal Revenue Collector for Wyoming Territory by General Ulysses S. Grant.

Harlan and some others agreed that after the end of the line in Utah, after the Golden Spike connected Union Pacific and Central Pacific into a single railroad, they would return to Cheyenne. The little tent town had grown. Just since they'd worked the Bitter Creek cut, Cheyenne could count 600 people. Dakota's territorial legislature had granted the town a permanent city charter. Maybe Carr would find his Jeanee there.

While they jawed, Carr reminisced about hunting in the Republican River valley. "It's fantastic. Wildlife spilling over."

"How big are those buffalo herds?" Harlan asked. "A couple hundred?" He'd never lived in the West until he agreed to go from Illinois to Wyoming in 1868.

"More than that. One day a herd clomping by woke me at sunrise. I watched it, to see how long it would run. I watched all day. The last one didn't leave until twilight."

"No!"

"Yes. You better believe it. This valley is world-class hunting country." *It would be the perfect place,* he thought, *except for those damnable Indians.*

By the time Carr and the other workers returned to Cheyenne in 1869, more than 4,000 people lived in the mushrooming town. Folks called Cheyenne the "Magic City of the Plains," because of the way it had popped up. A variety of people lived there now, not just railroad folks and soldiers.

Harlan, revved up from Carr's descriptions of the Republican River valley, decided to see for himself. He and five other men boarded the train in Wyoming and headed for Nebraska, no longer a territory but a state.

Carr, who hadn't joined them, waited for Harlan's scouting party to return.

PART II

Victor Vifquain

⌁ CHAPTER ⌁
6

MAL DE MER

Victor Vifquain, sixteen, staggered down the gang plank of a many-masted schooner in 1852, relieved to feel American soil beneath his feet.

"Christophe Colomb," he cursed as the solid dock rolled beneath him. Would he never get his sea legs, not even on land?

He scoffed when an old image popped to mind: himself in bell bottoms and blue jacket, his stiff-brimmed hat decked with ribbons, as he paced the deck of a French naval ship. He'd been so sure he'd be a French sailor.

Victor stumbled, then righted himself. That rolling Belgian ship behind him had kept him hanging over the rail all the way to New York City. He hated to admit it, but Papa had been right. Victor would never be a seaman.

As he walked, the rolling sensation ebbed.

"Hey, kid!" A tall skinny gent in a bowler loped alongside Victor. "Watch out for them Swamp Angels. That gang likes to pick on newcomers like you." The man merged into the crowd, his slender cane tapping.

Victor Vifquain

Victor picked up his pace. The ground beneath his feet felt solid enough. He caught up with the last of the crowd leaving the ship.

～

Victor yearned to be like his father, Jean-Baptiste Vifquain, who had led flashing French troopers into battle for Napoleon. But his father wouldn't hear of a military career for his young son.

"Go to America," Papa said. "Plenty of adventure there. Be a mountain man in the West. Trade beaver pelts with the natives. Take an Indian wife."

When Victor grimaced, his father shrugged. "Or become an entrepreneur, establish a Belgian colony. Bring over businessmen first, then their families."

So Victor decided to come to America and establish a colony, but he wanted to locate it in the old Louisiana Territory. That's what he called the area between the Missouri River and the Rocky Mountains, that vast country that Napoleon sold to support his troops, that strange land Papa described.

In fact, Victor would help settle just such an area, a place in the Republican River valley that would be called "Harlan County." But now he traveled west.

Time seemed to collapse. He had no idea how huge America was. Two years passed, and he'd just reached John Veuleman's successful cattle ranch in the rolling plains of central Missouri. Veuleman's ranch lay west of St. Louis near a tiny town, Round Hill, full of Germans and a general store run on the barter system.

Like Victor, the energetic Veulemans spoke French, so he felt at home in their family. Victor planned to leave for the old Louisiana Territory next, to found a Belgian colony there, but he couldn't part from the Veulemans. Their seventh daughter, fifteen-year-old Caroline, appealed to him. She moved like a colt. He liked her energy, her tomboy streak.

She liked him, too, and why not? He was an attractive young man. His chiseled face held deep-set eyes, and his mop of dark curly hair reigned over what would be a bushy mustache.

So he stayed, a regular at their dining table, listening to family stories of travel down the Mississippi in a flatboat they'd made, of their life in the unhealthy Natchitoches.

"Don't settle there," they warned Victor. "The climate's so rotten folks have to import a lot of slave labor. White folks can't take the humidity. Or the yellow fever."

Caroline, two years younger than Victor, showed him her parents' wooden chests. Victor rubbed his finger over the "1814" carved on one lid.

"They brought them all the way from Antwerp," Caroline said.

"Antwerp. That's not far from Brussels, where I live. Maybe thirty miles north."

"I never lived there," Caroline said. "I was born in Louisiana."

"So you're American, not Belgian."

"Don't tell Mama!"

Victor went berry picking and fishing with Caroline, chaperoned by her much older sister, Joannes. Caroline knew all the good spots, where to find wild strawberries and red mulberries, where to snag catfish and how to clean and cook a squirrel.

Or so she claimed.

Then after two years in America, Victor received a letter bearing news of his father's death, and he again found himself hanging over the railing of a ship, this time headed back to Belgium.

∼ Chapter ∼
7

Doubling Back

W hen Victor arrived in Brussels that fall of 1854, he went first to his childhood home. As he rounded the last street corner, he started. His mother's house looked so much smaller than he remembered. He eased the front door open.

Marie de Vuyst, his mother, stood with her back to him. He watched her lower a lavender taffeta gown over her wickerwork mannequin. She had stitched fine clothes for wealthy women as long as he could remember. When he cleared his throat, she turned and regarded him, a cluster of straight pins clenched between her teeth.

"Carry on!" he said.

Later they sipped tea. Marie sat so quietly that Victor, nibbling a *madeleine,* thought she'd stopped talking. Then she said, "Well, you know you have no birthright, don't you?"

Victor gulped. "What do you mean?"

Her teacup clattered. "You're illegitimate, you and Isabelle."

"So what? I have his name."

Marie turned around. "But you weren't born a Vifquain." She twisted her dish towel. "I had to register you under my name."

Victor gripped his tea cup. He knew he had both his father's names, not just Vifquain but also Jean-Baptiste. Jean-Baptiste Victor Vifquain. "But he named me after him."

"True. And we called you 'Victor' so no one would confuse you." She spoke loudly, over the noise of dishes rattling in the pan.

"So when did I become Victor Vifquain?"

She dried her hands. "Just a minute."

When she returned, she spread a roll of paper on the table and flattened it. "You were eight."

Victor read the official document that gave him and his little sister, Isabelle, the right to bear their famous father's surname "Vifquain."

He struck the document with his index finger. "And this doesn't make me legitimate?"

"No. Only marriage does that." She turned away from him. "Jean-Baptiste refused to marry me." Her voice sounded strained.

The next morning at breakfast, they talked again. Victor found out that although Jean-Baptiste wouldn't marry Marie, he had married Françoise in 1817. That marriage had produced Pierre and Louise and Anne. It lasted seventeen years until Françoise died and Marie met Jean-Baptiste.

"So," Victor said, "they're all legitimate?"

"Their children? Yes."

"How about Papa's stepdaughters?"

"Françoise's girls. Your father isn't their father. Their father was a rich Parisian industrialist. His death made Françoise a 'person of independent means.'" She brushed crumbs off her lap. "Handy for Jean-Baptiste."

"Handy?" He nibbled a slice of Gouda.

"I mean your father married Françoise for her money."

"Her money!" Victor slapped his thigh and laughed. "Papa didn't need her money."

"Well, he did then. He couldn't even muster up tuition for that fancy Polytechnic School in Paris he worked so hard to get into. His Uncle Louis had to bail him out."

"Do I know Uncle Louis?"

"No, no. He was way before your time. Filthy rich because he married a wealthy woman. That's what gave your father the idea."

"To marry Françoise, you mean?"

She nodded and picked up some breakfast dishes.

"With Françoise, he got a purse full of francs. But with me? Well, he said heaven made our love."

Victor flinched.

She shook her apron at him. "Go on, go on! Don't you have an appointment at the Big House this morning?"

～

Later that morning, Victor traveled to his father's house in the French quarter near the city's Botanical Garden. The house lay only a municipality away, but it seemed like a continent. He'd forgotten how big it was until it loomed ahead, surrounded by formal gardens, more castle than home.

Victor climbed to the portico, uncertain of his reception. The two stepdaughters, in their forties now, wouldn't be there. They'd long since married. So had Jean-Baptiste's daughter, Anne. But Louise, now thirty-nine, and his father's other son, Pierre, thirty-four, had stayed on.

Victor asked to be announced and waited until Louise greeted him. "You're looking fit! America must agree with you."

They sat on white upholstered chairs in the sunroom, light streaming in the windows. Louise looked at her lap and spoke rapidly. "A nervous breakdown. A nasty one." She glanced up. "You probably don't remember it; you must have been ten when it started. He just wouldn't stop working. He wouldn't let go."

"He seemed okay to me," Victor said, remembering their arguments.

"Well, he was, for quite some time, more or less himself." Louise fished in her pocket, dug out a handkerchief. "But edgy. Never able to settle down. When he retired, he didn't know what to do with himself." She glanced up again. "It got worse after you left."

Significantly worse. Victor was startled to hear that his father had died in Paris under the direct care of Doctor Esquirol, a physician famous for treating psychoses.

Victor waited, watching Louise twist her handkerchief, uncertain how much more he wanted to hear. Her voice turned brisk. "So of course he died in a state of prohibition and intestate."

"What does that mean?"

"He didn't have a will when he died." Louise stuffed

her handkerchief back in her pocket. "So the court will decide who gets what." She stood. "You know how French courts are."

"It'll take months," Victor said.

"More likely years."

~

On his way out, Victor stopped to look, no doubt for the last time, at Jean-Baptiste's medals, a whole case full. When Victor was young, he loved to play with them. As he aged, the military medals fascinated him more than the engineering decorations. The boy particularly liked the animals carved in some medals: "The Red Eagle of Prussia" and "*Chevalier* of the Lion *Merlansois*."

As he aged, he tried to imagine his father's war stories. How would it feel being trained and mounted as one of 22,000 troopers in Napoleon's cavalry?

By the time Jean-Baptiste fought in the Battle of Eylau in 1807, he'd been promoted to second lieutenant. That battle, fought between Russia and France during two days of heavy February snowstorms, threatened to stall as a draw. Then Napoleon unleashed his cavalry.

Jean-Baptiste and his fellow troopers swept through the Russian infantry, then divided into two wings, one attacking cavalry, the other plowing through infantry again, wheeling, storming right through the Russian center, then pivoting once more to cut down the gunners. What a cavalry charge! Never before had French *chasseurs* risen to such heights. Few would ever match them.

Jean-Baptiste leads the charge!

Then, on the battlefield, Napoleon called Jean-Baptiste forward. The "Little Corporal" removed his big two-cornered black hat. Wisps of hair fell across his damp forehead as he lifted his personal medal, the prestigious "Knight of the Legion of Honor" cross, off his breast.

"For outstanding acts of bravery." He lowered his medal over Jean-Baptiste's head and positioned it on his chest.

Napoleon's own medal. The highest decoration given in France. On Papa's chest. When he was eighteen, Victor's age now.

Victor tore himself away from the case. How, he wondered, could such a father die?

HIS FATHER'S FORTUNE

Surrounded by bolts of cloth, Victor Vifquain sat in his mother's house and thought, *How should I pass my time while I wait for the slow motions of the courts? How long would it be? Years, perhaps. What if the court rewards me nothing? After all, even mother called me illegitimate. How would I earn a living?*

As long as he could remember, Victor dreamed of fighting for France. He had planned to join the French navy until seasickness taught him otherwise. But his desire to fight for France remained strong.

He decided to pick up the military studies he'd abandoned when he sailed to America. Now, with no father to stand between him and his dreams, Victor returned to the Belgium Military School, finished his studies, and graduated.

Then, defying his father's wishes, Victor followed in Jean-Baptiste's footsteps by applying, in 1854, to one of Napoleon's prestigious military schools, *Ecole Speciale Military School of St. Cyr.* Highly selective, St. Cyr chose only 3 percent of its applicants.

The school picked bright, well-educated Victor as one of eight young men admitted from 350 applicants. He moved to the St. Cyr campus, located west of Paris.

Two tumultuous years followed. Victor, fond of hijinks, eclipsed the school's rascals. He loved escapades, preferring wild and reckless stunts despite rigorous discipline. As a result, he spent ample time in the guard house.

However, on May 25, 1856, he did graduate as second lieutenant of cavalry, a position his father once held in Napoleon's army.

Weeks later, on August 12, 1856, the French court divided Jean-Baptiste's enormous inheritance. Victor's father had amassed an immense fortune as a talented civil engineer, building railroads, canals, bridges, boulevards, streets, and a theater. Many of his projects were "firsts" in Belgium, Europe, or the world.

The court split Jean-Baptiste's fortune into three equal parts, one each to Louise, Anne, and Pierre, the three legitimate children of Jean-Baptiste and Françoise. Victor felt stomach punched.

"Wait a moment," Louise said. "We can't leave you and Isabelle with nothing. We're talking about it."

So Victor waited while the three legitimate heirs sold Jean-Baptiste's living quarters to the Jesuits who planned to install their House of Bollandistes in his father's house. In his adjoining garden, they planned to build a church and a convent.

Then the three legitimate children decided, without rancor, to redivide the estate. They each agreed to receive 13/45ths while Victor and Isabelle would receive 3/45ths each.

Victor's portion of the estate seems small, but Jean-Baptiste's vast fortune made Victor independently wealthy. He could do whatever he liked.

He stayed in the military a while, then resigned. In May 1857, Victor crossed the Atlantic again. When he disembarked, he headed west, keen on finding a place to establish a Belgian colony. First he stopped in Missouri to visit the Veulemans. That September he and their daughter Caroline married. She was nineteen and he twenty-one years old.

~

On May 1, 1858, Victor and Caroline set out to find a place for his Belgian colony. They rode through Missouri, too settled for their plans, and into Bleeding Kansas, still riddled by guerrilla warfare. They couldn't bring Belgians into such turmoil, so they angled northeast, following the beautiful, fertile Big Blue River. It took them right through the Otoe-Missouria reservation, but no one seemed to mind. They rode on north across the undeveloped Nebraska Territory, noticing how the Big Blue trail hooked up with the Oregon Trail.

Then they rode east along the Platte until they met Salt Creek, which flowed into the Platte from the south. Salt Creek got its name from the creek's shallow groundwater full of common salt. Once the greedy hoped to mine it, but no such luck. Railroads could transport Kansas salt cheaper than local salt could be produced.

Victor and Caroline followed Salt Creek south as it diminished, then rode in large circles between Salt Creek

and the Big Blue River, searching. The land was amazingly
varied. Sometimes it stretched out in level plains, and then
broke into wide, flat valleys. Sometimes the couple rode up
and down graceful hills. They scrutinized it all until, near
the point where the West Fork of the Big Blue empties into
the main river, they found the perfect spot. On July 11, they
squatted on it. Miles of unclaimed land surrounded theirs.
Just right for a Belgian colony.

The government allowed squatters to buy up to 160
acres of federal land at less than $1.25 an acre. To qualify,
a squatter must head a household, be a U.S. citizen (or
expecting to become one), live on his land for at least
fourteen months, and work toward improving his property.
Squatting on federal property became such a popular way
to own land in Nebraska Territory that folks nicknamed
Nebraskans "Squatters," not "Cornhuskers."

Without knowing it, Victor and Caroline were the first
white persons to settle in Saline County, which the territorial
legislature had created in January 1855. The Vifquains'
chosen land lay in the northeastern corner of the county.
To reach Nebraska City, the nearest town where they could
pick up mail or send for supplies, they traveled 75 miles.
Their closest white neighbor lived 25 miles away.

~ CHAPTER ~

9

300 INDIANS & ONE FAT OX

A large population of Kiowa and Comanche Indians overran Saline County at the time the Vifquains arrived. Those two tribes, once enemies, had made a lasting pact of good will with each other.

At first glance, the two seemed similar. Both nomadic, they shared the Plains Indian culture that revolved around horses, buffalo, tepees, and the Sun Dance. Since they lived in tepees, they could dismantle an entire camp in thirty minutes. They hunted, particularly buffalo, for food. Well-known riders, they enlarged their herds through far-flung raiding until each man averaged thirty-five horses and mules.

For ten days early each summer, the Kiowa and the Comanche danced their great tribal Sun Dance. They understood the sun as a spirit force—one of many—and they danced to catch a vision. The Sun Dance also brought the two together as individuals worked to prepare a lodge, to set up a post for the dancers, and to participate in a mock battle before dancing started.

These two tribes also shared calamities. Wave after wave of smallpox and cholera had infected many Plains Indians, but thousands of Kiowa and Comanche died from the infections. Epidemics had killed more than half of the Kiowa's people, leaving them smaller and weaker than the Comanche.

Bright, the Kiowa used a calendar to keep track of time. Many artistic women brought prestige to their families. Famous for beadwork, they also quilled and painted geometric designs.

The men cut a piece of hair short over their right ear. It facilitated the flight of their arrows but also served as a tribal symbol. Their legend maintained that the first Kiowa burst out of a hollow cottonwood trunk high in the Rocky Mountains.

The Comanche led a more mobile life, raiding horses and cattle. They often had a surplus of 100,000 horses. Long known as the Plains' finest riders, they loved to raid when a full moon gave them enough light to illuminate their way.

Fierce, the Comanche embraced warfare as a major part of their life. Widely known for recklessness, they fought with every other Plains Indian tribe at one time or another.

However, the first Indians that Victor met were neither Kiowa nor Comanche. They were Pawnee who once lived in the Saline County area.

Unlike any other Plains Indian, the Pawnee loved Americans, so when the United States asked them to give up their land, which covered most of Nebraska, and move into a reservation, they complied. Theirs was the first reservation on the plains.

Excellent hunters, the Pawnee possessed finely honed abilities with the bow and arrow. They hunted raccoon, quail, skunk, and prairie chicken, but they primarily ate buffalo meat. The Pawnee used every part of the buffalo in some way; they used even the buffalo's stomach lining for water pails.

Victor met the Pawnee during his first summer. The Indian agent in charge of their village had allowed them to leave the reservation to scout for buffalo, so they were traveling to their old Republican River hunting grounds to search for the big beasts.

When he heard horses approaching, Victor turned and looked. A small group of dark men rode to greet him, but Victor saw on the horizon more mounted Indians than he could count. He cursed himself for not yet planting explosives in his home so he could blow himself and Caroline up rather than face capture. He'd heard enough about Indian forms of torture to know what he'd prefer.

The Pawnee rode closer. Each wore a large black-tipped white feather sticking up out of the back of his dark hair. When Victor greeted the men in his broken English, to his astonishment, one Pawnee replied in French. Frenchmen had been among the first white men to trade and live with the early Pawnee; Peter-nash-arrow, a Pawnee chief, had recognized the French in Victor's English. The two became strong friends.

Victor let the Pawnee—all 1,900 of them—make his farm their headquarters. They camped in his timber as they rode back and forth to the Republican River valley where herds of bison covered acres of land, their brown hair undulating like a rug under the radiant sun.

As time passed, settlers arrived and Victor took on
an official role. It would be the first of many during his
lifetime. For this initial role, he became a justice of the
peace so he could marry two new settlers, Orion Johnson
and Isabella West, who located their claim close to Victor's
farm. He couldn't be a Saline County justice of the peace,
for that county had not yet been organized. So, according
to territorial law, he became a justice for Otoe County, the
nearest organized county to the east.

That marriage was on March 25, 1859, but another
marriage was pending in Belgium. Victor's little sister,
Isabelle, planned to marry a merchant from Tournai, Eugene
Duvergnies, on July 22, 1859. Victor wanted to attend
Isabelle's wedding, see his mother, and perhaps persuade a
few Belgians to join the colony he was planning.

Victor had no reservations about adventuring in
Belgium while Caroline stayed behind to protect their land.
He left Caroline pregnant, but he didn't leave her alone. By
this time, Victor had hired a man, Thomas Elon, and a girl,
Sarah Jones, to help them.

While Victor made himself scarce, the Comanches and
Kiowas clashed with the Pawnees in Saline County, easily
driving the Pawnee back toward their reservation with no
loss of life.

Caroline knew nothing of this until 5 p.m. July 28, 1859,
when she heard the cowbell clanking. This surprised her.
The cattle never came home so early.

She looked up and saw 300 armed Indians on horseback, stampeding the cattle. They ran the cattle into the Vifquain's yard, then stopped. At a signal, they dismounted, thrust their spears into the ground and tossed their reins over their spears.

The warriors wore "gaudy head dresses, ornamented with half dollar pieces, beaten to three or four inches in diameter," Caroline wrote later. "These were fastened to their scalp locks and hung down about three feet and glistening in the evening sun made a pretty sight."

To her surprise, below their gaudy head dresses, the warriors wore regular white-men's clothes and low leather shoes.

The Kiowa chief and his braves

A tall savage-looking Comanche chief, a heavy set Kiowa chief, several braves, and an interpreter came to Caroline's door. From the neck of Yellow Buffalo, the Kiowa chief, hung a large crucifix. When Caroline saw this, she lifted her own crucifix and showed it to him. This, she believed, spared her, for Yellow Buffalo said, "Good. Very good," as he pressed his crucifix to his breast.

"We're hungry and want an ox," the interpreter said.

Caroline brought out sacks of flour and meal, but the interpreter shook his head. Then she offered several sides of bacon, but that wouldn't do.

The chiefs kept pointing to a large fat ox.

A prairie plow had crippled the fat ox's mate, so Caroline offered the mate to the chiefs.

"Not fat enough," said the chiefs.

So she tried barter: "Give me a pony for the ox."

They shook their heads.

"We need all our ponies to bring back Pawnee prisoners," the interpreter said.

Caroline considered. She and her two servants stood alone against 300 Comanches and Kiowa. They could, she knew, take anything they wanted. So she gave them the big fat ox.

The Comanche chief shot the ox, which rolled down the bank to the river's edge. The Indians built fires. While the ox cooked, braves sharpened knives and tomahawks on the Vifquains' grindstone and hung the ox hide on the fence to dry.

When the cooks had transformed the fat ox into entrée, the chief gave Caroline a choice piece of meat. Then the braves rode past her house, each holding a cooked chunk of ox and calling, *"Bueno, Bueno good, good,"* before they settled down to eat.

The Indians spent the night in the yard, fires burning. About nine p.m., the Comanche chief got on his soapbox and ranted for several hours. Then drumming began, and braves danced to the hypnotic beat. Caroline, unable to sleep, watched from her window.

In the morning, the Comanches and Kiowas feasted on ox remains. Then they rode north. Caroline knew they rode to the Pawnee reservation to continue the fight. There the Pawnee lived in big oval earth lodges housing thirty to fifty each, but Caroline had watched the Pawnee braves head to the Republican River valley to hunt buffalo. She knew that in the reservation only women, children, and old men remained to fight or be captured.

"We'll be back in ten days," the interpreter said. They departed quietly, leaving only smoldering fires and mounds of bones scraped free of meat.

To Caroline's immense relief, they didn't return.

When Victor came back and heard about the Comanche-Kiowa visit, he taught his wife how to fire a shotgun and how to make bullets. An owl dropped dead with her first shot. She soon handled her gun like a seasoned sharpshooter. She wasted no ammunition either. One day she shot a single bullet through two wild turkeys who wandered into her garden.

Or so she said.

~ CHAPTER ~
# 10

THE THREE MUSKETEERS

South Carolina couldn't wait to pull out of the Union. Then, like a line of dominoes toppling, went Mississippi, Florida, Alabama, Georgia, Louisiana, and Texas. By February 1861, they'd adopted a constitution and elected a president: Jefferson Davis.

After the Fort Sumter firing, war news swept the continent. It fired up Vifquain, just as the call to war had roused his father, or so Vifquain believed.

"There's no turning back," he told Caroline, now seven months pregnant.

Vifquain agreed to wait for a Nebraska regiment to form, so he stayed home June 20, when Caroline gave birth to their second son, Elmer. In July, with no Nebraska regiment in sight, he sped to New York to join a French-speaking outfit.

In September, Vifquain, now twenty-five, enlisted as a private in the 53rd Regiment, New York State Volunteers. It bulged with Franco-Americans and Frenchmen, but the ill-fated unit fell apart February 26, 1862. How disappointing! A long cry from fighting with Napoleon.

Rather than look for a new outfit, Vifquain and several friends dreamed about *The Three Musketeers*, that popular French adventure novel of fights, duels, battles—and kidnapping.

Vifquain and his friends—Alfred Cipriani and Maurice de Beaumont—decided to be modern Musketeers and live by their motto: all for one, one for all.

But whom should they kidnap?

They agreed: the Confederate President, Jefferson Davis.

What if they carried it off! Vifquain wished Papa weren't dead.

Before they left Washington, the three friends—all French citizens—persuaded the French ambassador to write them letters of introduction. They left on foot March 30, carrying pistols and swords, their pockets stuffed with money. Their destination: Richmond, Virginia, capital of the Confederate States of America, 100 miles south. Davis should be there.

After they'd walked three miles, they stopped and slept in the bushes. At sunrise, off they went. Folks might have mistaken them for French tourists except for their Yankee officers' fatigue dress: light blue trousers and jackets.

By the next afternoon, walking had become boring. They bought three horses from a reluctant rebel farmer for $300 in gold, and they weren't polite about it. The farmer spotted them as Union soldiers.

In Occoquan, Virginia, twenty men tried to stop them. "Go back to Yankeeland!"

"We're Frenchmen," Vifquain said, "not Yankees."

The men ran toward their horses. "Dismount or we'll pull you off."

"Stand back," Vifquain said, "or we'll fire."

The crowd pulled back. Beaumont began to sing, in pure French, *La Marseillaise*. His remarkable voice possessed the crowd.

"So you see, we're not Yankees."

"Give us another!" a voice in the crowd cried.

Beaumont sang another verse, and the throng parted, letting the Frenchmen pass.

On Sunday afternoon, April 6, the Musketeers reached the yellowish waters of Aquia Creek. Holding pistols and swords overhead, the three rode into the stream.

Vifquain heard a voice cry, "Halt." When they rode out of the stream, they saw across from them on top of the bluffs six Confederates holding muskets.

"Halt," one cried.

The three Frenchmen turned toward the stream. The Confederates fired a hail of bullets.

The three friends grasped pistols and swords, intending to fight, but a troop of twenty cavalry arrived.

"Surrender," the commander called.

"No need," Vifquain said. "We're already captured."

The three prisoners marched to a ramshackle Confederate camp whose soldiers jeered, "French Yankee," until they arrived at Colonel Fitzhugh Lee's quarters. The colonel, twenty-six, a strapping fellow, spoke French.

The three Musketeers presented the ambassador's letters of introduction. Col. Lee, impressed, sent them to Maj. Gen. Smith in Fredericksburg who received them like ice and sent them to General John H. Winder in Richmond. Gen. Winder, a profane man, headed up the city's military prisons.

The three Musketeers cooled their heels in Richmond's Libby Prison until Captain George Alexander, Richmond's French provost marshal, moved the three to a better room. But instead of facing trial, Vifquain and his friends got out free. Short-tempered Gen. Winder couldn't find Walker, the farmer who sold them horses and then accused them of being spies and horse thieves.

At last, the three Musketeers could focus on their real reason for being in Richmond: capturing Jefferson Davis.

The newspaper reported that Davis took a regular run on his tugboat to Norfolk Navy Yard. There, Davis checked on *Virginia*.

Virginia, a strange ship built from the Union's *Merrimack*, had been sunk by Union forces when they withdrew from the Norfolk Navy Yard. Confederates then converted the ship into an ironclad ram, a new type of warship. Immune to gunfire, *Virginia* used her ram as a lethal weapon.

Now Davis visited Norfolk like clockwork to hurry repairs on his ironclad ram so he could send her out again to keep Union forces from advancing toward Richmond.

The three Musketeers saw the perfect plan. They would hop on the boat with Davis aboard, run it past Norfolk to Fortress Monroe, and turn it over to the federal government.

They just needed an invitation from Davis to come aboard.

"Why are you looking at me?" Beaumont asked.

Davis's ironclad ram

"Let's get an invitation to Secretary Benjamin's reception. He said Davis would come. You can sing for him, get in his good graces, ask him to take us with him to see the *Virginia*."

What a foolproof plot! No one could resist Beaumont if he sang for them.

On Tuesday, May 6, they received invitations to Benjamin's May 9 reception. Then Union forces landed 100 land miles from Richmond. Confederate forces retreated, staying just ahead of Union troops. Richmond panicked.

On Friday, reception day, the Confederates planned to abandon the Norfolk Navy Yard. Now Davis would have no reason to take his tugboat there. The Musketeers watched their plot to capture the Confederate president collapse.

The young Frenchmen felt insignificant. Vifquain tore up a letter to Belgium that he'd started. Jaws set, the three acquired passes and money, dressed in blue uniforms, and bought horses.

As they slipped out of Richmond May 11 before dawn, they heard an ear-splitting explosion. The entire eastern horizon blazed with light. Their faces glowed.

To avoid capture, *Virginia's* crew had run the ship aground and set her on fire. Flames ignited her supply of gunpowder.

Captivated, the mute Musketeers gazed until the flaming sky faded to predawn gray.

OH, GLORIOUS!

After failing to capture Jefferson Davis, Vifquain went to Springfield, Illinois, June 1862, to join the new Illinois 97th Volunteer Infantry Regiment. As he drilled, he thought about the news he'd heard of Santee Sioux who had gone wild in Minnesota. They attacked settlements along the Minnesota River valley, week after week after week. Just when it looked as though nothing could stop them, U.S. troops did. Arrested 2,000 warriors for killing 800 whites. Tried them. Sentenced 303 to be hanged.

Vifquain felt strained. Here he played soldier in Illinois, ignoring Caroline's safety. *What must it be like on their homestead where Comanche and Sioux and Pawnee roamed loose, enraged by news of mass arrests and hangings?* He tried to calm himself, but the drums played and he walked on, his thighs trembling. *He could never forgive himself if ...*

That winter, the now battle-ready 97th Volunteer Infantry Regiment moved 500 miles south, to the half-deserted town of Arkansas Post, located above the confluence of the Arkansas River with the Mississippi.

Nearby, on high bluffs overlooking the Arkansas, the Confederate Army had constructed a massive earthwork fortification: Fort Hindman. From the fort, the Confederates blocked Union ships and seized military supplies.

Of course, Union forces decided to capture Fort Hindman.

On Friday, January 9, 1863, a Union fleet of 30,000 Union infantry, including Vifquain and the 97th, moved up the Arkansas to face 5,000 Confederate soldiers in the fort.

The Union infantry landed and overran Confederate trenches; soldiers retreated to the fort. Sunday afternoon a fierce gunboat barrage resulted in white flags waving along the Confederate line. The Union captured 4,800 prisoners plus guns and supplies. The army destroyed the fort and torched Arkansas Post.

The Union now could move soldiers and supplies down the Mississippi all the way to Vicksburg. That city, well fortified and located on high ground, dominated the last section of the Mississippi River that Confederates controlled.

~

That spring, Major General Ulysses S. Grant shipped twelve barges down the Mississippi River right in front of Vicksburg, losing six to Confederate guns. On the six remaining barges, Grant ferried 23,000 Union soldiers from Louisiana across the river to its east bank, 40 miles from Vicksburg. Vifquain, along with the 97th Volunteer Infantry Regiment, joined Grant's Union army.

The army worked its way inland, first Port Gibson "too beautiful to burn" with its flowering white magnolias; then

Champion Hill, 30 miles east of Vicksburg. Bitter fighting pushed the Confederates toward Vicksburg until Union forces trapped them inside the city.

A forty-seven-day siege followed. Shells pounded the city. Vicksburg, under constant bombardment, had no way to import food. Troops and civilians soon had to eat mules and horses. On July 4, 1863, the city surrendered.

The day after Vicksburg's surrender, Vifquain asked for a twenty-day leave of absence to go home. When he received his leave, he didn't return to his homestead by the Big Blue. He went to Missouri where Caroline and the two boys lived with her mother. Once there, Vifquain collapsed, in ill health from the fighting. He requested an additional month's leave and got it.

In Tipton, where he and Caroline had picked berries, caught fish, and courted each other, Vifquain recovered. Before he left, he and Caroline conceived their third child.

Vifquain returned to fight with the Illinois 97th Volunteer Infantry Regiment. His time with Caroline must have revived him, for November 3, 1863, in southwest Louisiana, Vifquain made two outstanding saves during the Battle of Carrion Crow Bayou.

In this battle, the Confederates outnumbered the Union army, 6,000 to 1,625. The Union's Brigadier General Stephen G. Burbridge had marched his troops 90 miles north across southwestern Louisiana from the Gulf of Mexico. By November 3, they had scattered over a wide area trying to avoid the local bayous, or marshlands, near Opelousas, Louisiana.

When the Confederate commander, Major General Richard Taylor, spotted the disorganized Union troops, he sicced Brigadier General Thomas Green on them. Gen. Green charged out of a ravine and, using both cavalry and infantry, attacked Gen. Burbridge's camp.

In the midst of this chaos, Vifquain took two squadrons of Union cavalry and successfully defended a bridge. His action saved a regiment.

Then Vifquain saw how, in the heat of the battle, the Confederates had all but captured a large caliber Union cannon, a 12-pounder Napoleon, a favorite of Vifquain's for its sleekness and its power. Plus, of course, its name. The Confederates had killed the draft horses that pulled the cannon, so Vifquain hitched his horse to one side of the gun's big wheels and had his soldiers tug on ropes on the wheel's far side. Then away they went, Vifquain mounted on his steed, the soldiers pulling at their wheel. They dashed across a marshy area, dragging the gun with them. The Confederates, not even 50 yards away, fired like blazes, hitting Vifquain's horse several times. But Vifquain survived, and so did the cannon, which could no longer be turned and fired on Union soldiers.

In the meantime, Gen. Burbridge tried to battle his way out of this mess. He managed to reform and fight vigorously until Green and his troops pulled away. The Confederates had killed 25, wounded 129, captured 562 soldiers and taken one 10-pound cannon, but not the 12-pounder Napoleon that Vifquain saved.

When Brig. Gen. Burbridge ordered a retreat, he found that many of his soldiers had headed out before him, fleeing to the safety of another camp. Such a vexing defeat!

But Vifquain would be rewarded for his actions during the Battle of Carrion Crow Bayou. That December, he advanced to lieutenant colonel in the 97th Volunteer Infantry Regiment.

~

On Sunday, August 7, 1864, the dreaded event happened. Sioux, Cheyenne, and Arapaho struck ranches along the Little Blue River. The Indians killed with bullets and with arrows. When the raids stopped, thirty-eight settlers lay dead, nine wounded, five captured.

This began what's called "the worst Indian raid in Nebraska history."

Hundreds of warriors struck along a 300-mile stretch of the Oregon Trail, from Julesburg in Colorado Territory all the way down Nebraska's Little Blue River. Attacking thirty stagecoach stations, 150 ranches, innumerable homesteaders' cabins. Men killed and scalped. Women and children taken captive. Soldiers, gathering plums by the river, surprised, killed, scalped.

Wires hummed from coast to coast with stunning news of butchery in Colorado and Nebraska territories. Travel became perilous unless guarded. Mail and stagecoaches were irregular by intent.

Frantic, Vifquain tried to find out if Caroline and the children had survived. He knew they had left her mother's house and returned to their homestead on the Big Blue River. Just twenty-five miles separated them from the Little Blue.

He agonized. *Why am I in Louisiana fighting Southerners? I should be on the plains fighting Sioux and Cheyenne and Arapaho.*

He tried to resign, but no one would approve his application. Desperate, he wrote Major General Edward Canby, "I pray you on my knees, Sir, to let me go and fight the Indians and to protect all that is dear to me, my wife and children, or die with them in the attempt."

But Vifquain did not go to Nebraska.

Instead he walked into the most memorable battle of his life.

~

Soldiers once called the Confederate's Mobile, Alabama, one of the most fortified places on Earth. But now since the Union victories, Mobile had no stronghold left to protect her but Fort Blakeley.

Fort Blakeley lay 10 miles north of Mobile. Cannons guarded every approach; 4,000 men, including a Confederate elite combat unit, readied to fight the arriving 45,000 Union troops.

The formidable fort stood surrounded by a barrier of nine earthworks or redoubts. Redoubt #4, the strongest, lay behind a barrier of tree limbs with sharpened branches interwoven with obstructions including torpedoes detonated by trip wires. Union military engineers had been disarming mines for days.

Near Redoubt #4 Vifquain, leading the 97th Illinois, readied for battle. His commander told him to bring the 97th into action in a preliminary battle at 5:30 p.m. April 9, 1865. At the hour, dark clouds rolled across the sky and distant thunder rumbled. Vifquain ignored them. He drew his sword, held it aloft, and cried: "Forward, Ninety-Seventh! Charge!"

His regiment cheered and leaped forward. Soldiers attacked the edge of Redoubt #4 on the run. A shower of bullets reached them; several men fell. But Vifquain's soldiers rolled "down the hill like an avalanche" and poured across a deep ditch.

Above them a parapet or wall protected the fort. Vifquain leaped on it, drew his sword, and deliberately exposed his body in order to draw Confederate fire away from his men. That gave them time to reload before they stormed the fort.

When the Confederates used up their ammunition and stopped to reload, Vifquain cried again, "Forward, Ninety-Seventh! Charge!" His armed men scaled the parapet and swarmed into the fort.

There Confederates fought the 97th Infantry hand-to-hand with bayonets and musket butts. Soon sheer numbers breached the earthworks, compelling the Confederates to surrender.

The storming of Fort Blakeley

The Union forces had taken Fort Blakeley in twenty minutes.

Three days later on April 12, Mobile surrendered.

So had General Robert E. Lee on April 9, the day Vifquain leaped upon the parapet.

Except for some mop up, the Civil War had ceased.

~

Vifquain must have returned home happy to be reunited with Caroline and the children but also satisfied that he hadn't tarnished his father's military reputation. On June 8, 1865, President Abraham Lincoln gave Vifquain the highest military decoration awarded by the U.S. government: the Medal of Honor. The award, given to U.S. armed force members for heroic action in battle, went to Vifquain for his "gallant charge" and his "conspicuous bravery" at Fort Blakeley.

Lincoln also promoted Vifquain to brevet brigadier general for "meritorious and gallant conduct" in the same battle. Brevet, an honorary rank, lacked authority, but Vifquain, now twice honored for his valor, became known as General Victor Vifquain. He had just turned twenty-nine.

PART III

Unscrupulous Models

A COLICKY BABY

Both General Victor Vifquain and William Parker Carr seem, in retrospect, destined to play significant roles in settling Harlan County. Before they could, Congress had its own role to play, organizing what was still Unorganized Territory.

Harlan County would become a county in 1871. The creation of Harlan County required a state, Nebraska, and creation of the state of Nebraska required a territory, Nebraska Territory. Government officials at all levels provided Harlan County settlers with plenty of unscrupulous models to use in their bitter war to locate the county seat.

Unscrupulous Model #1: Stephen A. Douglas.

The Kansas-Nebraska Act of 1854 created the new Nebraska Territory. Congress passed this act, and President Franklin Pierce signed it, but the Kansas-Nebraska Act belonged to Illinois Senator Stephen A. Douglas. It was his baby.

Douglas was peculiar. Short-legged, he stood five feet four inches with an overlarge head and massive chest and

shoulders. Resembling a boy, he exhibited the boundless
energy of one. Some called him a steam engine in breeches.

In Illinois, he'd risen up the ranks of the Democratic
Party to become a twenty-nine-year-old member of the U.S.
House of Representatives. Three terms later, Illinois sent
him to the U.S. Senate where he became chairman of the
powerful Committee on the Territories. Wildly popular and
widely reviled, he became known as the "Little Giant." He
was thirty-four.

Like many Senators, Douglas envisioned a railroad
running to the West Coast, speeding across the Great Plains
via the flat Platte River valley. To accomplish that, he needed
to create a territory so he could rid it of buffalo and natives.

Eventually his moment arrived: a bill to create a Nebraska
Territory appeared in his Committee on the Territories.
Douglas pruned the bill so it would pass Congress. Since
one huge territory would never get the Southern vote, he
split the territory into Kansas and Nebraska. Even more
shocking, he repealed the old way of deciding whether a
territory should be slave or free. Instead, citizens of the two
new territories would choose by popular vote.

Douglas's bill satisfied the South, but horrified the North.

The Senate debate lasted four months with Douglas
"a ferocious fighter, the fiercest, most ruthless, and most
unscrupulous that Congress had perhaps ever known."

Beginning late on March 3, 1854, the Little Giant made
a five-and-a-half-hour speech defending his bill. On March
4, the exhausted Senate passed it, 37 to 14. All but two
Southerners supported it.

The House clashed more rudely over Douglas's bill. Legislators filled the large square chamber, and the balcony galleries rustled with visitors coming and going. The Representative from Ohio, Lewis D. Campbell, stood on a white platform beneath drooping flags. Since he had the floor, he had the right to unlimited debate.

At first Campbell argued for passing the Kansas-Nebraska bill. That was several hours ago, and he'd run out of argument, so he read some recipes. The sun wandered its way across the floor, slanting down though the enormous skylight.

"He's filibustering!" cried a Southerner, twisting the term to mean, for the first time, making a long speech to hold up a bill.

The sunlight and the possibility for dinner disappeared, but Campbell kept right on, by now reciting Shakespeare. This set folks' tempers on edge. First one, then another, spoke out of turn. Southerners slandered Campbell while Northerners stampeded to his defense. Neither side gave way. Voices turned bitter, language turned violent, as the air turned blue with vilification, vituperation, and plain old backstabbing.

After thirty-six hours of this balderdash, a lumbering Representative from Virginia, *Unscrupulous Model #2,* Henry Alonzo Edmundson, could take it no more. He swigged some spirits, dried his thick beard, rose from his desk, and knocked over his spindly legged chair as he moved into the aisle.

"Where you off to, Henry?" He was off to a dirty deal of the lethal kind, but he said nothing. A Representative tugged the tail of Edmundson's frock coat, but Edmundson knocked the hand away and barged up the aisle toward the white dais where Campbell still performed. About halfway there, Edmundson pulled out his pistol.

A chorus of voices rose. Three legislators grabbed Edmundson before he could shoot Campbell.

"Sergeant-at-Arms! Sergeant-at-Arms!" voices called. The sergeant arrested Edmundson. Since the commotion quieted Campbell, everybody went home.

Despite the crisis, the House of Representatives passed the Kansas-Nebraska Act, 113 to 100 on May 22 and President Pierce signed it into law May 30, 1854.

Furious Northerners, irate that Douglas's "baby" had opened the West to slavery, hung and/or burned likenesses of the Senator. From Washington, D.C., to Boston to Chicago, Douglas claimed, he rode "by the light of his burning effigy by night and in sight of his hanging effigy by day."

Douglas believed he had created territories to allow a railroad to cross the plains. Instead, his bill would release a bloodbath in Kansas that, some say, triggered the Civil War.

That colicky baby of his opened up Nebraska for settlement—but not yet what would be Harlan County. Furious Indian raiders still dominated that area. Carr and Gen. Vifquain would have to wait their turn.

Douglas might have modeled a lesson or two, for Harlan County settlers, about using long-winded oratory to lever a courthouse. To my knowledge, Harlan County folk, despite a bitter fight, hung no one in effigy. They probably couldn't decide whether to hang Thomas Harlan for railroading the county seat location or the judge who let him do it.

13

RED BLANKETS

The newly created Nebraska Territory was huge. It encompassed most of today's Nebraska plus much of Montana as well as pieces of North Dakota, South Dakota, and Colorado. Its 351,558 square miles made up more than 40 percent of the old Louisiana Purchase.

(One might expect that men chosen to govern a territory so vast would provide an admirable model for settlers like Carr and Gen. Vifquain to follow in creating Harlan County. But the model those territorial lawmakers produced, while striking, remains far from admirable, as you'll see. Obnoxious, even.)

President Pierce appointed the territory's first governor, forty-seven-year-old Francis Burt, an active Democrat. Unfortunately, Burt suffered from digestive problems, and the grueling trip from his South Carolina home to Nebraska Territory did him in. He died there in Bellevue on October 18, 1854, two days after a judge had administered the oath of office to him.

Thomas B. Cuming

Residents of Bellevue, the only town to speak of in the territory, felt shattered. They had been so sure Burt intended to make their town his capital.

Unscrupulous Model #3: Thomas B. Cuming

While settlers waited for a second governor to arrive, the territory's secretary of state became its acting governor. In a nasty twist of bad luck for Bellevue, that secretary of state was Thomas B. Cuming, twenty-five. He had been secretary of state for ten days when Governor Burt died.

Born in New York and educated in Michigan, Cuming served in the Mexican-American War. Then he wandered into Keokuk, Iowa, where he lived for six years, working as editor of the Keokuk *Dispatch*.

To accept his secretary of state job, Cuming and his Keokuk bride moved 300 miles to Council Bluffs, Iowa, and settled down. Nebraska Territory had no suitable place for them to live. Bellevue bragged about her mission and her government agency, but she housed only fifty people. Nebraska City, 40 miles south, claimed one wagon and one house and big plans for the future. There freighter Stephen Friel Nuckolls was building a majestic two-story brick structure to be Nebraska's capitol. A bad case of "if you build it, they will come."

But Council Bluffs, a hub of activity, had 2,000 people. Her prosperous merchants outfitted Mormons and 49ers for travel on the Great Platte River Road.

Cuming made friends there. These friends had hired a surveyor to lay out 320 blocks in Nebraska Territory for a new town, Omaha City. The town sat directly across the Missouri River from Council Bluffs in a wooded area that fronted on the river.

Cuming's friends urged him to make Omaha City the seat of Nebraska's territorial government.

"We'll put up a two-story building for your capitol," they said.

Already Omaha City had a hotel built by the Council Bluffers, a postman who delivered mail from his hat, a newspaper called the *Omaha Arrow,* and a claim club organized to protect the Iowans' land. The club enforced its rule by mob violence; masked vigilantes rode at night to beat up claim jumpers.

Cuming became a member. When a man named Callahan filed an illegal claim on Cuming's land, claim club members chopped a hole in Missouri River ice and dunked Callahan until he saw the error of his ways—and contracted fatal hypothermia.

Here's how Cuming made Omaha City capital of the territory.

First, he ordered a census of the eastern territory from the Niobrara River to Kansas. The rest of Nebraska's huge territory, including Harlan County, remained unbroken wilderness.

The census takers counted 2,732 people. Of the total, almost twice as many (1,818) lived south of the Platte River as lived north (914).

The Platte served as a natural border through the territory. A person couldn't ferry it: too shallow. Or ford it: its sandy bottom too soft. Or bridge it: too wide.

Next Cuming created eight counties fronting the Missouri River. He ignored population in favor of geography, distributing four counties above and four below the Platte.

Then the acting governor numbered out legislators for each county. He gave the northern counties a total of twenty-one legislators, but only eighteen to the populous southern counties. One northern county, Douglas, received twelve legislators—more than any other county.

Why?

The new town of Omaha City lay in Douglas County. Cuming wanted his capital's vote to count. And he wanted the Republican legislators from the northern counties to outvote the southern Democrats.

FIRST TERRITORIAL CAPITAL, 1855

The two-story ramshackle capitol

Members of the territorial legislature met in Omaha City, January 16, 1855, for their first session. A ramshackle capitol, the two-story brick building Cuming's friends provided, had been readied for them. A thin coat of frozen ice and mud plastered the interior walls. The uneven floor threatened to topple the heedless.

The legislature consisted of a House of Representatives and a Council. The House, with twenty-six members elected for one-year terms, met on the first floor. The Council, with thirteen members elected for two-year terms, convened on the second floor.

The Iowa gang provided school desks for the legislators; they shared, two to a desk. Red and green calico curtains dangled at the windows.

What an odd bunch of legislators would inhabit those two floors! Settlers elected many members who didn't call Nebraska Territory their home, and most other members lived in the territory briefly. Nor were these men—many in their early twenties—long on experience. One had been elected illegally at nineteen.

The first day these legislators met, the South Platters, or legislators from counties south of the Platte, couldn't wait to express their outrage against Cuming and his Omaha City capital. They filled the streets and bellyached that they were not well represented, which they weren't. To dramatize their anger, each wore a bright red blanket tossed over his shoulder.

Liquor magnified the turbulence. Soon South Platters swore that they would not attend a legislative session. Then they swore they would move the capital from Omaha City to a town south of the Platte. Come hell or high water.

~

Eventually these feisty young, transitory legislators did meet. They couldn't be bothered to create a body of laws to govern the territory. They just copied Iowa's laws, all of them, civil and criminal, even though the laws prohibited selling or drinking alcohol in a territory where men used liquor freely. Omaha City rarely enforced the new Iowa regulation, judging from the number of legislators who patronized the saloons next door to the statehouse.

Instead of creating laws, legislators squabbled over whether a member should, while in his seat in a session, drink whiskey from a bottle. They spent hours locking horns on whether to build a windbreak to run along the entire western boundary of the territory. It would run along the Continental Divide from today's Colorado to the edge of Canada's British Columbia.

The stupidest thing these young legislators managed to do was to—accidentally—repeal all the territory's laws leaving English colonial law to preside.

Members spent most of their time arguing about moving the territorial capital from Omaha City and placing it somewhere—anywhere—south of the Platte. Boosters proposed various towns, most of them "paper towns"—that is, communities planned on paper but not existing in reality. Few settled communities existed.

No wonder at the settlers' passion. So much rested on securing a territorial capital besides renown. That town would also reap the benefits of a government payroll, multiple business opportunities, and the wealth that speculation could bring.

Tempers rose so high that, in the January 1856 session, young J. Sterling Morton proposed that the land south of the Platte leave the territory and join Kansas. The U.S. Congress could use the Platte River as Kansas's north boundary, he argued. This idea had strong support among the South Platters.

The Nebraska territorial House tabled Morton's bill, but his idea didn't disappear.

These legislative sessions, often discordant, lacked any kind of decorum. Take the behavior of these legislators in their January 7, 1858, session, for instance, a clear example of *Unscrupulous Model #4*.

One legislator, Mr. Decker, decided he should chair the meeting, instead of Dr. Thrall, the official chairman. Decker waited his chance. When the doorkeeper announced the arrival of a message, Decker didn't hesitate; he moved next to Thrall and positioned himself so he, not the chairman, would receive the message.

A member objected.

"I'll have that message," Decker said, "or die right here." He snatched the gavel from Thrall, grabbed the arm of his chair and tipped it. "Down! Leave!"

Before Decker could dump Thrall from his chair, another legislator, Mr. Murphy, intervened. He grasped Decker's arm and pulled him down to the bumpy capitol floor. They scuffled, with Decker gripping the gavel and Murphy trying to twist it away. Then a Mr. Paddock rushed up, and soon all three legislators clutched the gavel.

Finally a fourth legislator, Mr. Hanscom, sneaked up behind Decker, grabbed him around the waist and rolled him under the table, breaking him from Murphy and Paddock's hold.

Thrall, using a book for a gavel, struggled to create order.

Decker stood up and acted as chairman; he tried without success to dissolve the committee and adjourn the House.

Mr. Clayes, who had the floor, harangued. Technically, the floor had been his all this time, and he hadn't wasted a minute.

Decker, still fancying himself in charge, ignored Clayes and called on a Mr. Kinney to speak. Lacking the floor, Kinney did his best: he stood on a desk and ranted.

"Get down, you," cried Thrall, still legally in charge. "You're not even a member."

Kinney dutifully clambered down, but Decker wouldn't give up. He talked his friends into creating as much disturbance as possible by strutting around the room wearing their hats.

~

Twenty-six members of the thirty-nine-member legislature, a majority, left Omaha City the next day, January 8, 1858, to meet six miles north in the town of Florence. The minority remained in Omaha City and met in the capitol. Both groups approved bills.

In Florence, legislators passed a bill to move the capital to a place at least fifty miles west of the Missouri and no more than six miles, north or south, of the Platte. The South Platters favored a settlement named Neapolis, south of the Platte, of course.

When townspeople heard Neapolis would be considered for the Nebraska Territory capital, they turned into a bundle of energy. Settlers broke the prairie, built houses, and operated a sawmill. They imagined a capitol towering 40 feet above the valley when Neapolis became "Queen City" of Nebraska.

But a new governor, the third, William A. Richardson, arrived January 12, 1858, in the middle of the Florence secession. He said in effect, "A pox on both your houses." He refused to sign bills passed in either Florence or Omaha City during the few days the lawmakers met separately. So, having accomplished nothing, the legislators went home until Richardson called them back for a special session to deal with the great confusion caused when they had abolished all the laws.

In the meantime, Morton's idea of seceding remained alive. In 1859, he called a convention in Brownville, saying that annexing South Platte with Kansas is the area's "only hope—our salvation."

By the time the territory's fourth governor arrived that May, the South Platters had become so bitter they swore they'd no longer live in the territory.

At an open meeting in Nebraska City, the south-of-the-Platte legislators decided to act. They would ask Congress and Kansas to change Kansas's northern border to the Platte River.

Soon delegates arrived in Washington, D.C., with a resolution to transfer the land south of the Platte (including what would be Harlan County) to Kansas.

Congress declined.

In Kansas, a Representative floated a bill to annex southern Nebraska, but it died in committee. So twelve South Platte delegates went to Kansas in July to argue their case. They presented thirteen pages of argument, including their strongest, that increasing the size of Kansas would make her an important state.

However, Kansas legislators feared they would import a bunch of Democrats if they incorporated southern Nebraska. Besides, they said, increasing the size of Kansas would push the center of the state north. That would not favor Topeka or Lawrence. Both settlements hoped to become Kansas's state capital. So Kansas, too, declined.

The North and South Platters continued to fight about the capital. They fought right up to the last meeting of the territorial legislature—a fierce battle where legislators again brandished both guns and fists on the capitol's floor.

So one might say that in Nebraska Territory, legislators set a strong precedent for fighting. They seemed able to do little else.

~ CHAPTER ~

14

SLAVE OR FREE?

Nebraska Territory's young legislators argued day after day about whether Nebraska should be a slave territory or free. Why? Well, when the Kansas-Nebraska Act gave settlers the right to choose or reject slavery, Nebraska legislators took that choice seriously. Knowing they must decide, they debated the topic again and again, even though in 1855, just thirteen of Nebraska's 2,732 residents were slaves.

Southern farmers who settled around Nebraska City brought most slaves to Nebraska Territory. Stephen Friel Nuckolls, who once hired Carr to freight corn, owned two slaves he'd brought from Virginia.

Nuckolls wasn't the only big slave holder. Alexander Majors of Russell, Majors and Waddell—the plains' largest freighter that soon would be famous for its Pony Express— lived in Nebraska City, and so did the six slaves Majors brought from Kansas City, Missouri.

Clearly those imported slaves didn't cotton to their lives here.

On November 25, 1858, both Nuckolls's women ran away. Nuckolls raged, offered $200 reward, and, with a U.S. Marshall's help, searched for them. One slave, Eliza, escaped to Chicago. There a mob rescued her from arrest. She fled to Canada. Nuckolls never saw either slave again.

On June 30, 1860, all of Majors's slaves disappeared and never came back, even though the freighter offered $1,000 to return his six.

Majors's and Nuckolls's slaves probably escaped via the Underground Railroad, a path used by runaway slaves on their way to Canada. They may have stopped on the Allen Mayhew farm near Nebraska City. There Mayhew had built a cabin from hand-hewn cottonwood trees. Then he dug a room beneath the main cabin; the only way to enter was through a tunnel from a nearby ravine.

Mayhew's Underground Railroad cabin

As many as fourteen slaves could hide by day in Mayhew's underground cave. After resting, the runaways cut across the Missouri River and headed to Tabor, Iowa, where a community of abolitionists supported another stop on the Underground Railroad.

By 1860, Nebraska's territorial population had shot up to 28,841. That included eighty-one Negroes, but only ten were slaves.

Soon after this, the slavery question became moot in Nebraska Territory, for in January 1861, the legislators, after debating for six years, passed an act outlawing slavery in the territory.

~

Who wouldn't want Nebraska Territory to become a state?

Quite a few people, oddly enough, despite the fact that to become a state and play on the national stage was quite the thing to do. Even Nevada became a state.

And Nebraska looked like today's state. Her once huge territory had been sharply reduced in size as Colorado, Dakota, and Idaho territories bit into it.

But many people opposed statehood. Democrats, for instance, swung out against it. "Becoming a state's an expensive luxury," they argued. "Can we afford it? Think about it. We'll have to pay a bunch of new state taxes, and on top of them, a heap of federal taxes."

Even so, late in 1859 both Republicans and Democrats declared for immediate statehood. In January 1860, Nebraska's territorial legislature called a special March 5 election to decide whether to call a convention to create a state constitution.

The closer election day came, the more second thoughts arose in politicians of both stripes. They loaded up the ballot with so many additional propositions and questions that even a sharp-witted lawyer would flounder.

Nevertheless, voters dutifully selected convention delegates. Republicans won 40 of the 52 delegate slots. But Nebraska's citizens didn't much cotton to a constitutional convention. They defeated it by 638 votes: 2,732 to 2,094.

So Nebraska's first attempt at statehood failed.

Yet, help sprouted in Chicago when a dyed-in-the-wool Republican, Alvin Saunders, met Abraham Lincoln. A man with deep-set eyes and a Greek nose, Saunders became an avid Lincoln booster. That enthusiasm paid off when Lincoln, just after he became president, named Saunders governor of Nebraska Territory. He became the fifth territorial governor.

However, the new governor's first proclamation in 1861 had nothing to do with statehood. Instead, he called to Nebraska's counties to muster regiments to fight in the Civil War.

In January 1864, Nebraska's territorial legislators asked Congress to pass legislation that would make their statehood possible.

This request stirred interest on Capitol Hill. The Radical Republicans there, our *Unscrupulous Model #5,* needed the votes of new states to reelect Lincoln, a Republican, in November. They required extra support because of Lincoln's moderate policies for reconstructing the South. He had just approved a policy allowing plantation owners to hire their former slaves to cultivate plantations again.

Nebraska, with its strong well-known Republican governor and a Republican majority in its legislature, seemed an ideal candidate for a new state. So these Radicals pushed a bill that authorized Nebraskans to form a new state. The bill, called the Enabling Act, passed April 19, 1864.

In it, Congress directed the territory to hold a constitutional convention to hash out statehood questions, so Governor Saunders ordered a June 6 election to choose 52 convention delegates. Statehood opponents worked feverishly to endorse a slate of antistatehood candidates. Their strategy worked. When the elected convention members met in Omaha in the territorial capitol July 4, they voted only once, 37 to 7, to adjourn immediately without framing a constitution.

This second defeat surprised only the naïve.

With the end of his first term in sight, Governor Saunders announced that he would not seek a second term. The territorial legislators didn't want to see him go. He was the only Nebraska territorial governor who had not died or resigned while still in office. The legislators unanimously petitioned President Lincoln to reappoint Governor Saunders.

The President signed the requested reinstatement paper and left his office to go to Ford Theater to see the popular play *Our American Cousin*. Fatally shot there by John Wilkes Booth, Lincoln never returned to his office. But the paper he'd signed lay on his desk bearing what's believed to be his last signature.

Governor Saunders stayed on for a second term.

In his second term, Governor Alvin Saunders—only forty-nine despite his snowy white hair and beard—decided to push Nebraska Territory to become a state. When he spoke to the Assembly of Council members and Representatives on January 9, 1866, he parted his tight lips to devote a portion of his message to that subject.

"We can't delay statehood forever. Our territory is filling up." Governor Saunders's stony eyes wandered over his young audience, some twisting in their seats. He sped up his delivery. "When we're a state, we'll become part of a national community. Our senators and representatives in Congress will give us an influential voice in policies and legislation that affect us. So why should we deny ourselves advantages of statehood and equal representation in Congress?"

A few days later, the Republican governor met in his office with a couple of Republicans he could trust. These territorial Republicans become our *Unscrupulous Model #6*. Their meeting might have gone like this:

"You made a stirring argument for becoming a state, Alvin," said Clayton, the governor's number one ally. He tugged on his shiny black silk vest and lowered himself cautiously into a chair.

"Really? Sometimes I think those legislators can't see beyond dollars. 'More state taxes, more federal taxes,' that's their song."

"Gus," standing by the window, guffawed, "'Their song.' That's a good line." At thirty-one, Gus was at least a decade younger than Alvin and Clayton. He was given to outbursts, but he could be useful, with his Democratic friends, so Alvin had invited him, too.

The governor spread his hands on his desk. "Congress says we must call another constitutional convention, but you know and I know a third convention would be as dead in the water as the first two."

Clayton nodded as Alvin continued. "Now those monkeys in the Assembly..."

"Current gentlemen excepted," Clayton's voice ended in a slight squeal.

"Of course." Alvin tugged on his white beard, flat as a pancake. "We can't trust those monkeys to write a constitution. They'd have us living under English colonial law again."

Gus laughed. "So what are we going to do? Write a constitution ourselves?"

Alvin and Clayton swiveled to look at Gus standing by the window in his flashy patterned vest, his auburn sideburns plowing into his mustache.

Alvin slapped his leg, "By God, Gus, you've read my mind! Not you and me, exactly."

"Someone's got to do it," Gus cried.

"The three of us could do it, all right, plus a couple of lawyers good with words."

"A good idea." Clayton shifted in his chair and crossed his plump ankles. "But then what are you going to do, Alvin? Try to send it through the legislature? Can't trust those legislators any further than you can toss a buffalo."

"Maybe we'll have to force it through."

"Candle to the devil," Gus cried. "That's a spanking good idea!"

The two men stared at him.

"Finagling would never work with those legislators. We got to ram that thing through. Those monkeys will never know what hit them. I'll talk to J. R. He'll help us. He's a master of persuasion. Doesn't even twist an arm."

Gus was right about J.R. Porter's persuasive powers. Porter was also the only Democrat of prominence in the Council, and the Republicans had to have a Democrat on their side.

~

So these men, or some like them, plus some lawyers—a self-appointed committee—met secretly in Omaha in Experience Estabrook's office to create a state constitution.

Experience Estabrook, what a name! In 1855, President Franklin Pierce appointed Estabrook the first District Attorney for the newly organized Nebraska Territory. This year, Governor Saunders had just appointed Estabrook, now fifty-three, to codify Nebraska laws.

These territorial Republicans didn't spend much time drafting a new constitution. They just modeled their new state constitution on the outdated territorial one, changing a word or two here or there to bring it up to date.

"We got to be careful," Alvin said. "It's not enough to push this constitution through the legislature. We've got voters to persuade, after that."

"Damned if I'm going to be beaten again by frugal voters afraid of the cost of state government." Clayton pushed his little round glasses up his nose. His cheeks turned red.

"I think you're right. A respectable state government would scare folks. We've got to give them their government cheap."

So they did. They created state government taken directly from the territorial model of the Kansas-Nebraska Act. They added not one office more than the territory had. The state's executive officers—governor, secretary of state, auditor, and treasurer—were the same as those in the territory. The judicial system remained three members serving as district judges and as a supreme court. The legislature was a thirteen-member Senate and a thirty-nine-member House of Representatives modeled after the Territorial Assembly with its Council and its House.

Clearly statehood would involve no great dislocation, not even in salaries.

New state legislators would get $3 a day for up to forty days a session, and salaries for the government officials, even by 1860s standards, were minimal.

"The constitution's so primitive," Experience observed. "Can't be very workable."

Alvin thought a bit. "You may be right, Experience, but we can deal with that after we've become a state."

Next the secretive Republicans had to take care of J. Sterling Morton. He presided over the Nebraska Democratic Party and had for decades, ever since he'd led the South Platters' struggle to leave Nebraska and join Kansas. Like most local Democrats, he was dead set against statehood.

Morton also doggedly opposed voting rights for African Americans (as we say today). He couldn't stomach that national Republicans on Capitol Hill wanted to pass a civil rights act giving voting rights to every man born in the United States, without exception. If that act passed, every man could vote just as though he were white.

So for Morton, the Republicans made one more change in their constitution. They limited voting rights to "free white males."

~

Now to ram that constitution through the Territorial Assembly.

Governor Saunders gave their document to Gus's friend, J. R. Porter. He introduced it in the Council (the upper house) February 5. The Council referred the constitution to a special committee of Porter and two other legislators. They reported it back the same day, but early enough so the legislators could pass it before adjourning. They passed the constitution by a 7 to 6 vote, with the president breaking the tie.

On to the House it went. The House didn't bother to refer the constitution to a committee. Four days later, the representatives approved it.

Had the Republicans rammed it through the Assembly?

Consider this. Oddly enough, few legislators had more than a foggy notion of the constitution's provisions, for they voted on a constitution none of them had read. No printed version existed. And legislators could offer no amendments; the Republicans permitted none.

On February 9, Governor Saunders signed the bill. Only the election remained: the last hurdle for the local Republicans.

Cautiously, legislators presented the question of a state constitution to Nebraska Territory voters in a June 2 election.

The voters kicked it out again.

Oh, wait a minute! Get this. Here comes an election outcome determined by those who count the votes rather than by those who cast them.

Those Republicans in Cass County, the board of canvassers, checking to see that all was in order, chucked all the votes of one precinct, the Rock Bluffs precinct. Threw out 157 votes. On technical grounds. Just so happened that 107 of those votes were Democratic.

But canvassers let the heavily pro-Republican vote at Plattsmouth stand, even though it exhibited the same technical irregularity.

Then there was nothing they could do but accept the soldier vote from Fort Kearny—almost unanimously Republican.

Surprise! Those changes reversed the territorial vote from a Republican loss to a Republican victory. Voters had now magically "ratified" the constitution 3,938 to 3,838.

Indeed, Republicans won almost all the entire re-counted ticket. The new count reversed the election for state governor. Now Republican David C. Butler, who had been trailing popular J. Sterling Morton, the Democratic candidate, amazingly won by 109 votes.

When the Republicans announced results, civil war nearly broke out in Nebraska. Democrats shouted, "Fraud! The Republicans stole this crooked election!" But the hue and cry availed nothing. No one ever offered an adequate defense of what happened. However, the Republicans now could submit the "official" constitution to Washington, D.C., and bring Nebraska into the United States as a Republican state.

~

Nebraska's state constitution, now "ratified" by voters, barreled to Washington for approval. It arrived to find Capitol Hill in shambles. Andrew Johnson, Lincoln's vice president and a Democrat from Tennessee, had become president. The Radical Republicans who dominated Congress despised their new dour, rigid, combative president. They fought like cats and dogs.

Johnson intended to carry out Lincoln's plan of reconstruction, a plan that would bring Southern states back in the Union with full rights, as if the war had never happened, but the Radical Republicans sought harsher terms. They wanted Southern states to become territories again, each ruled by a military government.

In May 1865, Johnson pardoned all the rebels but the leaders and restored their property, except for slaves. He called upon each rebel Southern state to assemble a convention of white representatives to write a new constitution and plan its government. Then the states could seek permission to return to the Union. Like the Nebraska constitution, none of these state constitutions granted black men the right to vote.

The Radicals in Congress fumed. Unlike Johnson, these Republicans favored voting and other rights for the newly freed slaves. In February 1866, Congress passed a bill to distribute land to ex-slaves, create schools for their children, and use military courts to protect their rights. Johnson, who was, after all, a Southerner, vetoed it. Congress attempted to override his veto but failed.

On George Washington's birthday, a few days after his veto, the president spoke to a crowd gathered outside the White House. He accused "rebels" in Congress with plotting to take over the government. And he named names.

His speech solidified the Republicans. They whispered "impeachment."

The following month, Congress passed the Civil Rights Act of 1866, which granted citizenship, including the right to vote, to every male citizen no matter what his race.

Johnson, who didn't believe ex-slaves should vote, claimed the bill violated state's rights and vetoed it.

Then, to the amazement of many, Congress did what had never been done before in all ninety years of American history. It overturned a presidential veto.

Congressional powers rose. That summer, Congress sent the Fourteenth Amendment, which they had passed, to be ratified by state legislatures. The Amendment included their Civil Rights Act, granting every male, including ex-slaves, the right to vote.

"Impeachment" whispers became talk. The Radicals counted their votes. With just two more votes, they'd have the two-thirds majority needed to impeach Johnson.

Then into Congress came a bill that would admit Nebraska as a state, a Republican state that would add two more Republican Senators to Congress.

Democrats weren't enthusiastic about admitting a Republican state. However, in the last hurried days of the session, the bill passed both houses of Congress.

Johnson, dead set against bringing in a state that would give the Republicans two more Senators, enough to impeach him, vetoed the bill, so Nebraska didn't become a state in 1866.

In the next year, the Nebraska bill returned to Capitol Hill. This time, the Radical Republicans noticed that the state constitution limited voting rights to white males.

So eager were the Radicals to get Nebraska's two Republican votes that they rewrote our state constitution—a highly irregular act—so it included the vote for black males. They sent the revised constitution to the president to sign.

Johnson, fighting for his political life against the growing movement to impeach him, argued that Congress had no right to tell a state what its constitution should be. He vetoed the bill.

Congress promptly overrode Johnson's veto. Then the Radical Republicans asked Nebraska if it would rather have its original "white male" vote. Or statehood.

Governor Saunders called a meeting February 20, 1867, to consider the question. Some of Nebraska's territorial legislators put up a fight—can you believe this?—against accepting the Radical Republicans' terms, but eventually chose statehood.

Or at least the local Republicans chose it; they had the majority.

Then President Johnson had no choice but to proclaim, on March 1, 1867, that Nebraska was the nation's newest state, the thirty-seventh.

Was President Johnson impeached?

You bet.

On February 24, 1868, the House of Representatives voted to impeach Johnson, listing eleven examples of his "high crimes and misdemeanors." Never before had a U.S. president been impeached, and it would be the last time until Bill Clinton 131 years later.

The Senate tried Johnson, who didn't appear in person. Conviction would mean his removal from office. The trial began March 5 and continued for eleven trying weeks.

During that drawn-out stretch, the president's enemies had time to reconsider his impeachment. One Radical Republican, Edmund G. Ross, age forty-one, a "Free Stater" from Kansas, decided to change his vote to not guilty. You can imagine the monumental pressure Ross received from fellow Radical Republicans. "A vote to acquit Johnson," they warned, "will end your political career."

But on May 16, when the Senate called on Ross, he stood up and said, "Not guilty." His voice reverberated in the packed room.

So Ross's single vote ended Johnson's impeachment. Despite those two additional Republican votes from Nebraska, the president remained in office.

And did Ross's vote end his political career? No way. He became a Democrat and went on to be governor of New Mexico's territory.

PART IV

Taming the Wild Tribes

15

THE "FIGHTING PARSON"

Even though Nebraska had become a state, men like General Victor Vifquain and William Parker Carr couldn't settle yet in what would be Harlan County. Why not? It was overrun by and surrounded by many angry wild tribes of the Great Plains.

Take, for instance, Tall Bull. That leader of the Cheyenne Dog Soldiers, those fierce plains warriors, wouldn't give in.

"Just sign this paper," White Man said. But Tall Bull refused to write away his freedom.

"Go to the reservation with us," Chief Black Kettle said, but instead Tall Bull and his soldiers took their 165 lodges and broke away from Black Kettle's Cheyenne tribe.

Tall Bull, of course, claimed the White Man started it. Remembering put the Cheyenne leader in a nasty mood.

The wild tribes—Cheyenne, Arapaho, and Sioux— hadn't minded when trappers, explorers, and traders showed up on their land. Some trappers became husbands for their women; traders introduced fire water and guns.

Tall Bull, Cheyenne leader of the Dog Soldiers

But the three tribes did mind when White Man set in motion the twin scourges of smallpox and cholera. The Arapaho lost so many people that the Sioux's losses seemed slight by comparison. But the Cheyenne lost 2,000, more than half its population.

And the wild tribes certainly minded when government agents rounded up bands and stuck them on reservations.

In 1854, when the Kansas-Nebraska Act opened Nebraska Territory to settlement, would-be settlers pounded down the Great Platte River Road. Immigrants stole tribes' horses and hunted on their grounds. The frequent wagon trains split the massive buffalo herds in two, making the huge animals difficult to pursue.

Every year the Great Platte River Road traffic got heavier, from hundreds to thousands to tens of thousands of people: immigrants in wagon trains, stagecoaches full of travelers, freighters, Pony Express riders, soldiers. Along the road, white men built hundreds of ranches and stagecoach stations to accommodate these voyagers.

Tall Bull could hardly ignore such belligerent behavior.

Then it got worse.

Enter the "Fighting Parson," John Milton Chivington. A revival meeting swayed Chivington, twenty-one, to join the Methodist Episcopal Church; he became a minister. As a preacher in Missouri before the Civil War, Ohio-bred Chivington angered his congregation. He held fire-and-brimstone antislavery views while his pro-slavery members did not agree. When they sent him a threatening letter, telling him to stop preaching or they'd tar and feather him, Chivington came to church packing a Bible and two pistols.

"By the grace of God and these two revolvers," he cried, "I am going to preach here today!"

Preach he did. Afterward, folks dubbed him the Fighting Parson. Some called him "a crazy preacher who thinks he is Napoleon Bonaparte." The church sent him to safety in Omaha, Nebraska.

In Omaha until 1860, Chivington then moved to Denver City, a two-year-old mining town in Indian Territory on civilization's brink. There he founded a congregation. When the Colorado First Regiment tried to name him their chaplain, he refused, insisting on fighting rather than preaching. Soon he replaced the colonel for the Colorado Volunteers.

After a Denver newspaper advocated exterminating Indians, those red devils, Col. Chivington sang the same song.

Col. John Chivington

"Damn any man who sympathizes with Indians!" he roared. "I believe it is right and honorable to use any means under God's heaven to kill them." And he meant it.

~

Black Kettle and White Antelope, Cheyenne chiefs, wanted peace with the whites. So did some Arapaho chiefs. So they met with Col. Chivington and John Evans, governor of Colorado Territory, at Camp Weld near Denver City September 26, 1864. There the Indian chiefs promised to give up land deeded to them by the U.S. government and move to Oklahoma to live on a reservation along the Arkansas River.

As part of the bargain, the Indians traveled 200 miles to a key military post on the Santa Fe Trail. At Fort Lyon, believing the whites also wanted peace, they turned in their arms. Then the 800 Indians, Cheyenne and Arapaho, moved 40 miles from the fort, to Sand Creek in the southeastern plains of Colorado Territory. There they waited for the day they would move to Oklahoma.

Over his Sand Creek lodge, Black Kettle hung a massive American flag given to him by Abraham Lincoln who had promised it would protect the Indians from harm. Black Kettle also flew the white flag of surrender to mark his camp as friendly and to prevent careless attack by passing soldiers.

When the camp ran short on food late that November, a band of Cheyenne and Arapaho men rode off to hunt buffalo. They left behind chiefs Black Kettle and White Antelope with women and children plus men either too young or too old for the hunt.

At the same time in Denver, Col. Chivington rounded up a company of 700 cavalry, mostly claim jumpers, street toughs, and assorted riff raff. He rode with them 200 miles to Fort Lyon. There, ignoring fort officers' protests, Col. Chivington commandeered several hundred more soldiers. They all set out for Black Kettle's camp, only 40 miles away, the men riding and drinking, repeatedly toasting their anticipated victory. They rode much of the night.

Before dawn November 29, Col. Chivington positioned his troops, now 1,000 strong, and his four howitzers in a circle around Black Kettle's campsite. Soldiers loaded the cannon with grapeshot, which is made of small round balls joined in clusters, Napoleon's favorite. Grapeshot, when fired, spreads out, spraying a chosen area. It's superb at short range against a mass of people.

The soldiers' activity woke the Cheyenne and Arapaho; fearful, they bounded from their lodges half-dressed. Shivering in the icy morning air, the Indians gathered under the massive American flag above Black Kettle's lodge.

Old and young braves surrounded the huddled women and children while Chief White Antelope, at seventy-five a respected elder, ran toward the soldiers. He held up his hands and cried, "Stop! Stop!" in his impeccable English. When the white men failed to stop, White Antelope folded his arms and waited.

The howitzers, aimed at the cluster of people, fired. The grapeshot battered men, women, and children.

After the smoke cleared, soldiers leaped from their horses and charged, shooting and slashing, hunting down those still alive like rabbits.

"Okay to kill the children?" a soldier asked.

"Yes," Col. Chivington famously replied. "Nits breed lice." He wanted victory, not prisoners, and so his soldiers killed every Indian who hadn't escaped.

When dawn turned quiet, soldiers readied knives. In a bloody frenzy, they scalped the corpses, they carved them, they disemboweled them no matter whether they were women, children, or infants, mutilating each in some way.

Soldiers severed fingers, noses, and ears. They sliced off women's breasts. They knocked out brains. They carved off sex organs—women's, children's, and especially men's.

White Antelope's body lay in the creek bed. One of Col. Chivington's street toughs had sliced off the chief's nose, his ears, and his testicles, which the soldier waggled, "I'll make 'em into a tobacco pouch!"

By the time Col. Chivington and his men finished hacking, the sun had risen. They adorned their weapons, gear, and hats with scalps and body parts. Some displayed female trophies on sticks. Some wore rings they'd stolen from dead fingers. Some exhibited fetuses.

Before the soldiers left, Col. Chivington's men liberated the contents of the tepees, stole the horses, and set fire to the remainder of the camp.

No one knows how many Cheyenne and Arapaho the soldiers killed. The conservative say only seventy, but other estimates are in the hundreds with the highest at 600 dead. Ten soldiers died, most by friendly fire from besotted companions.

When Col. Chivington and his gang reached Denver, they hastened to the Apollo Theater and saloons, presenting their battle trophies and bragging.

"We took on the Dog Soldiers and whipped them," Col. Chivington lied.

That impressed his listeners who knew the fierce Dog Soldiers, those notorious raiders and killers of white settlers.

But Tall Bull's Cheyenne soldiers weren't in Colorado. They had pitched camps in the Republican River valley in Nebraska or in the Smoky Hill valley in Kansas, hunting buffalo and planning plunder.

Slowly, word of the Sand Creek Battle spread: the Denver soldiers had scalped and disemboweled hundreds of Cheyenne and Arapaho, mostly women, elderly, or children. It was not a victory but an atrocity.

Col. Chivington resigned from the military.

The Colorado governor quit.

Congress held an investigation.

And the Sand Creek Massacre, as this savage dirty deal became known, infuriated the wild tribes so much that they launched a full-scale payback.

~ CHAPTER ~
# 16

PAYBACK FOR SAND CREEK

Sand Creek survivors, plus those who had hunted buffalo and been saved, fled 200 miles north. Early in December, they stopped in Cherry Creek valley at the Arapaho's favorite campground. Their camp lay so near Denver City, Indians heard player pianos; miners, trollops, and gamblers, departing through a saloon's swinging doors, saw tips of Arapaho tepees jutting above the prairie grassland.

Runners, bearing the Arapaho's war pipe, sped from Cherry Creek to Tall Bull's Smoky Hill River camp in Kansas Territory. There Tall Bull and Pawnee Killer, chief of a Sioux band, learned about the massacre and smoked the pipe, sending criers to other camps to announce a plan for war.

On short notice, some 3,000 Indians—Cheyenne, Arapaho, Sioux—gathered in the Cherry Creek encampment.

By New Year's Day, the chiefs had set their goal. They ignored the nearby tough little mining town of Denver City as insignificant. Instead, they located their payback in much more valuable Old Julesburg, 200 miles up the South Platte

River. Several overland routes intersected at Julesburg and a large stagecoach company headquartered there, making the town an important transportation center. Julesburg also boasted a telegraph office, a warehouse, and a large store.

January 7, 1865, a thousand warriors, ablaze with war paint, set out from Cherry Creek. They systematically burned stagecoach stations along the South Platte River all the way to Julesburg. That halted overland communication.

Before they attacked Julesburg, the warriors stopped at its neighbor, four-month-old Camp Rankin. The fort held a modest number of military troops, but from its depot flowed government supplies for a region that stretched 150 miles along the South Platte River.

Camp Rankin's sod buildings

The camp's jumble of sod huts hid sixty men behind a sod wall 18 feet high. Rather than attempt to attack this impenetrable fort, the warriors planned to ambush. They picked ten men to act as decoys. The ten charged the fort, and then retreated.

Soldiers poured out of Camp Rankin and chased the decoys 3 miles, or almost to the planned point of attack. Then some trigger-happy young braves couldn't wait to fire at the soldiers. When their guns blasted, the army captain spotted a formidable group of Indians half-hidden behind the bluffs. He wheeled his horse; so did his soldiers. Warriors swarmed from the bluffs, in hot pursuit.

By happy chance for the soldiers, warriors tended to aim their rifles and revolvers so high, they often missed their shots. However, bows and arrows proved deadly. The Indians cut off and killed a few men who had dismounted to defend themselves. Altogether, eighteen soldiers failed to return to the fort.

"We killed sixty Indians!" the soldiers claimed. No, they killed none, insisted the warriors.

Outside the fort, camp civilians ran a stage station, store, and warehouse. The wild tribes looted these buildings; civilians, sheltered in the fort, watched Indians carry off an impressive amount of plunder. Then the warriors headed for nearby Julesburg.

Fifty men lived there, fifty men "armed to the teeth" to protect their property. Certain that Indians never fight in winter, the white men couldn't believe their initial view of Indians.

And Indians there were! A thousand warriors poured from the bluffs, filled the valley. Stampeded livestock. Shattered windows, smashed doors, demolished furniture. Robbed the stagecoach, left bullet holes in its sides. Attacked a mule train. Fought for six hours.

Still, the wild tribes persisted. They raided all along the South Platte River, to the east, to the west. More ferocious than ever, they attacked a ranch or a stagecoach station every few miles.

Then, toting their loot, the warriors returned to the Cherry Creek encampment. The Cheyenne and the Arapaho, still in mourning for the loss of so many of their people, took heart when they saw warriors bringing badly needed goods.

When the sun set, the warriors portrayed their victory with a dance. They circled and stamped, yelling and whooping their war cry, becoming tumultuous as they danced. Then they gestured to show how they had carved up the enemy. Finally they ground their teeth, hissed and gurgled to mimic the sounds of death in battle.

Women had prepared the scalps the warriors brought to the camp by stretching them and mounting each on a frame. The Plains Indians believed that every piece of skin and hair contained the spirit of the man who'd lost his scalp. The women hung the skins on top of poles to prepare for their dance, a ritual ceremony of cleansing, a lively cheerful scalp dance, performed after the victory dance.

Dancing and feasting continued by the gleam of lighted staffs. The young people in particular danced until dawn, celebrating the victory and thanking the spirits for their support.

A cheerful scalp dance

Still the payback for the Sand Creek Massacre continued.

Early in February, warriors returned to Julesburg. There fifteen soldiers and fifty civilians hid in Camp Rankin as the Indians helped themselves to the town's remaining supplies, then set each building on fire. Soon all of Julesburg blazed until their buildings burned to the ground.

The Julesburg telegraph station, no longer in Julesburg, escaped the firestorm. When the warriors found the station, now located near Camp Rankin, they invaded it.

Batteries replenished by nitric acid powered the telegraph. When the Indians spotted jars full of extra nitric acid, they assumed those jars contained alcohol. Of course they chugalugged them.

What potent fire water!

It burned their lips, mouths, and throats! The Indians smashed the jars on the floor. There the acid ate through their moccasins. Dashing outdoors gave them no relief nor did their high-step dancing.

Once the nitric acid wore off, the warriors went home proud of themselves. They never could win back the Cheyenne and Arapaho who died at Sand Creek, but they surely killed as many as they had lost.

(Their payback for Sand Creek proved, of course, to be a massive dirty deal for white military men and civilians. Dirty deals often prove one-sided like that.)

~ CHAPTER ~
# 17

INCANDESCENT GLORY

William Parker Carr and General Victor Vifquain soon would settle in the Republican River valley. First, however, the military had to get rid of the valley's wild tribes. But the army couldn't do that until it cleared out the larger, more important Great Platte River Road that followed the Platte River. Washington gave that task to Brigadier General Robert B. Mitchell.

Poor Brig. Gen. Mitchell. The rascal so wanted to make a name for himself. He'd fought in the Mexican-American War, but only as a second lieutenant. He'd led a regiment in the Civil War only to be shot from his horse. And now, in the winter of 1864, too injured to return to the Civil War, he'd been named commander of this God-forsaken back country, the army's Nebraska district.

April 1864, the army tagged him for a "Big Talk" with the Great Sioux Nation, to persuade the Indians to stop plundering travelers on the Great Platte River Road.

Brig. Gen. Mitchell anticipated no trouble. Telling the Sioux to keep clear of the Platte River valley, how hard could

Brigadier General Robert B. Mitchell

that be? As a brigadier general he knew how to command. So he mounted his horse and rode west from his Omaha headquarters to Fort Cottonwood, nearly 300 miles. The fort, a year old, lay halfway between Fort Kearny and Julesburg.

An aid described the general as "dashing," but at forty, he showed signs of wear. A receding hairline exaggerated his high forehead. Tiny close-set eyes gazed out of a badgerlike face, but his beard, a wide waterfall of dark hair, remained magnificent.

So, that April 17 at the fort, he had talked with several Sioux chiefs, heard their tedious complaints. They didn't like the way alcohol flowed into their camps. They didn't like the way U.S. surveyors crawled around the Niobrara River. Who could negotiate with such barbarians?

Chief Spotted Tail

Brig. Gen. Mitchell discovered that he could not stand Indians. Perhaps he could have tolerated them if they had decent manners, but they did not. Underfoot at Fort Cottonwood, the Sioux grabbed shiny objects, begged, and of course stole. And stared. He had ordered fort soldiers not to copulate with the filthy squaws, but that stopped no one.

At the "Big Talk," when his turn came to speak, the general barked out: "Steer clear of the Platte River valley."

Instead of embracing Brig. Gen. Mitchell's order, Chief Spotted Tail said, "We're willing and able to give the white men all the war they want."

That puzzled the general. "Why did he threaten?"

"You've shredded their pride," the fort commander said.

Their pride. How disgusting!

The commander's feast cooled tempers, but the conference, Brig. Gen. Mitchell knew, had been an abysmal failure. He had won nothing but a promise to meet again.

So on May 26, he rode again through the prairie wasteland to Fort Cottonwood, knowing he must struggle to polish his tarnished reputation as a negotiator. This time he agreed to withdraw those Niobrara surveyors, and he ordered additions to the Sioux payment: molasses, hard bread, bacon. But again, matters spiraled downward.

The chiefs demanded that white men get out of Sioux hunting grounds between the Arkansas and the upper Missouri rivers. What kinds of fools were they? That would mean abandoning the Great Platte River Road with its telegraph lines, mail routes, stagecoaches, immigrant wagons, and gold seekers. Impossible!

So Brigadier General Mitchell upped his demands: not only stay out of the Platte River valley, but also keep your young braves in line.

"An incentive might work better than a threat," the fort commander said, but the general disagreed.

The upshot? Brig. Gen. Mitchell had to negotiate a third time. It would be his last. On this visit, the general brought with him a troop of Pawnee scouts. Frank North, a young clerk at the Pawnee Agency store, had organized the scouts. North spoke the Pawnee language and acted as an interpreter, while the Pawnee, keen fans of the United States, scouted for the army.

The general needed the extra clout. The Sioux had joined with two other more hostile "wild tribes," the Cheyenne and the Arapaho, who encouraged their young braves to raid up and down the Great Platte River Road.

Frank North and his Pawnee scouts

But as Brig. Gen. Mitchell rode to the fort, he sensed he was on a fool's errand. And he was. Nothing, it turned out, could have been worse than bringing Pawnee to face their long-established enemies, the Sioux.

The moment they saw each other, both bands harangued and threatened until the fort commander had to separate them by a line of troops.

When neither tribe would stop its tirade, the general ordered the Sioux to clear out. As they left, he realized that he had pushed the Sioux deeper into the grasp of the belligerent Cheyenne and Arapaho. That failed day burned like salt on an open wound.

As Brig. Gen. Mitchell saw it, he now faced a hopeless situation: to protect the overland mail route along the Great

Platte River Road. To do this he had strung out along that 500-mile route only 680 soldiers, thanks to the Civil War, but he faced thousands of Sioux, Arapaho, Cheyenne, Apache, Comanche, and white outlaws.

When the war department, responding to the Indians' "payback" on Julesburg, told Brig. Gen. Mitchell to lead a stalking expedition into Republican River country, to find and deal with those Cheyenne, Arapaho, and Sioux, he must have felt ecstatic at the possibility of warfare rather than negotiation.

The general knew that many Indians, some said 4,000, lurked in the Republican River valley. The river, which ran catty corner across what would be Harlan County, provided excellent hiding places. Its numerous spring-fed tributaries, creeks we now call Sappa, Spring, and Turkey, sliced so deeply into the earth that their steep banks created concealed shelters. These the Indians considered ideal for thwarting unexpected enemy attacks or ambushing the heedless.

The general's opportunity to prove himself seemed simple enough. He and a hundred or so soldiers would leave Fort Cottonwood, angle south into Kansas, follow the Republican River back into Nebraska, and scatter the wild tribes.

His goal: to keep the Sioux, Cheyenne, and Arapaho on the run so they couldn't mount an offensive on the Great Platte River Road. Chasing the Indians would be more effective than engaging them. Their horses could outrun government mounts; Indians often carried better arms than Brig. Gen. Mitchell's soldiers had.

At Fort Cottonwood, the general pulled together 640 cavalry, some howitzers, and 200 supply wagons. He and his men departed January 16, 1865, expecting to be gone twelve days. He marched his troops south and west, determined to flush out those redskins who burned Julesburg.

From early each day until nightfall, soldiers searched for hostile tribes but found none. Oh here and there, they spotted a lone Indian acting as a scout. After three days, they discovered the Arapaho camp on Cherry Creek near Denver City, but no one lived there, and hadn't for several days. Later one night, a small Indian band rode through Brig. Gen. Mitchell's camp, shot into the tents, and left before the soldiers could catch anyone. And the soldiers saw plenty of Indian trails crisscrossing theirs, hopelessly tangled trails. Stopping to untangle them felt asinine.

Instead of savage wild tribes, soldiers encountered brutally cold weather. Temperatures hung low on the trail both day and night, once dropping to minus twenty degrees Fahrenheit. Frostbite incapacitated more than fifty soldiers. Even the horses shivered; their hides quivered like flags against their bones. Soldiers, chilled to the marrow, trembled under their uniforms. Men crept from their pup tents to squat near campfires. Some nights they sat until dawn rather than freeze to death.

When Brig. Gen. Mitchell realized he could not execute the war department's order, he brought his shivering soldiers and horses home early. Damn! He'd fizzled out again.

Back in Fort Cottonwood, the general stewed. What sort of frontier soldier was he that he couldn't find those Indians? He plunged into depression, but not for long. Instead, he justified his actions. What sort of hardship would it be for the wild tribes if he had kept them on the move? Not much. They were more used to blasts of frigid air than his men were. Even being moved around would be a mild penalty for their depredations along the South Platte River.

Soon he hit upon a better solution.

Fire.

He would burn them out.

January 27, Brig. Gen. Mitchell launched his incendiary plan. He telegraphed military commanders from Fort Kearny in Nebraska to Julesburg, Colorado, and ordered them to set the prairie on fire that evening at sundown.

As the sun slipped out of the sky, soldiers at Fort Kearny, Fort Cottonwood, the Station Post, and the post at Julesburg, fired the prairie along 300 miles. The men kindled the grass a variety of ways, but most chose to set a bale of hay on fire and drag it across the prairie behind a horse.

Among the grasses they ignited was Little Bluestem, now Nebraska's state grass. Then it carpeted the prairie. When dry, as it was that January, bluestem is highly flammable. Combustion must have seemed instantaneous as splashes of radiant splendor trailed the bales.

The fires raced across the prairie, coaxed by a strong northwest wind. Soon the separate conflagrations joined in one huge blaze. It "rolled as a vast confluent sheet of flame to the south," Eugene F. Ware remembered. He rode out from Fort Cottonwood to watch the impressive scene. The fire spread, as Brig. Gen. Mitchell planned, until it enveloped the Republican River refuge of the Sioux, Cheyenne, and Arapaho.

The Indians no doubt saw it coming. A fire that size burning on the edge of night is visible for miles. "Lightning," they must have thought since lightning commonly ignites prairie fires. At any rate, they split.

Moving on is what a nomad does best. If the general could have seen the fleeing Indians, he would have felt pleased that, at last, he'd budged them. However, knowing his hatred of the wild tribes, he no doubt wished the fire would roast them alive.

The brilliant flames that burned over most of southern Nebraska kept right on sizzling. Blazing bluestem leaped high to embrace the wind, and the wind stayed true to Brig. Gen. Mitchell. It blew the conflagration south until fire gleamed along the Arkansas River in Kansas and Colorado. Flames even reached the Texas panhandle in spots.

I suppose this magnificent combustion provided a sense of incandescent glory for Brig. Gen. Mitchell. However, I did wonder what the war department said when it realized that the general had torched a major section of the Great Plains, filled not only with Indians but also with settlers.

By spring, the wild tribes who beat a hasty retreat in the face of Brig. Gen. Mitchell's galloping wall of flames had returned to hiding out in the porous Republican River valley. Indians overran what would be Harlan County. Only small parties of hunters and trappers dared enter the area; some would die for their audacity. Even military commanders, who prefer to fight on a level field of slaughter, avoided the place. No one yet dreamed of settling the still unorganized land.

~ CHAPTER ~
# 18

THE BLACK-BEARDED COSSACK

Late in May 1869, Tall Bull and his Dog Soldiers left their Republican River camp to raid settlements in north-central Kansas. Along the Republican, the Solomon, and the Saline rivers, they killed, looted, and burned. They stole horses, derailed a train, raided homesteads, killed more than two dozen people, and captured two women.

Tall Bull's warriors snatched the first woman not far from today's Denmark, Kansas, as three German immigrants—Fred Meigheroff and the Weichels—rode to inspect a farmstead they might buy. Maria Weichel, wife of well-to-do George, glanced over her shoulder to see a dozen Cheyenne warriors dashing toward them.

The immigrants bolted and sped south along Spillman Creek, the men firing at the Indians. After a couple of miles, the Germans exhausted their ammunition. Then the Cheyenne warriors killed both men and seized Maria, a radiant twenty-year-old who spoke only German and who owned, it was said, twenty-four silk dresses.

Before long, the Dog Soldiers caught the second woman outside Michael Healy's home near the Saline River. As the Cheyenne arrived, they fired guns in the air. Those inside the house heard the racket and panicked. Three adults fled on horseback, leaving two mothers and their children to fend for themselves.

The women attempted to hide in thick brush along the Saline River's far bank. Bridget Kine clutched her two-month-old daughter, waded across the river and hid. But pregnant Susanna Alderdice and her four children didn't make it.

When the Cheyenne caught them, Susanna sat on the ground with her two youngest—Frank, two, and Alice, eight months—in her lap. The Indians shot five arrows into Frank and bashed his head on the ground. John, five, got bullets; Willis, four, received arrows, bullets, and a spear in his back. For some reason, the warriors didn't kill little Alice or her mother.

(A distinctly dirty deal for the captured women. But wait! It gets worse.)

~

The war department renamed Fort Cottonwood in 1866. It became Fort McPherson. The fort still sat midway between Fort Kearny and Julesburg, so its soldiers could protect Oregon Trail travelers—and pursue Indians, of course.

In May 1869, the army brought to the fort a renowned Indian fighter, Major General Eugene A. Carr (not related to our earlier Carr, William Parker Carr). An 1850 West Point graduate, Maj. Gen. Carr fought Indians until the Civil War, then he fought Confederates, and after that he fought Indians again. He had been pelted by bullets, pierced by arrows, and threatened by cholera, but he lived and moved up the ranks, often promoted for bravery and gallantry.

His courage in the Civil War Battle of Pea Ridge had earned him a Medal of Honor, which made him—and his beard, massive and black—nationally famous. A bold commander, Maj. Gen. Carr earned the nickname of "The Black-Bearded Cossack."

On May 21, he rode into Fort McPherson with 800 men on horseback, the eight companies of the U.S. 5th Cavalry. Plus Frank North and his fifty Pawnee scouts, each wearing two large upright black-and-white eagle feathers tucked into thick hair. The scouts wore the U.S. Cavalry's blue uniform, decorated with porcupine quills.

In addition to scouts, the Black-Bearded Cossack brought along, to act as Chief Civilian Scout, his friend, William "Buffalo Bill" Cody. Cody had recently earned his nickname by killing 4,280 buffalo in eighteen months after the Kansas Pacific Railroad hired him to supply workers with buffalo meat. Cody's fans claimed he "never shot an animal but once and not one buffalo escaped."

The buffalo killer's hair hung to his shoulders. He wore a thick mustache above a thin black goatee. His buckskin trousers and shirt displayed gaudy fringe, and he liked to wear his wide-brimmed hat at a jaunty angle. Already one of the Old West's most colorful figures, Buffalo Bill had just turned twenty-three.

What a troupe! The Black-Bearded Cossack brought these performers to Fort McPherson to go boot Tall Bull and his Dog Soldiers out of the Republican River valley.

The general also brought his pet dogs. Greyhounds. He showed the skinny, narrow-nosed creatures to Cody.

"Look at those wiry legs," the general said. "And those barrel chests. For speed, only the cheetah can beat them."

"Not the antelope?" Cody knew how fast antelopes sprint on the open prairie. Since they can't hide from predators, they rely on speed—and endurance. And spectacular leaping skills.

"No. No. These dogs can outrun antelopes easy, easy."

The next morning, before they left, Cody tagged along with Maj. Gen. Carr to watch his greyhounds outrun an antelope. A fabulous animal, the antelope, Cody knew. Eyelashes as long as a camel's. And nimble. Not at all like the sluggish buffalo.

Before long, the men spotted a scattered herd of antelope grazing, and the general let his dogs loose.

When the greyhounds moved, the twelve antelope turned, sizing up the situation. They didn't run right away. When they did move, the herd seemed to accelerate as one, tawny hides blending with the prairie, white rumps flashing.

For a few minutes, the race looked close, and Cody thought Maj. Gen. Carr's greyhounds might win. But no. As the chase continued, the dogs—not known for endurance— lagged far behind the antelopes that disappeared over a hill.

Cody's eyes crinkled as he looked at the Black-Bearded Cossack. "Sir," Cody said, "if anything the antelope is a little bit ahead."

On June 9, the colorful Republican River expedition swept out of the fort. The Black-Bearded Cossack and his troops headed southeast to the river, passing through what would be Harlan County on their way to Prairie Dog Creek and Kansas.

When they didn't find Tall Bull, they reversed direction, heading west along the Republican and its tributaries. On the way, the expedition had brushes with Cheyenne scouts, but the Pawnee scouts blocked their attacks.

When the troops reached Frenchman Creek, they turned northwest toward Colorado Territory. Still no sign of the Cheyenne chief.

At last, twenty-five days after the group left Fort McPherson, the scouts picked up a trail. They followed it to a recent Tall Bull campsite where they found a woman's shoe tracks; Maj. Gen. Carr felt sure that the Cheyenne chief held the two Kansas women captive.

The scouts lost the route, but everyone kept pushing up Frenchman Creek, certain they would find Tall Bull as they headed from Nebraska Territory into Colorado Territory.

Then the Pawnee picked up a trail so warm that the general knew they had to be close to a Cheyenne village.

"They'll expect us to come from the east or the south," Maj. Gen. Carr figured, "so if we come from the northwest..." He reversed the direction of his troops.

When he turned downstream along Frenchman Creek, the Cheyenne scouts who were watching believed he had retreated. They stopped pursuing.

On July 10, a month and a day on the trail, Maj. Gen. Carr positioned his soldiers northeast of Tall Bull's Cheyenne village with its eighty-four lodges and 500 Dog Soldiers. The Cheyenne had pitched camp in a favorite Plains Indian spot: Summit Springs with its fresh spring water. Buffalo also favored the remote treeless valley in the northeast corner of Colorado Territory. Fresh water, plenty of bison. What else did a village need?

When the time came for the final push, the Black-Bearded Cossack led 244 soldiers, fifty Pawnee scouts, the North brothers, and Cody, all riding horses.

Rolling sandhills provided such excellent cover that Maj. Gen. Carr led his men to within two miles of the village. Pawnee scouts stripped to prepare for battle, but they left on enough blue clothing so Maj. Gen. Carr's soldiers wouldn't mistake them for Dog Soldiers.

When the trail broke up three ways, so did they, planning to attack the village from three sides. North and his Pawnee scouts arrived first. When the Cheyenne heard the Pawnee firing, Tall Bull's people thought that their Sioux friends had come to visit. The sight of Pawnee flabbergasted them.

Striving to avoid shrieking Pawnee, the Cheyenne rushed to grab ponies. Tall Bull caught an orange pony with a silver mane—not his usual white war pony—and boosted his little daughter, his favorite woman, and himself onto its back. They rode into a narrow, steep ravine. He settled his daughter and woman with twenty other hidden Cheyenne and rode back to the opening. He watched as, outside the ravine, the cavalry and the Pawnee crushed his soldiers.

He turned to his woman, who'd followed him. "I can't bear to live after this." He grabbed his knife, plunged it behind his pony's foreleg and straight into its heart. The pony slumped to the ground.

Frank and his brother, Luther North, closed in on the ravine with a group of Pawnee. Tall Bull's head popped up over the ravine's ledge as he fired a shot. His head dropped out of sight. Frank aimed and waited. When Tall Bull's head popped up again, Frank killed the Cheyenne chief with a single bullet.

The fierce battle lasted not quite three hours. By then, Maj. Gen. Carr's men had killed fifty-two Cheyenne and captured those who hadn't run away, mostly women and children. The Cheyenne wounded only one of Maj. Gen. Carr's soldiers; arrows scratched his forehead, glanced off an ear.

During the fight, a Cheyenne had escaped on Tall Bull's white war pony. Cody shot the Indian off the well-known horse and felt certain he'd killed Tall Bull. But Frank North and an enlisted man, Daniel McGrath, both swore they had killed the chief.

"McGrath killed Tall Bull," Maj. Gen. Carr said. "The fact that he captured Tall Bull's pony proves it."

"Not so!" Luther North replied. "I myself watched my brother put a bullet through Tall Bull's head. Frank killed him."

Round and round they went.

The Black-Bearded Cossack searched the village, hoping to rescue the two women captured in Kansas. He knew that if German-speaking Maria Weichel and pregnant Susanna Alderdice had lived the typical lives of women kidnapped by Indians, they had been repeatedly raped, fed little, and worked to the bone.

He didn't know that Susanna had watched her eight-month-old daughter, Alice, choked with a bowstring, her limp body hung in a tree.

When the general and his men had attacked the village, the Cheyenne tried to kill both women. They succeeded in killing Alderdice; Maj. Gen. Carr found her dying. A Cheyenne woman had smashed the pregnant mother in the face with a tomahawk.

Weichel survived. Tall Bull's pistol ball shot through her back had glanced off a bone, hit her rib and lodged in her left breast. Painfully wounded, she would recover in less than a month at Fort Sedgwick, the new name for Camp Rankin near Julesburg. Afterward, or so it's said, she married her hospital attendant.

Late that afternoon, an unexpected lightning and thunder storm pounded the area with rain and hail, drenching everyone including the Cheyenne fleeing from what had been their home.

The next morning, the soldiers kept what they wanted from the village. They found clocks, watches, photographs, shawls, kitchen and household utensils, mules, horses, rifles, revolvers, knives, and axes. They also found 1,500 dolls, 9,300 pounds of dried meat, and more than ten tons of Indian clothing, equipment, and food. When they found cash, almost $900, they gave it to the wounded Maria Weichel.

At last the soldiers burned the village to the ground. It took 160 fires to destroy what they didn't take.

The success of the Black-Bearded Cossack's victory, a total rout, exhilarated the soldiers. They talked nonstop about how they trounced the Cheyenne, thrashed the Dog Soldiers and put them to flight. How easy it had been!

To these men, no dirty deal existed. Only Susanna Alderdice's death soiled Maj. Gen. Carr's clean sweep.

But the Cheyenne experienced a dirty deal of a tall order. Those who fled owned only what they wore or carried, and the horses they rode. The soldiers had killed their charismatic leader, killed or captured more than 100 people, and destroyed their village and its contents. Even worse, the Black-Bearded Cossack had obliterated their once terrifying power.

STAKING THE LAND

S oon Nebraska's Republican River wilderness would be transformed into counties. However, before Harlan County could be home to William Parker Carr, General Victor Vifquain, and dozens of settlers, the river valley had to be safe enough to survey. Major General Eugene A. Carr's overwhelming Summit Springs victory had rid the locality of Tall Bull and his Cheyenne Dog Soldiers, but that didn't render the valley without risk. Far from it. Chief Pawnee Killer and his Sioux tribe still dominated the area.

Earlier surveyors had figured out where the border between Kansas and Nebraska lay, a boundary that would mark Harlan County's southern border. That wasn't easy.

The first Kansas-Nebraska border, designed to fall on the 40th degree of latitude north of the equator, didn't. Instead, the boundary zigzagged so badly that the territorial governor called in the U.S. Army to help.

Army engineers arrived with some decent surveying instruments, the best available, they said. They chose a spot on the Missouri River's west bank to observe the movements of the sun and the stars. At last they calculated exactly where the 40th degree of latitude fell on a tall bluff that overlooked the Missouri valley.

To make sure other engineers didn't lose that spot again, they built a tall monument there and inscribed "Nebraska" on one side and "Kansas" on the other. I hope they were correct, for all subsequent Nebraska surveyors used this monument as a starting point.

David C. Butler, when elected Nebraska's first governor in 1867, hired civil engineers to survey south-central Nebraska, along the dangerous Republican River valley. Crews had already laid out a framework for a guide. However, townships (6 miles square) and subdivisions (1 mile square) had to be completed.

Engineers typically measured the Earth and marked boundaries in the middle of Indian country since surveying opens the way for settlers. Every season from 1863 to 1877, surveyors in Nebraska fought Indians. The crews soon learned to pack rifles along with their measuring chains, compasses, levels, and telescopes.

Indians easily spotted surveyors. Crews had to pound stakes in the ground to mark each portion of land so that settlers could claim their homesteads. Indians grimaced when they saw white men driving wooden posts in the ground. They knew stakes meant men would come to seize Indian land. Whenever the wild tribes could, they pulled up stakes and drove off the white men.

When Governor Butler put out a call for surveyors, Nelson Buck from Pontiac, Illinois, applied. Sixty-one years old, Buck counted thirty-four years in the surveying business plus letters of recommendation from distinguished men, including Abraham Lincoln. Governor Butler offered Buck a contract to survey in south-central Nebraska, in an area west of what would be Harlan County.

In June 1869, Buck left Pontiac for Chicago with his crew: five men, all under twenty years old. From Chicago, they rode a train to Kanesville, Iowa (now Council Bluffs); then they tramped down the east side of the Missouri River. A rope ferry carried them across to Plattsmouth, Nebraska.

"I'm no more prepared to be killed by Indians than other men," Buck said. He planned to buy, at Fort Kearny, enough firearms to protect his party, so he bought none in Plattsmouth. However, he did hire six more men, including a scout and a teamster.

Buck had accepted this job not just for profit but as a tourist. He wanted to see the West. Fear of Indians, he said, had "little or no weight in the matter."

On July 4, Buck and his boys set out for Fort Kearny, 150 miles away. They had a single wagon loaded with their goods and a team that could barely pull it, so the men all walked. Rain fell almost incessantly. The crew spotted some Indians, Pawnees, supposed to be friendly. When they encountered a group of sod houses, they learned they'd arrived in Grand Island.

By the time they reached Fort Kearny, Buck had acquired more wagons and horses. He applied for arms at the fort, expecting he could get six Spencer rifles, breech loaders, not slow muzzle loaders. Plus 200 rounds of ammunition for each rifle. Besides arms, Buck wanted an escort, but Fort Kearny couldn't supply Buck. He left without escort or arms.

Buck did have a fine rifle, but a muzzle loader. One of his boys carried a rusty shotgun, another an old army revolver, and a third had an army Springfield carbine but with only ten cartridges.

The crew didn't mind. H.B. McGregor, the youngest member, would describe their attitude: "Harm. It was all a dream with us and we thought little of any danger."

Ten days later they were in what would be Red Willow County, pitching camp on a curve in Beaver Creek about a half mile north of the already surveyed Nebraska-Kansas border.

Uneasy about their lack of arms, Buck sent two men— John Nettleton and young McGregor—back to Fort Kearny for an escort and guns.

Then about August 20, everything unraveled.

While Buck surveyed near the border, two of his scouts, away on the lookout, spotted four Sioux warriors. The scouts must have reasoned that "the only good Indian is a dead Indian," for without delay, they killed three of the four. Exasperation that the fourth "got away" would have deepened to terror if the scouts had known that the escaped Indian belonged to the renowned Pawnee Killer's tribe. When Chief Pawnee Killer heard about the unexpected slaughter, he rounded up 200 warriors and led them to attack the surveyors.

A commotion caught Buck's attention. He looked up to see a mass of Indians galloping toward him. The approaching warriors, their famed white feathered headdresses stirring to the rhythm of their horses' hoofbeats, must have made him think, for just a flash, *Ah! The real Wild West.*

Then Buck leaped on his horse and galloped up Beaver Creek with five of his crew. They easily lost the Sioux who stayed behind to capture two horses and Buck's rations. Then the Indians burned his wagons and killed half his crew: five young men.

Buck and the other five men raced 50 miles along Beaver Creek. *With any luck,* the surveyor thought, *we can make it back to Fort Kearny. Only about 70 more miles.*

Then they heard horses gallop. Soon they found themselves in the midst of a running gun battle with well-armed Indians.

The Sioux picked off the white men, one at a time, one after another, until only Buck and a single other surveyor hadn't been caught. These two crossed Beaver Creek near its fork with Sappa Creek, not far from today's Harlan County, and continued to ride northeast. The Sioux rode hot upon them.

When one killed Buck's horse, the surveyor slipped off his mount's flank. His rifle, that fine muzzle loader, had dropped under his horse. Buck landed alongside a sizable thicket of plum shrubs and, just for an instance, he flashed on the plum thickets of his Illinois childhood, sanctuaries for quail and rabbits. Then he plunged into the bush. He crawled under crisscrossing little branches sagging with the weight of summer plums until he found a good hiding spot. Then he froze, stiff as a rabbit, and listened to Sioux riders leave.

Around Buck, petals and plums carpeted the ground. The once white petals had turned brown, and many juicy plums had cracked open. Buck could hear bees or wasps humming; he knew the insects loved the syrupy sweet taste of the wild fruit.

A breeze picked up and rippled leaves. Buck heard some plums drop of their own weight. He watched a yellow jacket land on a split plum and suck the juice. The wasp shimmered as golden as the plum's exposed flesh. Sunlight flickered overhead. Buck relaxed a bit and drew a slow breath.

Then a Sioux warrior stamped through the branches. They stared at each other for a split second, before the warrior killed Buck.

By the time the Sioux finished, only two members of Buck's surveying crew escaped death—the men Buck had sent back to Fort Kearny for arms.

~

Only the Sioux knew about the eradication of Buck and his crew. Even so, the military understood that someone had to stop Chief Pawnee Killer and his Sioux raiders, holed up in the Republican River valley waiting to plunder settlements or slaughter surveyors. Most commanders would rather not risk their lives—except General Thomas Duncan, "a jolly, blustering old fellow."

"An Indian bullet can't hurt the General," one Fort McPherson recruit said. "He's been shot in the head with a cannon ball, and that didn't hurt him one bit."

"Right," another replied. "The way I heard it, the ball glanced off his head and killed one of the army's toughest mules."

At Fort McPherson, tough-headed Gen. Duncan gathered an expedition similar to Maj. Gen. Carr's Republican River expedition. He enlisted companies from the 2nd and 5th cavalries, plus two groups of Pawnee scouts including Frank North, and that civilian scout, Buffalo Bill Cody.

Gen. Duncan's expedition left Fort McPherson on September 15, 1869, and headed straight for the Republican River valley. At dusk eleven days later, the company arrived and set up a temporary campsite.

The next morning North and Cody woke at daybreak and headed out. Maybe they could kill a couple of buffalo or spot a place for a more permanent campsite. However, after messing around awhile, the men agreed that the early morning exercise had proved too much for them. North stretched out to rest while Cody, curious to see if the expedition had awakened yet, rode over a hill to look.

Cody saw the cavalry riding toward them, but so far off that he figured he had time enough to mimic North and take a snooze. Before could find a good spot, he heard shots and whirled to see North galloping toward him. Behind North raced a bunch of screeching Sioux firing rifles. Cody chased them; they shot his whip from his hand and put daylight through the crown of his hat. Or so he said.

Gen. Duncan's advance guard, twenty cavalry soldiers strong, took up the chase. The Sioux retreated. Then North and the Pawnee scouts lit out after the warriors.

Gen. Duncan and his cavalry advanced more slowly, hoping to find the Sioux campsite. Then John Y. Nelson, a scout for Gen. Duncan, spotted a trail that veered off from the retreating Indians. "Maybe somebody headed home to give warning."

Gen. Duncan, his guards, and Nelson followed the trail. Sure enough, it ended in a village of fifty-six lodges. They looked recently abandoned; some fires still burned.

Nelson, who spoke Lakota, one of the Siouan languages, captured an Indian fleeing the village and interrogated him. To Gen. Duncan's delight, the Sioux said they stood in Pawnee Killer's village. "The chief headquarters here," Nelson said. Gen. Duncan grinned. The very village he'd hoped to find.

The general ordered his soldiers to trash the village. In the process, the men found some curious objects: surveyor tools, measuring chains, compasses, levels, and telescopes. Could the tools belong to that Buck and his men, missing since August?

Near the village, a soldier found an old Sioux woman and brought her to Gen. Duncan who called for his translator. When Nelson saw the woman, he cried, "I know her! She's related to my wife. She's Pawnee Killer's mother."

Nelson and the woman spoke. Then the scout said, "When she couldn't keep up with them, they left her behind. To die. It's the Sioux custom with old people."

"Ask her what she knows about these." Gen. Duncan showed her the surveyors' tools, shaking a telescope under her nose.

The old woman nodded and, through Nelson, described how whites on Beaver Creek had killed three young Sioux, how in revenge Pawnee Killer and 200 warriors followed the white men, took their horses, destroyed wagons. Battled all afternoon. Some warriors wounded. All the whites killed.

"Buck," said Gen. Duncan. "Must be Buck and his men."

After destroying Pawnee Killer's village and leaving his mother to fend for herself, Gen. Duncan's expedition galloped off to find the fleeing Sioux. The Pawnee scouts who had ridden ahead, hard on the Sioux's heels, noticed that their trail showed no sign of halting until after they'd ridden in haste for 90 miles. The Pawnee scouts hunted until nightfall, but the Sioux had vanished.

Gen. Duncan and his men looked for Pawnee Killer and his tribe for nearly a month before they gave up and turned back to Fort McPherson.

This may sound as if they accomplished little. However, their destruction of the Sioux village so soon after the Summit Springs battle gave the military an upper hand in the Republican River valley. Indian troubles there stopped almost entirely.

The expedition also served Buffalo Bill well. From it, he created an excellent scene for his Wild West Show. He called it "Last Stand of the Indians."

PART V

Harlan County's Bitter Birth

~ CHAPTER ~
# 20

VIFQUAIN'S BUNCH

When blustering, jolly old General Thomas Duncan drove Pawnee Killer from the Republican River valley, he liberated what would become Harlan County for white settlement. At that time, William Parker Carr and Thomas Harlan still called Cheyenne, Wyoming, home. General Victor Vifquain lived in eastern Nebraska with Caroline and their children on their farm near the Big Blue River.

Gen. Vifquain made the first move. When he heard that Gen. Duncan had burned and chased the Sioux out of the Republican River valley, he rejoiced. At last he could see for himself that sportsman's paradise with its shaggy nut-brown hump-backed bison, its statuesque bull elk sporting their winter trees of antlers, and its startling abundance of skittish deer, black-tailed and white-tailed.

Within a few days Gen. Vifquain rounded up a band of gunmen, keen to try their luck in that still unorganized river valley. They rode out from Gen. Vifquain's home in early November 1869.

The men found a valley teeming with wildlife, as claimed, except for buffalo. When William Parker Carr had hunted along the Republican River in 1863, he found an abundance of buffalo because millions of them still roamed free on the plains. Six years later, that had changed.

Paid marksmen, like Buffalo Bill, killed bison for meat, providing food for railroad workers or army troops. When the army noticed the Indians' dependency on buffalo for food, clothing, and shelter, it urged hunters to eradicate herds to persuade Indians to move to reservations.

When owning a buffalo robe became stylish, slaughter heightened. Slaying buffalo turned into an industry, with gunmen killing 250 buffalo a day. The gunners marketed the hides and left the rest to spoil.

Soon offing buffalo became a sport. Ranchers bragged about how many buffalo they could polish off before

Buffalo robes

breakfast. Tourists shot buffalo out train windows, firing until their guns heated or ran out of ammunition.

Before long, towering heaps of buffalo carcasses rotted on the plains.

When Gen. Vifquain brought his sportsmen to the Republican River valley, plains buffalo numbered in the thousands, not the millions. In thirty-five more years, they would total just 200.

~

Once the Blue River hunters arrived in what would be Harlan County, Gen. Vifquain chose a campsite situated on a high bluff south of today's town of Orleans. The camp overlooked the Republican River, which flowed diagonally past on its long eastward trek into Kansas.

When not hunting, Gen. Vifquain explored the numerous creeks that fed the river. By the time he returned to camp, he'd examined eight fine streams that crisscrossed the land. Spring fed. Most eroded the earth so deeply that they carved out caves, caves that once sheltered a hornet's nest of Indian raiders. But Gen. Vifquain didn't know that.

The richness of the land near the river astonished the general. Narrow belts of trees, especially cottonwood but also ash, elm, box elder, hackberry, walnut, and oak, lined the river and its creeks. Beyond the river's flood plain, broad, slightly rolling uplands stretched, their wild grasses rippling in the wind.

Next, Gen. Vifquain inspected prairie soil. Would crops flourish here? To his joy, he found plains mantled heavily with rich, wind-blown deposits of silt called loess. This made the valley as fertile as any land he knew.

His excitement spiraled. Silent as a dream, his idea rose: Might this rich land be the place to organize a colony? Not a Belgian colony, not anymore. He didn't want another seasick journey to Europe looking for men to join him. No, he'd scout for settlers along the Blue rivers or in the Nebraska City area, as he had for hunters. Surely he could find men who would benefit from taming such a flourishing world.

That summer, August 1870, Gen. Vifquain set out from eastern Nebraska for the Republican River valley with a party of forty men, whose names appear at the back of this book. None came from Belgium. Most had English, Scandinavian, or German backgrounds. Only two besides Vifquain bore French names and one was Irish.

The forty men traveled overland with nine covered wagons loaded with supplies they thought necessary for settling in an unknown land. At some point along the way, Joseph W. Foster from Nebraska City joined them.

(Keep an eye on Foster. He crossed the prairie with the Gen. Vifquain party, but he never became part of that community. Instead, he became the first "Alma man," as you'll see. The split between the settlers started early.)

Gen. Vifquain led his men to the high bluff where he and his hunters had camped, and they pitched tents. The camp became their headquarters, which they called Fort Melrose, although why I don't know. The name "Melrose" refers to a tiny Scottish town that dates to the early 1300s, but none of Gen. Vifquain's settlers claimed to be Scottish.

As Vifquain and his men settled into Fort Melrose, a familiar person visited: Andrew Ruben, a burly guy with skin darkened by outdoor life. Ruben, whose Swedish name was Anderson, had come to the Republican River area as one of Gen. Vifquain's hunters and never left. Instead, he built a dugout and stayed over the winter to become the first settler.

"Feast on buffalo all winter long?" Gen. Vifquain asked.

Ruben laughed. He had a reputation as a buffalo hunter. Fearless and persistent, he'd killed more buffalo last fall than all of Vifquain's men combined.

"Yeah. But ate turkey and rabbit, too," he said. "Still, it beats plastering. Or working on the railroad."

"I s'pose you've killed a thousand buffalo by now," little Squire Guillet said.

"Three hundred is more like it. I got a mighty fine scar from this last fellow." Ruben yanked up his shirt. "Big-horned guy," he rubbed a sizable scar near his belly button, "damn near gored me to death. Had to slit his throat with my hunting knife to get him off."

Slitting a buffalo's throat took gumption. And skill. Settlers would talk about Ruben's feat for years. They admired the man so much that they would name a township for him (spelling or misspelling its name): "Reuben Township."

~

Abraham Lincoln's Homestead Law of 1862 allowed settlers to own government land for free. All you need is a shack and a well, one writer said. And ten acres plowed and planted.

Well, almost.

You had to live on the land and work it for five years. You had to head a household. You had to count at least twenty-one birthdays. You did have to fork over some money: $10 plus surveying and registration fees. And the government nixed the whole deal if you'd ever borne arms against the U.S. or committed any of a roster of other offenses.

Homesteading had drawn Gen. Vifquain's men to the Republican River area. At Fort Melrose, on August 31, 1870, those men chose claims by casting lots.

Frank Sullivan and little Squire Guillet's wagon won first choice. They chose what looked like a prime spot, but had to leave the spongy land for a better claim. Today we call their first choice "Elm Swamp."

Guess who showed up at the fort to cast lots? Slick Mr. Foster from Nebraska City. He won second choice, but shook his head. "Can't do it. Already staked a claim further east."— Now that was fast!—"You can give my choice to Hofnagle."

So Gen. Vifquain did.

Frank Hofnagle, a German immigrant from Westphalia, chose a place west of today's Orleans on what would be called Hofnagle Creek. There he built a dugout that would be the site of a rescue by God. More on that later.

Ruben settled where he already was, to the north in what would be Reuben Township.

And so it went. These early colonists, like most settlers, chose claims near the river or on one of its tributaries. All of them also chose claims in the west near Fort Melrose—all but Foster.

~

A county seat became Gen. Vifquain's next concern. For this, the group needed a town, so Vifquain chose a few others to help him select a site.

The "few others" may have included Franklin A. Bieyon and Little Squire Guillet. Both men would play an active part in county affairs, but Vifquain probably chose them for their French backgrounds. He might need them to support the controversial French name he had in mind for the town.

For their townsite, the men selected a half-section, or 320 acres, which lay southeast of today's Orleans, not far from Fort Melrose.

Then Vifquain named the town "Napoleon." Settlers with English backgrounds could not have been pleased. Englishmen despised Napoleon, they called him "The Ogre." But the general loved "The Little Corporal."

Of course Gen. Vifquain would. His father won medals fighting in the Napoleonic Wars, including Napoleon's own prestigious "Legion of Honor." Nothing, Vifquain would argue, could tarnish Napoleon's glory.

Naming this Nebraska townsite Napoleon indicates the nature of Vifquain's dreams. Surely he hoped his town would become the county seat. Indeed, it would be a contender for county seat in the county's first election.

Foster dreamed big dreams, too. Shortly after he staked his claim near today's town of Alma, Foster returned to Nebraska City. There he bought enough timber to build a house. He hired carpenters and teamsters who loaded lumber in wagons, drove to the Republican River area, and built Foster's residence.

By early September 1870, Foster moved into his 14-by-15-foot house, the first wooden building in what would be Harlan County. Foster's palace, I call it.

A palace, certainly, compared to Ruben's dugout—then the only other dwelling in the area.

Foster's residence sat on the eastern side of today's county where the river and what we now call Cook Creek intersect. It would be the hub of the Alma colony.

General Vifquain's camp and his Napoleon townsite lay in the west, the heart of what would become the Orleans contingent.

Already the settlers had splintered.

How different history might have been if Foster had not branched off, if he had built his home on the west side of the county with everyone else.

But he didn't.

~

That fall, Gen, Vifquain and twenty-six of his forty men returned to their homes near Big Blue River, but fourteen remained at Fort Melrose for the winter. Together they tackled the sort of venture that a military man like General Vifquain might envision: they built a fort near today's Orleans, which they called the Melrose Stockade. Under Franklin A. Bieyon's leadership, they erected a 40-foot-square stockade as a shelter against the plains' fierce storms and Indians. Inside the stockade walls, the men erected a log cabin that they would call home.

Outside, a barrier of cottonwood poles 10 feet high surrounded the stockade's walls. Made of sod, the walls measured two-and-a-half feet thick. The men left loopholes to shoot any Indians who might contest the settlers' right to be on the Sioux hunting grounds.

The government issued a Spencer repeating rifle, a powerful new weapon, to Ruben. Ruben prized this gun, which could fire twenty rounds per minute as opposed to a muzzle loader's two or three. When a large Sioux tribe settled about 25 miles west of the stockade, Ruben felt sure he'd have to fire the rifle at one of them, but he never did. The Sioux camped and hunted on the river, but they ignored the tiny group of settlers in and around the Melrose Stockade.

Having Sioux so nearby upset some settlers. They no doubt remembered the heavy fighting seven years ago with the Sioux. That hundred-mile trail along the Platte had been "one continuous string of dead, both white men and Indians—dead stock, burned trains and ranches."

So when two of Nels Peterson's white horses disappeared from his claim, naturally he blamed the Sioux, but no other settler reported troubles.

THOMAS HARLAN'S BOYS

Thomas Harlan knew he must see this Republican River valley that William Parker Carr so prized, even though traveling there might prove challenging. So early February 1871, in Cheyenne, Wyoming, he and his scouting party waited to board the Union Pacific train for its 360-mile ride to Nebraska.

That is, Harlan and four of his five men waited. Those four—Mark Coad, Thomas Murrin, Thomas Mullally, John Talbot, all of Irish extraction—could be trusted. But Painter! Where was Mr. Joseph H. Painter, the only other Englishman?

Harlan, a lawyer turned tax collector, now faced the loss of his job, thanks to Congress. When the lawmakers let the temporary Civil War income tax expire next year, he'd have no tax to collect, no property to seize, no slackers to prosecute.

An unexpected Chinook wind persuaded Harlan to hitch his collar higher and his hat lower.

"You'd think the UP would have built a depot by now," he told Mark Coad, one of his party. "Railroad's already five years old. Passengers still shiver in the winter. Even the agent has to conduct his business in a tent."

"Typical," Coad said.

They turned to see Painter jump onto the platform just as the train screamed into the station. Harlan glared at the maverick, but Painter shrugged, reached into a bulging jacket pocket, and pulled out a handful of pemmican or dried meat. "I nearly forgot it. Elk and cranberries."

He offered some to Harlan, but the party leader shook his head. "Indian food."

Painter patted his lumpy pockets. "Might come in handy." And indeed, it did. The party ate the last of it on their train ride back to Cheyenne.

Nightfall beat the travelers to Grand Island, their stop. About a thousand people—half American, half German— lived in the town. The community had originated fourteen years earlier when thirty-five German immigrants settled on a long wooded island in the Platte River. Many of those settlers relocated to shore when the Union Pacific placed its station there. The UP named the new town "Grand Island," after the original island.

Harlan and his men ate dinner at a nearby railroad eating house. That evening, Harlan located an experienced guide, Richard Sydenham, and hired him to lead the scouting party on its 100-mile trip to the Republican River valley.

Early the next morning, the men piled into Sydenham's wagon. Mark Coad tugged on the driver's jacket. "Did you say your name's Sydenham?" The men watched Coad's round face jerk, his broad nostrils flare and his tongue dart in and out of his mouth.

Harlan stared. "What the devil are you doing?"

But Sydenham threw back his head and howled. "He's honoring my ancestors. One of them, a doctor, discovered St. Vitus Dance."

The men laughed, then piled out of the wagon when Sydenham stopped in front of the O.K. Store for supplies. The store sat inside a large sod stockade featuring a six-pound cannon. One of the two proprietors, Fred Wiebe, greeted them.

Harlan stroked the cannon. "Ever use this?"

"No, sir, we never had to. Our fortifications are so good, the Indians never attacked us."

"Maybe we should stay here."

"Why?" Fred asked. "Where you going?"

"Republican River valley."

"Yes, sir, I heard Indians down that way are a wild blood-thirsty lot. But they should be wiped out by now."

"I sincerely hope so." Harlan turned to shop. Soon he walked to the counter and set down the supplies he'd chosen. As he paid Fred Wiebe, Painter came back into the store. "Oh, Mr. Harlan. There's a U.S. land office across the street."

Harlan picked up his bundle. "So?"

"Well, that's where we'll file our claims, isn't it?"

"Looks like you got the cart before the horse. We haven't even seen the place, and already you're homesteading it." *Damn fool.*

Sydenham drove the party out of town and over a bridge that spanned the Platte River. He stopped in the middle and faced the men. "Ain't it a beauty? Cost $15,000 dollars. It's so new we're almost the first wagon to cross it."

The men stared at the bridge spanning the flat river. Its water barely moved. Little river islands floated like pancakes, and along the shore, leafless trees bumped into each other.

After a while Sydenham stopped again. "Look what our surveyor found." He gestured east. The men looked. The driver seemed to point to empty pasture land. Then something moved. And again. Soon they saw fuzzy tan heads bopping up out of holes, then plump furry bodies scampering. The men gazed at the largest prairie dog village any of them had ever seen.

"Ten miles of it," Sydenham said. "Thousands of them. Don't dare ride a horse in there; it'd break its leg. The ground is just riddled with holes."

"Okay." He clucked at his horses. "Enough sightseeing." And off they went. Five Union Pacific workers and Harlan, now thirty-six. *Thought I'd be a lawyer.* He suppressed a snort. *Trained in Illinois. Married Elizabeth. That was ten years ago. But I made friends with Abraham Lincoln there; fought in his Civil War. That changed everything. General Grant named me Internal Revenue Collector for Wyoming Territory, which is where I met William Parker Carr. Now that job is winding down. Time to move on. Maybe to this Nebraska place. Elizabeth, she hates Wyoming, wants to go back to Illinois, but she's a tough Vermont schoolteacher. She can adjust to most anything.*

Harlan and his men bounced all the way to the Republican River valley where, as Carr had described, the river curved up and the creeks streamed down. The land around them, teeming with wildlife, measured up to Carr's boasts.

But could they find good land to homestead? And what would it be like to live in such a remote place?

The party stopped at the Melrose Stockade, attracted there by smoke curling from the chimney. Inside the cabin, burly Thomas Fly and the Peterson brothers crouched by the fire making rope. Fly scoured a buffalo hide, Truls Peterson sliced rawhide into thin strips, and Nels braided them. They set their work aside to point out, to their visitors, the stockade's virtues: its thick walls of sod, its enclosure of cottonwood poles, its loopholes for shooting Indians.

"Have you shot many?" Harlan said as they gathered back around the fire.

Fly laughed. "Haven't even aimed at one."

Truls picked up the hide and sliced it. "We've scared them off."

"Don't forget my white mustangs," Nels said. "Indians stole them two."

"Those nags!" Truls scrutinized his brother. "What sensible Sioux would want them?" "For food. They might have ate them."

"Not likely. Them two must of wandered off when you forgot to hobble them."

Nels, silent, stared at the strips he'd braided.

Harlan gestured at his party. "Supposing we want to take claims around here. What would you suggest?"

"Claims?" Fly tugged on his wispy beard. "Let's see. There was forty of us came, and most of us took claims close by here. So there aren't hardly any left within musket range, and those that are usually aren't good ones by the river or a stream."

"But that doesn't mean you can't find a good claim, if you look." Truls said. "It'd be nice to have the seven of you settle nearby."

"The six," Sydenham said. "I'm just the driver."

After Harlan and his men left, they drove east until chubby Coad spotted Foster's new house. "Take a look at that! Wood. Looks like wood, and not cottonwood, neither. Let's angle over that-a-way, Mr. St. Vitus."

Foster welcomed them. He boasted about how he'd gone back to Nebraska City, hired teamsters to drive him, his carpenter, and enough lumber to build the house. He showed off his property, including a fine cottonwood grove, and paraded his visitors along the creek and the Republican River that flowed by two sides of his claim.

"Yes, sir," Harlan said. "This is a mighty fine setup you have. But what about Indian troubles?"

"Indian troubles?" Foster laughed. "A thing of the past." He didn't mention the fifty or so Indians living 25 miles away. Instead, he changed the subject to describe the idyllically mild winter weather, which he thought typical. Slender new shoots of bright green grass had already pushed up among winter's yellowed stems.

Delighted to find such a balmy, beautiful, game-rich, Indian-free country, most members of this Cheyenne scouting party selected claims—ones that lay close to Foster's palace.

By February 17, the railroad workers, who had returned to Cheyenne, broadcast glorious accounts of the valley. Harlan resigned his revenue collector job and, in March, led a colony of men from Wyoming to the Republican River. Five of Harlan's original scouting party joined him plus twelve others, including William Parker Carr.

Carr, now forty, homesteaded a rich quarter section about two and a half miles southeast of today's Alma. Partially river bottom land, Carr's 160 acres included the beauty that had drawn him to this area, especially the wide variety of trees, the prodigious flocks of birds, and the gleaming river.

That spring, Nebraska's first great stream of immigration began. Thousands poured west in search of free homes. As Addison Erwin Sheldon describes it, "They came in all possible ways, some up the Missouri River in steamboats, some on the railroads across Iowa, but more came in covered wagons, or 'prairie schooners' as they were called, drawn by horses, mules or oxen. In these came the pioneers with their children; often with a box of chickens tied on behind, while a few cattle and the family dog brought up the rear. All the roads leading into and across Nebraska were white with these land ships, and soon the valleys and prairies…were dotted with dark spots, where they had anchored and the men and women in them had begun to break the prairies and build homes."

Many of those immigrants came to what would be Harlan County.

Women and children now arrived, plus oodles of Civil War veterans. Under the liberal Homestead Act rules, a Union soldier could count the time he'd served in the war toward his five years of residency.

New immigrants found the best river bottomlands taken. However, feeling they could live in safety from Indians, these pioneers took claims along the river's tributaries instead. By June 1, at least one homestead had settled along every Republican River creek. Settlements soon scattered all over the area.

Homesteaders Joseph Gould, a Civil War veteran, and his wife, Mary, wagoned into the valley one day with Garvin and Albert, their sons, and Albert's wife, Hattie. The creek they tried to cross, one with banks steep enough to hide an Indian, resisted. The Goulds pushed and they pulled, groaned and they cursed, but they just couldn't get the wagon to cross that creek.

"Let's rest a while, Joe," Mary said. "Build up our strength." The five sat on the bank, dangling their legs, singing the chorus to James Bland's "Oh, Dem Golden Slippers," a new song they'd learned on the road. Then they sang, "There'll be a hot time in the old town tonight," about Mrs. O'Leary and her lantern and the Chicago fire. Then Joe bet Garvin he couldn't remember all the verses to "Little Brown Jug," which he almost did, which amused everyone so they forgot about their predicament.

Then they got up and gave the wagon one final push. It was a good push. The wagon creaked and groaned and screeched and rasped. Just as they thought it would fly over the water to the other side, it cracked like a clap of thunder. The wagon's tongue had split off.

"We've got to fix it, otherwise we can't go nowhere," Joe said.

"Maybe if we pool our money," Mary said.

Everyone gathered their coins, but found they had only twenty-five cents among them, not enough to fix much of anything.

They stood staring at the wagon. It looked like a coffin, and they felt like mourners at a wake. Then Hattie, Albert's wife, spoke up. "Why can't we forget fixing the broken tongue and homestead right here?"

So they did, taking out their claim southeast of today's Alma.

They repeated their story so often that folks named the stream "Tipover Creek," in honor of that broken wagon.

Gen. Vifquain's settlers, who'd wintered in the stockade, built living quarters that spring. Most scooped pits, called dugouts, in the hillside or ground. So many Scandinavians settled around the Melrose Stockade that folks called it the "Swede Stockade." It became the largest, most effective settlement in the county.

A second townsite, in addition to Gen. Vifquain's Napoleon, popped up. Two of Harlan's scouts—Mark Coad and Thomas Murrin—plus a newcomer, a New York lawyer named Nathan Cook, selected a site that adjoined both Foster's claim and Cook's new homestead up the creek from Foster.

The threesome named the new townsite "Alma City" after Cook's young daughter, Alma. On Alma's name, the founders flew the word *City* like a kite's tail, hoping to make the town sound important. Most new Western towns flew just such a tail in infancy and later dropped it, as Omaha City had and Alma City would.

Alma City's founding created an eastern rival to western Napoleon for the county seat. Indeed, both would seek that prize in the county's first election.

All these settlers—some independent pioneers and others led by Gen. Vifquain or by Harlan—lived in what would be Harlan County when it was formed. The bulk of Vifquain's party settled around Napoleon and the Melrose stockade, southwest of what would be the county's center. Most of Harlan's Cheyenne group settled south and east of Vifquain's group, around Foster's palace and the townsite of Alma City.

Altogether more than two hundred people lived in the county. They included men, women, and children but mostly men. All this settling took place in less than a year, from August 1870, when Gen. Vifquain's party cast lots for claims, to June 1871, the month when the battle for the Harlan County seat began.

~ CHAPTER ~
# 22

CHICANERY 101

During the late winter and early spring of 1871, settlers near Alma City spent many long dark evenings at Foster's palace, sprawled on his high-back chairs, his deacon's bench, and even on the seat of his big hall rack. Bit by bit, the settlers shrank to a core group: Foster, of course. Harlan and his new lawyer friend, Cook. Three from Harlan's scouting party: Coad, Murrin, and Painter. Plus a newcomer, James O. Phillips, a Pennsylvania shoemaker with a sharp sense of politics.

The settlers had been quick to decide that a party of Alma City men would visit the Lincoln capital to form a new county as soon as warm weather permitted. But what should they do once they got there?

Foster filled them in on local politics, so they knew that the Democratic South Platters and the Republican North Platters had been playing tug-of-war ever since Nebraska became a territory in 1854. Seeking power, each party fought the other's proposed counties. By 1870, the legislators had nearly tied in organizing forty-six counties: twenty-two north of the Platte, twenty-four south. These counties had established local governments in most of the eastern third of the state.

Now the North Platters had placed their money on six north-of-the-Platte hoped-for counties: Antelope, Boone, Greeley, Howard, Sherman, and Valley. The South Platters, with less land but more people, had only a possible Thayer County in the wings. Would the North Platters stomp all over Thayer in their eagerness to hammer out their six counties? Would the South Platters refuse to recognize all the proposals, including Thayer, in order to avoid organizing the six North Platters' counties? How would an Alma City proposal fare?

Talk in Foster's palace must have revolved around such issues.

"Let's take our case to a South Platte representative," Harlan might have suggested.

But not everyone agreed.

"How can we know which legislator has the most power?" Phillips said, "We should go higher."

"Higher?" Cook shifted in the deacon's bench. "You mean Governor Butler?"

"Right."

"But do you think he'd listen to us?"

Murrin paced the room. "Everyone knows how congenial he is. We might have more luck contacting him than trying to get cozy with a Democrat we've barely heard of."

"Let's make our case bullet proof," Cook said. "So strong he can't refuse us."

"We could rename Alma City Butler City," Painter said.

But Cook, Coad, and Murrin, who had selected the site and named the town Alma City, loudly refused.

"Let's keep that idea in our back pocket, to take out only if we need to," Phillips said. "Butler's been a Republican, you know, ever since the Grand Old Party began. In 1854, I think. And he's the only governor we've ever had. This is his third term."

"Beloved," Harlan said. "That's what folks call him."

"Well, he's genial, all right. Always patting his bosom and saying, 'I thank God from my heart of hearts,'" Phillips laughed. "But he's cagey. He would have lost that first bitter election, it was so close, but some of his Republican friends in Cass County helped him out. Tossed out 107 Democratic votes. Enough to give Butler the election. He didn't object."

"So we choose between contacting a congenial cagey Republican or a Democrat we don't know?" Harlan dropped in a chair with a thump. "Some choice."

"Let's name the new county 'Butler County,'" Cook said.

Painter stood up and thrust his arm in the air. "I second the motion."

~

Governor David Butler's first task, after his crooked election in 1866, was to locate the state capital. This proved simpler than one might think. The South Platters, who had long fought for a capital south of the Platte, were no longer a minority. Thanks to their increasing population, they had won a majority of legislative votes in the 1866 election. They easily passed a bill to remove the capital from Omaha and relocate it. The only question was where.

Governor David Butler

Oh, one Omaha Senator, a Republican, snarled about the vote and moved to name the new capital "Lincoln" after the late president. The Senator knew Lincoln's name would torment the Democratic South Platte leaders who had opposed the president. He figured the Southerners would give up their city south of the Platte before they'd name it Lincoln. He was wrong.

To choose a location for the new capital, the legislature named popular Governor Butler to head a three-man commission. On July 29, 1867, the three men (Governor Butler, Secretary of State Thomas P. Kennard, and State Auditor John Gillespie) selected the tiny village of Lancaster with its handful of log cabins. Lancaster sat between Salt and Antelope creeks in the middle of open prairie, which included salt flats and marshes. Salt, precious on the plains, preserved meat well. Indeed, salt set the little village apart.

Lancaster settlers, and the three commissioners, expected great wealth from the basin. Already local settlers sold bags of salt in Nebraska City. They harvested salt that formed as a crust on the ground, and they pumped vats full of brine and boiled the water away to reveal salt.

Not everyone embraced the commissioners' salty choice of Lancaster for the state's capital.

"No one will go there," a newspaper reporter warned. "It's too isolated. It has no river, no railroad, no steam wagon, nothing."

To hush protesters, Governor Butler broke precedent and assigned three plums to the little village: the state university, the penitentiary, and the lunatic asylum. Most governors scattered such perks among several towns.

Only one small matter remained: the Great Seal of the State of Nebraska. The secretary of state keeps the seal; only he or the governor may use it. But Governor Butler didn't possess it. It had remained in Omaha in the territorial capitol. Without it, he couldn't stamp important documents, making them official.

Governor Butler turned to his Republican secretary of state, Thomas Kennard, for help. Kennard, happy to oblige, hitched up a team on a Sunday, drove to the Omaha territorial capitol, and quietly "acquired" the seal. He wrapped it carefully, stuck it beneath his wagon seat, and rode home.

In the meantime, Governor Butler left Omaha to go to Pawnee City. In his home there he drafted an announcement about the seal's removal.

On Monday, both went to the capitol in Lincoln. Kennard arrived with his heist, just in time to stamp a piece of paper for the governor. That paper, drafted by Governor Butler in Pawnee City, proclaimed that he had opened the new capital of Nebraska, in Lincoln, now ready for business.

By January 1869, Nebraska's "Ship of State" with its new Lincoln capital had been safely launched.

~

In May 1871, off went Harlan, Phillips, Murrin, and Coad to the state capital, firm in their resolve to see Governor Butler.

The two-story state capitol

As the men approached Lincoln, they noticed the central cupola of the capitol visible above the horizon. Soon they could see that Lincoln itself had blown up into a boomtown. In the four short years since the village of Lancaster became the capital of Nebraska, its population had expanded more than eighty times, from thirty people to 2,500. (Look what winning a seat of government can do! I'll bet Harlan and his gang took notice of that.)

The crumbling two-story capitol seemed flabby after the robust new town. At the capitol's entrance, the Alma City men spotted clues that the three-year-old limestone building had begun to disintegrate, thanks to poor construction and inferior quality stone.

Inside, Harlan and his men found Governor David C. Butler's suite only to discover, to their dismay, that the highly regarded Nebraska governor had been booted out of office. In March, the Nebraska House of Representatives had brought eleven articles of impeachment against Governor Butler. They charged that he had dipped his hand deep into the government till.

William H. James sat where Governor Butler should have been. Poor James! He hadn't served three months as secretary of state when the Senators catapulted him into governorship on March 3, 1871. The Alma City men peered through the open door at the acting governor. Nearly forty years old, he had a baby face that made him look young despite his heavy beard, solid black from his ears and bottom lip to his collar.

Harlan and his men found a free room where they could sit in empty school desks and discuss what to do. Governor

Gov. WILLIAM H. JAMES.
(E. G. Clements collection.)

William H. James, acting governor

Butler had no power, but Governor James didn't have much either. Should they look up a South Platte legislator?

Instead, the men decided to wait for Governor Butler's May 30 trial, on Tuesday, only a few days away. The Senate decision on impeachment should clarify matters.

The morning of Governor Butler's trial, settlers packed the Senate chambers. The Alma City men, having arrived early, had good seats. They saw Governor Butler for the first time. As usual, he wore his dark hair in a pompadour, combed up to emphasize his high forehead, but his startling appearance didn't seem to matter to his many friends. They had elected him governor three times: in 1866, 1868, and

1870. And why not? Courteous but friendly, he seemed bright enough, despite his limited education, and as governor, he understood how to get things done. That, indeed, proved to be his downfall.

The Alma City bunch must have attended every day of the four-day trial. A lot rested on the legislators' decision. If Governor Butler won, Harlan's group would, as planned, deal with the easy-going governor. If not, they would do business with the unknown Governor James, rumored to be a serious man.

On Thursday, June 1, the impeachment court rendered its decision. The Senators acquitted Governor Butler of ten of their eleven charges, but they booted him out of office for his misuse of $16,881 of Nebraska's school funds.

Governor Butler's supporters became bitter. They saw his impeachment as a dirty deal. Historian James C. Olson wrote that many never required "rigid honesty in the handling of public affairs." In the eyes of his friends, Governor Butler's "borrowing" $16,881 of school funds for his own use was only a "trifling transgression."

Even the Senators must not have expected "rigid honesty," for they overlooked Governor Butler's real estate speculation in the capital's lots and blocks, his kickbacks from architects and contractors hired to plan and build state buildings, and his selling of appointments. One could say that honesty was not the custom in Nebraska's capital at the time the Alma City men visited.

After the Governor Butler trial, the legislators, worn out by the trial, itched to shut down. But before they could, the Alma City delegation contacted Governor James. For nineteen months, he would act as governor until Nebraska inaugurated its next elected governor in January 1873.

When Harlan and his men asked Governor James to establish their county, such a request must have been his first, possibly his only one. He began immediately to produce the special legislative act that would create the county.

"What's your county's name?" Governor James asked.

Phillips hadn't time to say "James County" before Coad spoke: "Harlan County."

Governor James inscribed the name in the legislative act. "For James Harlan," he said. "U.S. Senator from Iowa and Secretary of the Interior. A nice choice."

Coad started to object, but Phillips interrupted. "Thank you, sir. We thought it an excellent choice, too. Didn't his daughter marry Lincoln's son a couple of years ago?"

"Yes, the two families were quite friendly."

Outside the acting governor's office, Coad lit into Phillips. "How could you agree to name our county after James Harlan? When I said 'Harlan County,' I didn't mean James Harlan, that shaggy old guy, his eyebrows as rumpled as his beard. I meant Thomas Harlan. Our Harlan. Not James. That stupid man. Fired the poet of the little people. You know, 'O Captain! my Captain!' Said it wasn't worth reading. Not James Harlan, that pompous twit."

"Calm down, Mark, calm down." Phillips grabbed Coad's shoulder and gave it a shake. "You read what the governor wrote. It doesn't say 'James Harlan County,' it just says 'Harlan County,' it doesn't say Harlan who."

So Coad calmed down, and he and Phillips and Murrin agreed to reply always, if asked, that the county had been named for their leader, Thomas Harlan.

A dialogue like this must have caused the confusion about which Harlan gave our county its name.

Some do say the Alma City settlers named the county for Senator James Harlan. Others claim they named it for his nephew, but that's impossible. Senator Harlan's only nephews, according to his family's genealogical records, were sons of his married sisters, so none bore the Harlan name.

A few historians claim that the Alma City leader, Thomas Harlan, was James's nephew, but he was not. However, he was James's first cousin, according to Ruth Bartels, librarian for the State Historical Society of Iowa in Des Moines.

A formidable group of writers agree that Alma City settlers named Harlan County for their leader Thomas Harlan. John Thomas Link, known for his thorough research into Nebraska place names, wrote that settlers named Harlan County for Thomas Harlan who brought pioneers from Wyoming's Cheyenne Territory to the Republican River valley and who "contributed towards the development of the county."

Harlan and his boys must have felt stunned as they watched the legislators, before the session closed, pass the act to create Harlan County. That left the other counties, six north of the Platte and one south of the Platte, still knocking to be admitted.

Why had only Harlan County passed muster?

Luck, Coad maintained. Strategy, said Phillips.

Maybe Harlan County's western location kept her out of the north-south controversy. Or perhaps, as that venerable historian Andreas noted, legislators "did not always ponder over abstract right and wrong, nor even over policies in some cases."

Then again, Harlan County may have squeaked under the wire because legislators had more important actions to take—such as asking the U.S. Congress to move the national capital from Washington, D.C., to Fort Kearny, Nebraska, which they did request.

Relocating made sense to the Nebraska legislators. Not only was Fort Kearny situated in the middle of the United States and therefore well protected, they argued, but it also had plenty of land available to sell as town lots. (Those rascals.)

Congress declined, but the Nebraska petition shamed Washington, D.C., legislators into noticing their unremarkable, muddy, unpaved town. Fearing other, more enticing petitions to relocate, Congress turned Washington into one of the world's most beautiful capitals.

Anyway, on Saturday, June 3, 1871, the Nebraska legislature carved Harlan County's square area out of the then-large Kearney County. Some maintain that the state formed Harlan County from Lincoln County, but that's impossible. By 1871, Nebraska had redefined the once-large Lincoln County and moved it to its current location north and west of old Kearney County.

Nebraska also named three Alma City officers—Director James Phillips, Secretary Thomas Murrin, and Treasurer Marcus Coad—as temporary county commissioners. The state charged these men to call and oversee an election that would choose county officers and designate the county seat.

We know, now, that only Alma City settlers organized the county, because the legislative act creating the county makes no mention of any western settlers. So in the fight to locate Harlan County's seat, Alma clearly won Round 1.

~ CHAPTER ~
# 23

THE DIRTY DEAL ELECTION

Why hadn't Gen. Vifquain taken some Melrose settlers, traveled to Lincoln, and requested a county?

The answer's simple. The general had become involved in state politics.

As early as August 15, 1860, Vifquain attended Nebraska's convention of Democrats in Omaha, where he swore fidelity to the Democratic party.

In 1868, the Democrats nominated Gen. Vifquain, by acclamation, to run for the office of secretary of state. His Republican opponent, Thomas P. Kennard, up for reelection, currently served as Nebraska's first secretary of state.

In cahoots with the ever-popular Governor Butler, Kennard had produced surveys in Lincoln that helped Governor Butler's speculation in capital lots. The three commissioners, Kennard, Gillespie, and Governor Butler, built themselves imposing homes in the young capital city to encourage settlement there. They hired a twenty-seven-year-old Chicago architect who also designed the insane asylum.

Ox-drawn freight wagons hauled lumber from Omaha and Nebraska City for the three homes. Governor Butler's brown stone home was the largest, but Kennard's the fanciest, an Italianate mansion that featured a cupola on its roof. During construction, Kennard and Governor Butler lived in the just-finished state capitol.

Kennard, with his multiple Governor Butler connections, looked like a hard Republican to beat, and Gen. Vifquain did not.

Then in May 1871, about the time the Alma City crew headed to Lincoln, Gen. Vifquain's home county, Saline, elected him as a delegate to Nebraska's Constitutional Convention, also in Lincoln. The convention had been called so Nebraska could replace her current inadequate constitution. Republicans, who had rushed the constitution through the state legislature in 1866, had modeled it on a long-outdated territorial constitution.

So on June 13, ten days after the legislature created Harlan County, fifty-two delegates, among them Gen. Vifquain, assembled in the ramshackle state capitol to create a new state constitution.

Evidently state politics fascinated Vifquain more than county politics, or he would have requested a new county. No Melrose settler, preoccupied with hunting or with planting crops on his homestead, came up with the idea, either. In the spring of 1871, these settlers lacked even one lawyer. Warren Fletcher hadn't arrived yet and neither had Judge J. Thompson. What a difference these legal thinkers might have made, had they taken claims near the stockade a few months earlier. But they didn't.

No early records report what Melrose settlers thought when they learned that Alma City men had created a county that included the Melrose Stockade, Napoleon, plus all their claims, had named it after that quirky revenue collector from Wyoming, and were about to hold its first election. They must have been enraged.

Did they sense that creating counties and locating county seats in the Midwest could, and probably would, turn into a free-for-all?

Did they know that newly formed counties like theirs, with no one town more established than another, often become vulnerable? The practice of having only one winning county seat in a county, like Harlan County, makes the conflict intense, noted historian James A. Schellenberg. The prize cannot be divided between two towns. One town's victory is "completely at the expense of the other's interests," he wrote, which makes many county seat location fights spiteful, even vicious.

Perhaps the Melrose settlers understood their position. "People of that era," a *Smithsonian* reporter noted, "saw the rosiest future for a town selected as the county seat, but only dust and demise for any town that lost." This view had some justification.

The town that won the seat would benefit financially. Speculation alone could make it rich overnight. Venturers would buy a section of town land from the government for about $800, break the land into 5,120 lots, and resell them to individuals. Back East, such a lot would cost $100. Even if Nebraska lots sold for a fraction of that, the sales promised high profits for speculators.

The place that lost, by contrast, often lost all.

Walnut City, once a contender for county seat in Rush County, Kansas, exists no more, nor does Pleasant Hill, Nebraska, once a hopeful county seat candidate in Saline County where Gen. Vifquain homesteaded. DeSoto, which fought with Fort Calhoun for the Washington, Nebraska, county seat, shows up on no official state highway maps nor does Phelps Center, now entirely gone. It had vied with Holdrege for county seat of Phelps County, Nebraska. These once-active towns are just four of the dozens that died because they weren't chosen to head county governments.

Certainly the Melrose settlers hoped to avoid such an extinction.

~

Nebraska required the new Harlan County commissioners to hold an election within thirty days. The three state-appointed commissioners—Murrin, Phillips, and Coad—lost no time creating precincts, approving lists of candidates, and deciding on polling places.

Required to form precincts for the settlers' convenience, the commissioners established three: No. 1 south of the Republican River, No. 2 east around Alma, and No. 3 west around the Melrose Stockade.

Precinct No. 1 accommodated twenty citizens who had homesteaded south of the river. Many were independent settlers. Most lived near Prairie Dog Creek, the Republican River's largest tributary in Harlan County.

Citizens in Precinct No. 1, located closer to Alma City than to the Melrose Stockade, often supported eastern interests. Even that precinct's polling place, although located south of the Republican River, was in the dugout of James E. Ryder, an Alma City director.

Precinct No. 2, north of the river, encompassed the Alma City men. This precinct consisted of some forty citizens who would cast ballots south of the city at Foster's palace.

The third precinct, also north of the river, ran to the western boundary of the county and contained most of the Melrose area's legal voters, who numbered about thirty-five. Precinct No. 3 voters cast ballots at Squire Guillet's homestead, no longer in Elm Swamp, but at some drier location.

However, commissioners Murrin, Phillips, and Coad, so quick to fix polling places, dragged their heels when advertising the election.

Nebraska law required that twenty days before an election (June 13 in Harlan County), commissioners must post election notices. The commissioners did post notices before the election, but they lollygagged around so much that notices went up only a week in advance.

The state required that these notices be posted in five most public places. But where would "five public places" be in Harlan County? The infant county contained only the Melrose Stockade with its log cabin plus a scattering of homesteads, mostly dugouts except for Foster's palace and Cook's log cabin. Alma City and Napoleon, both "paper towns," lacked streets or buildings. Harlan County had no sign posts since, like most surrounding counties, it had no roads or bridges.

"When we wanted to go anyplace," an early pioneer remembered, "we started out in a general direction and went as far as we could, then around the head of a pocket or canyon, then in another direction. When we came to a stream of water we would ford it and we had to be on the watch out for quicksand."

Without five truly "public places," Alma City election workers posted their notices on trees.

William Parker Carr waited and watched as Commissioner Murrin lettered several notices by hand for Carr to post. When Murrin finished, Carr left with his stack of notices and tacked them on trees for the commissioners.

"Saw one on a tree near a creek over west," Carr reported later at Foster's place, "and one posted near Whiting's creek."

"Yeah," settler Joseph Crockford said, "I saw that one posted near Reverend Whiting's dugout, too. But the poster I put up yesterday is already torn down."

Were notices posted in the stockade? John "Big" Olson lived there but learned about the election from a neighbor two days in advance. Olson would testify that he saw no election notices at the stockade. Of course Olson read Swedish, not English, so he might not recognize a posted election notice, although he said, "But I think I could."

Harlan County's poorly publicized first election was held on July 3, 1871.

Forty-two men voted.

Alma City and Napoleon competed for the county seat. No one had officially entered either site as a "town" with the

U.S. Land Office, so ballots listed these "communities" as sites. Voters chose between Section 28 (Alma City's site) or Section 23 (Napoleon's).

Alma City won a lopsided county seat victory. The vote stood at 37 for Alma City, 5 for Napoleon.

That vote broke down this way: all fourteen voters in Precinct 1 south of the river voted for Alma City; all twenty-three voters in Alma City's Precinct 2 voted for Alma City; and all five voters in Melrose's Precinct 3 voted for Napoleon.

Was this election a dirty deal? Yes, it was a dirty deal. Or, if not dirty, certainly shady. A county created in secrecy, an election barely advertised.

The tiny Melrose vote of 5 should have been more like 35. At the end of December 1871, seventy-two of the 122 males in the county lived in the western precinct. Discounting twenty who hadn't yet arrived by July and seventeen Swedish immigrants not eligible to vote, the voting men in the Melrose precinct still total thirty-five, not five.

But that's not the worst of it. Think, then. Why did the Melrose area draw so few voters? Where were the other Melrose men? What were they doing?

~ CHAPTER ~
# 24

FIREWORKS ON THE 4TH

In 1871, the United States, although 95 years old, still felt quite new. The July 4th celebration of our country's birth had evoked festivities from the first Independence Day in 1776. By 1871, jubilant activities commonly included eating, drinking, waving flags, parading, ringing bells, shooting off fireworks, and firing guns. More solemn enterprises involved reading the Declaration of Independence, proposing toasts, giving orations, and unveiling monuments.

The day's popularity had become so time-honored that wagon trains that stopped for an entire day only on Sundays halted all day to celebrate the 4th of July.

In 1804, Lewis and Clark fired their keelboat gun and picked names for two local streams, Independence Creek and 4th of July Creek, to honor the occasion. The next year, more festively, their men drank the last of their 120 gallons of booze and danced to a fiddle.

In Harlan County, July 4, 1871, fell on Tuesday, the day after the county election. Fifty-six settlers assembled for "The Day We Celebrate," as they called it. They gathered at

Foster's place—not his palace but his nearby cottonwood grove. The previous year, only Ruben had lived in the locality. Melrose settlers had lived there ten months; Alma City members only four.

Gen. Vifquain, absent at Foster's grove, celebrated this Independence Day—in his fashion. Back in his campsite on holiday from the Constitutional Convention, he lived it up by tying a U.S. flag to a handy tree near a creek. Later folks called that stream "Flag Creek."

In the grove, tables bulged with food—and liquor, for toasts. An 1800s Independence Day wasn't complete, writer Dee Brown noted, "without a plentitude of toasts accompanied by suitable beverages."

Harlan County merrymakers probably downed the first toast to Independence Day, the second to the U.S. Constitution and the Declaration of Independence, then perhaps to George Washington, President Ulysses S. Grant, the army and navy, Nebraska, the Spartan mothers of the American Revolution, the ladies (Mrs. Kate Reynolds and Miss Susie Friday) who supervised the "sumptuous dinner," then to families in faraway states or countries, and so forth.

The county celebrants heard Thomas Murrin read the Declaration of Independence aloud, a common practice. Sometimes men read it in German or Spanish. Once a convicted prisoner read the Declaration at a prison. No matter where people heard it, they'd cheer for America's independence from Britain.

Then the one-armed Reverend John Whiting, who had delivered the county's first sermon in June, preached a 4th of July sermon. A Free Methodist minister who'd lost his arm in the Civil War, the Reverend Whiting had used the cottonwood grove near his home as his church. His congregation sat on the ground, and a tree stump held his altar.

By now, settlers, without a doubt, had heard the election news: that Alma City would be their county seat. They likely knew how lopsided the vote had been: 37 to 5. But the festivity continued as planned until, thanks to abundant liquor, the celebration in Foster's grove turned to conflict.

A quarrel broke out between William (or John) McBride and a soldier named Costello. McBride was a new settler from the Alma City area; Costello was stationed at the Melrose Stockade as a member of a U.S. cavalry company. The company patrolled the valley for "marauding" Indians, still common.

What McBride and Costello argued about we don't know (some say they just had a drunken brawl), but if their turfs indicate their loyalties, they might have disagreed about the election results. What we do know is that both men were royally drunk (many, too many, toasts), and that Costello deliberately drew, shot, and killed McBride.

Startled, Harlan County's celebrators witnessed the county's first death—death but not murder. The judge at Costello's trial called the shooting "justifiable" and ruled Costello not guilty.

Perhaps Costello had settled a score for the Melrose folks, for they must have been furious when they heard that, in the July 3 election, Alma City had won not only the county seat but also all the county offices.

If Melrose's voters had been devious, they might have secured the townsite title for Napoleon, renamed the town Alma City, and declared it the county seat. Boone County, Nebraska, citizens tried that solution when two paper towns wrangled. After Albion beat Boone, 67 to 21, for the county seat, Boone's citizens promptly surveyed their paper town, renamed it Albion, and declared it the capital of Boone County.

But the Melrose group didn't think that way. Instead, they charged that Harlan's men had stuffed the ballot boxes. Legal Harlan County residents hadn't cast all those winning votes, Melrose settlers said, but had imported them, perhaps from nearby Franklin County.

Perhaps. Importing voters to determine the outcome of important elections certainly had precedent on the plains. A well-known case of ballot-box stuffing occurred in Kansas in 1855 when 6,307 votes were cast in an election where only 2,905 Kansans were eligible to vote. The non-eligible voters, most from Missouri, exhibited revolvers as proof of their voting rights.

But why would Alma City import voters? The Harlan group didn't need imports to win. They had a more exciting plan of action.

On election day, or so it's said, some men from Alma City rode west of the Melrose Stockade and set the prairie on fire. Like the soldiers who fired the entire prairie in January 1865, the Alma City men purportedly rode horses that dragged bales of burning hay across the prairie.

When grass is dry, it doesn't take much to start a fire. In Nebraska early in July, the summer's heat can dry short grasses to their roots, leaving brittle leaves to act like tinder. A strike of lightning or a spark from a camp fire is enough.

Naturally, faced with a sea of fire, Melrose voters would choose to fight it rather than vote in an election. The women must have fought the fire with brooms and pails of water; the men plowed breaks and set fires between them.

But did Harlan's men really set a fire? Or is this a tale invented by the disgruntled?

Writers are silent on this subject. However, I've been told that, after the election, men found partially burned pieces of rope strung out all across the prairie west of the Melrose Stockade. Rope must have tied those burning bales of hay, even though rope was scarce then, laborious to braid.

Still, think of the risk involved for Alma City men. Prairie fires are notoriously difficult to contain. With prevailing westerly winds blowing, a fire west of the stockade could have threatened residents' possessions in the Alma City area, for no stream big enough to stop a fire lay between the Melrose and Alma City areas. Even a river can't stop a fire if a burning tumble weed blows across.

A prairie fire would have filled the air with ash and cinders at Foster's grove—or certainly at Gen. Vifquain's campsite—but no writer mentioned ashes. Likewise, no records list any property or animals lost.

Of course, that July 3 might have been a calm day, with hardly a breeze stirring, and the fire had no wind to help it on its way. Or perhaps the prairie's tall grasses, often green until the autumn frosts, inhibited the blaze. Or perhaps no fire was set at all.

Yet why did only five of the thirty-five voters in the western half of the county show up to cast votes for the Napoleon site?

Maybe a fire kept Melrose voters away, but maybe they didn't cast a ballot because they didn't know about the election. Maybe the Harlan men posted only one or two fliers on trees in the western county. Maybe they didn't post fliers in the Melrose Stockade as they later claimed.

But for some reason, 88 percent of the men living in the southern precinct voted, 68 percent of the men in the eastern precinct voted, but only 14 percent of the men in the western precinct voted.

Here's the sad part: even if all thirty-five Melrose settlers had voted for Napoleon, that still would not have topped the thirty-seven votes cast for the Alma location.

~

Costello's gunshot evaporated the thrill from the Independence Day celebration. So did the lingering election news. Alma City had won it all: county seat, three county commissioners, a county clerk, a probate judge, a treasurer, a sheriff, and a coroner.

Settlers shifted, then began to leave.

Wily lawyer Cook rounded up the three newly elected commissioners (Joseph Foster, Hugh Trimble, and Thomas Sheffrey), the clerk (Alexander Burke), and other officers.

Together they headed up the creek—Foster's Creek, they called it, since it bordered his property, but it ran right along Cook's homestead, too.

Burke nodded toward the water trickling south. "So is this still Foster's Creek? Or is it Cook Creek here."

Cook turned and stared at him. "You don't divide a creek in half. It's Cook Creek all the way to the river."

Foster stiffened but said nothing as Trimble and Sheffrey laughed at Cook's talent for stirring up a squabble.

The men stopped in front of Cook's new log cabin. They admired the chimney rising up one side and the log roof Cook had put together, but they decided not to meet inside the single room, it being July. Instead, they pulled up a couple of spare logs and sat on them to transact county business.

What business they conducted we'll never know in detail, for, lacking a bound book with blank pages, Clerk Alexander Burke recorded his minutes on loose sheets of paper. Those loose pages survived almost a year, then disappeared, lost or destroyed.

Making the July 3 election legal must have been the primary order of business. Election judges no doubt presented ballots from their precincts, ballots they had tallied the previous day. The commissioners scrutinized all forty-two ballots and certified them as required by law. Clerk Burke recorded these properly canvassed election results, preparing them to be filed with Nebraska's secretary of state.

To secure the county seat, some Alma City men had to submit, within thirty-one days after the election, a certified statement of the results of the election to the secretary of state. This they did, riding again down to Lincoln and on July 10 certifying the election as required by law. We know they did. The secretary of state's records tells us so.

Harlan's men had achieved what they intended: to form a county and claim Alma City for the county seat.

After this, however, county officials did nothing. None of them performed.

Of course, they had no supplies for their jobs, no bound blank books to record proceedings, no election book or stationery or the county seal. Perhaps they couldn't obtain a copy of Nebraska statutes to learn exactly what their duties were. Or maybe they just lacked interest in running a county. Perhaps, given that law still apparently rested with the sharpest shooter, the new officers felt it prudent not to fulfill their duties.

But county officials made a mistake when they neglected to serve. That gave Melrose settlers an opening to attack the election. Which they soon did.

HER BUFFALO SKULL

Harlan County changed quickly that election year.

A few weeks after the 4th of July celebration, a Dr. John McPherson, seventy-two, arrived. An Ohio Medical College graduate, he proved more businessman than doctor. That's because graduating from nineteenth-century medical schools turned out to be so easy that many became doctors for the prestige but made a living in other ways. Dr. McPherson, for instance, had manufactured linseed oil, sold lumber, managed a mercantile business, established a cigar factory, and directed a steam-powered flour and sawmill.

The doctor soon chose a 347-acre townsite of splendid flat land broken by a meandering creek. The site lay east of Alma City and north of the Republican River. He called his town by the unique name of "Republican City"; it is the only Republican City in the world.

Dr. McPherson named his town after the nearby Republican River, which, in turn, had been named by French fur traders in the late 1700s. Those traders discovered Indians living in spacious permanent lodges on bluffs overlooking a large nameless stream. The men traded muskets for buffalo hides, among other things. The French dubbed the Indians "Pawnee" for their "parika" or scalp lock.

These Pawnee fascinated the traders. "How like us they are, despite their *parika,*" the Frenchmen said. They supposed the organization of the Pawnee tribe, apparently dependent on the common man, to be identical to their own French Republic with its "liberty, equality, fraternity." So they mistakenly called this tribe "the Republican Pawnee" and the large river alongside the village "the Republican River."

After the doctor named his town, he left with his son and came back later hauling a dozen wagons piled high with lumber. Soon a wooden building, to be Dr. McPherson's new store, rose, but failed to impress Jason J. Drew, age nine.

"I thought Republican City was a big town," Drew said. When he and his father visited, all Drew saw was a stake and a store. The stake held a board reading "Republican City." The store, dug three feet into the ground, had been built up from logs covered with dirt.

"Where's the town?" Drew wanted to know.

Bit by bit, the town emerged. That summer, Dr. McPherson built a mill to crack corn, grind wheat, and saw timber. Now settlers could erect frame buildings from native cottonwood or walnut logs instead of hauling lumber hundreds of miles as Foster and the McPhersons had done. Mill business became so brisk that folks named the stream that twisted through town "Mill Creek."

In September, the doctor launched his general store. Later, two hotels and a drugstore started up. Hiram M.

Luce from Dobytown opened the drugstore. Dobytown, a nickname for Kearney City, was famous for its gamblers and prostitutes who, said Dr. C. M. Clark, spoke four languages: "Mexican, French, English ... and profanity."

When Luce came to Harlan County, he followed a stream toward the river. Near the creek's mouth, he spotted exactly the rich river bottomland he wanted. Delighted, he cried, "Eureka! I've found it; here is my home."

Luce, an educated man, surely knew that the ancient mathematician Archimedes, ecstatic when he solved the riddle of volume while taking a bath, had cried "Eureka!" as he ran stark naked through Sicilian streets. Even so, Luce dubbed his stream Eureka Creek, a name it still bears.

Next, Joseph Snyder and James Parker built a wooden shingle mill in Republican City. What a boon! Now local residents didn't have to travel to Alma City to buy shingles from William Parker Carr, the first in the county to produce them. Folks liked the wooden tiles. They stopped rain and snow better than sod roofs did. Sod leaked badly, but only after the storm when the water had time to work its way through the thick dirt.

Republican City flourished. Soon its main street ran two blocks long, impressive but not arresting enough to keep 4,000 stampeding buffalo from racing down it.

Unlike the paper towns of Napoleon and Alma City, Republican City became Harlan County's first actual town, the only town that existed on more than paper.

Indians continued to live near Harlan County settlers and sometimes visited them. However, neither Indians nor settlers exhibited much trust in one another.

One autumn evening, the Comstock family of nineteen worked near their dugout, some using sacks of seed corn as seats. Several children and two women wandered off toward the creek. Soon after, they returned shrieking, "Indians! Indians!" They piled into the dugout for safety as the menfolk grabbed their weapons and headed toward the stream.

The Comstocks in the dugout braced themselves, expecting to hear firearms' report any instant. But the night remained still, except for the reverberation of a slight breeze blowing.

After a while, one man returned. "Come on," he said. "You better show me what you seen."

The women and children obliged, walking close to the man.

"There!" they whispered, pointing. "Right there." They turned to flee, but the man grabbed one terrified woman by the hand and marched her toward the natives.

"Looks like a band of 'em, don't it?" the man said. "But see what happens when you get closer."

When the "Indians" failed to move, the woman crept closer until she watched their forms change into silhouettes of shocks of corn, tassels stirring in the wind.

Later that fall, Frank Hofnagle, a German immigrant, had a harrowing Indian encounter. He returned to his dugout to discover that someone (Indians, he felt certain) had ransacked it. Search as he might, he couldn't find his only sewing needle. How could he stay through the winter with no needle to repair his clothes? He'd have to return to Michigan.

The next morning, a Sunday, Hofnagle knelt inside his dugout to pray. Out of the corner of his eye, he noticed a shadow. When he turned, he saw an Indian momentarily silhouetted right outside his door, tomahawk raised.

Expecting certain death, Hofnagle turned back to his prayers.

When he finished, he glanced toward the now-empty doorway. And what did he see? On the dirt floor, sparkling in a narrow stream of sunlight, lay his missing needle.

Rejoicing, he leaped up, grasped the needle, and held it high in the sunlight. "It's a sign from God, for sure," Hofnagle said. "He's telling me I should stay through the winter!"

Which he did, and eventually proved his claim.

What a winter it was! A deadly snowstorm, one of the worst on record, hit November 16, 1871. That day had dawned warm and beautiful, one of a string of fine autumn days. By noon, however, huge snow-filled clouds rolled in, pushed by a high wind and releasing a blizzard that raged for four nights and three days.

The unexpected storm caught many outdoors. Settlers abandoned wagons, mounted horses, and rode for their lives. Two men saved themselves by rolling in blankets and lying down. The snow, drifting over them, insulated them and kept them from freezing. Others were less fortunate. The blast caught many buffalo hunters; some froze, others survived but suffered.

This blizzard proved to be the first of a siege of damaging storms and exceptionally cold weather. Deep snow remained on the ground until early February, but most settlers pulled through the cold. They cut ample fuel from the woods along the river's many tributary streams and killed buffalo, wild turkeys, and other game for food.

During that awesome winter, Lafayette Cady, forty-six, a man evidently not intimidated by weather, moved to Harlan County. But then he'd come from Vermont, one of the coldest states in the Union with an average winter temperature of 22 degrees.

In tiny Vermont, Cady had run a large-scale candy factory, a stoneware factory, and a store. After he relocated in Republican City, he built a hotel, ran a mercantile business, served as postmaster, and became active in the fur business.

The following spring, some businessmen founded a new town, Melrose. It lay a mile northwest of today's Orleans, or east of what had been the Melrose Stockade.

Had been? Yes.

In February, someone set fire to the stockade and its cabin, burning them both to the ground. Shades of the election battle? No. Settlers torched the stockade to kill the cooties (body lice) that plagued the place.

By this time, Napoleon also had expired. Gen. Vifquain neglected to file legal papers to secure his townsite. In fall 1871, William Gaslin, later renowned as a judge but then just an opportunistic attorney from Maine, discovered Vifquain's negligence. The forty-four-year-old lawyer promptly homesteaded one-half of Napoleon; his friend, Charles H. Carey, homesteaded the other half.

So the new community of Melrose seems to have risen Phoenix-like, from the dust of Napoleon and the ashes of the stockade.

Soon it mushroomed.

Because Melrose was a company venture, its men designed a wide business area for the town. In the area, the group erected many top-notch and costly buildings, including a "commodious" two-story store, a blacksmith shop, a doctor's office, a drugstore, a tin shop, a saloon, and The Melrose House, a two-story log hotel.

Mike Manning and his wife, Mary, ran the hotel. Folks considered Mike, with his thick Irish brogue, "quite a personage." He extended his hand to customers, promising them the "foinest" of everything, including "crame from the milk of the spickled heifer for their coffee in the marning."

When Gen. Vifquain discovered that Gaslin had homesteaded on Napoleon, the general left the Republican River valley forever, taking some Melrose area men with him. Vifquain, enamored of Napoleon Bonaparte, must have felt that Gaslin lacked honor. Who would want to spar with such an ungallant opponent? The general didn't fight like that. As one reporter noted, "General Vifquain *a Democrat* fights like an honorable foe. He never sneaks in the underbrush when he is out after republican scalps."

Although the general no doubt felt defeated when he left Harlan County, his legacy is secure. When he founded Fort Melrose, he established not only the first Harlan County settlement but also the first in the Republican River valley.

He brought settlers into the valley at his expense and located them on prime farmlands. So he did accomplish what he had intended, which was to help develop Nebraska.

Gen. Vifquain's Nebraska career would span forty years, during which he became "an important and interesting figure" in state politics, wrote historian Addison Sheldon. The general would live to regard his activities in Harlan County as one of his "important works."

Ironically, thirty-five-year-old Vifquain returned to his Saline County home only to witness a bitter county seat fight there, a fight that would last longer than fifty years, that would still be active in January 1904 when he died.

~

Buoyed by winning the 1871 election, Alma City became a sure-enough town.

Frank Shaffer put together Alma City's first structure, a log house. Prior to coming to Harlan County, he had helped lay out Parkersburg, Iowa, where he'd run a livery business and a hotel.

Alma City's townsite committee named Shaffer its president. The committee laid out 160 acres, staked off 40, and gave a lot to anyone willing to build.

Soon a Mr. Broadmore built a sod blacksmith shop, and George Moore and a Mr. Sappington erected the town's first store. Moore and Sappington proved to be opportunists. As soon as they noticed business booming in the west, they waved good-bye to Alma City. They rolled their store on logs, the standard way to move a cabin, all seven miles to Melrose.

Joseph Painter, once in Harlan's scouting party, still counted himself an Alma City man, but his tether to the community had weakened. He considered Harlan a feeble leader. The Illinois lawyer hadn't figured out how to govern. If he had, Alma City would have been the county's first actual town, not Republican City.

Even so, on July 14, Painter accepted a U.S. Postal Service appointment as postmaster in Alma City, the county's first post office. Before this time, mail distribution had been a private enterprise.

The tiny town's founders imagined "a bright and prosperous future," thanks to its county seat designation. The *Harlan County Journal* even expected Alma City to "become the metropolis of the county if not the entire Republican valley."

But despite its new post office, its blacksmith shop, and its fly-by-night store, Alma City, as a town, remained more fragile than Republican City or Melrose. Alma City had fewer businesses, and, in times of trouble, its citizens too often picked up and moved elsewhere, the way Moore and Sappington had.

At this time, Harlan County had progressed from having two paper towns, Alma City and Napoleon, to having two tangible communities, Republican City and Melrose, plus one almost real town: Alma City. Or, as Andreas put it, "Republican City and Melrose each had a store, a hitching post, and a clothes line, while Alma City had only her buffalo skull."

~ CHAPTER ~
# 26

SHENANIGANS GALORE

When Harlan County's first elected officers failed to knuckle down to business, they launched local gossip strong enough to undermine the 1871 county seat election. Citizens eager to snatch the seat huddled and talked. The county, they noticed, not only lacked active officers but also had no courthouse. "The election's dead," they all agreed.

Some settlers, eager to elect a new county government, met in secret at Joseph H. Painter's homestead. Why Painter's place? Perhaps its convenient location some distance away from Alma City. Or maybe because anti–Alma City voters felt comfortable with Painter's rebellious political views. Disgruntled with Harlan's leadership, Painter no longer served as vice president of the Alma City group.

On Painter's farm, in the spring of 1872, these citizens met in public to discuss relocating the county seat. Settlers swarmed from all over the county, some say, but like as not most represented Melrose or Republican City. These voters drew up a petition requesting an election and, in May, went to Lincoln and presented it to William H. James, still acting governor.

In the year since Harlan's group had requested a county, Nebraska legislators had given the acting governor a hard time. In January 1872, they tried to override his veto of their plan to call, illegally, a third constitutional meeting. "To call a convention," the acting governor argued, "Nebraska needs a vote by citizens, not legislators."

Angry, Governor James adjourned the legislature indefinitely, although he had no authority to do so. The Senate president obeyed the order and adjourned the Senate, but the Senators refused to leave. Instead, they elected a new president and declared the position of acting governor vacant. The Senators hoped that would drive the acting governor out of office, but it didn't.

Instead, he left for Washington February 6, on public business. He failed to tell the new Senate president, Isaac S. Hascall, to act as governor until his return. Maybe he forgot or maybe he didn't trust the president.

With good reason.

The instant the president heard that the acting governor had gone out of town, he decided to call a special February 15 legislative session. For that, he needed to use the state seal, so he "bulged" into Governor James's office. There President Hascall "whipped his proclamation under the seal of the state" and took the seal's impression. Then he telegraphed Senators to announce the meeting.

President Hascall hoped to pass, in his special session, a bill organizing forty-two new counties. Thirty-three lay north of the Platte but only nine to the south. By Nebraska law, each county, no matter how small, could send a delegate to the state convention. If Hascall's bill passed, politicians north of the Platte would dominate the next state convention.

The president's "flank movement," noted the *Brownville Advertiser*, "is so transparent a cheat that it will not hold water."

When Governor James heard about Hascall's plan, he stitched up his Washington business and sped to Lincoln. To prevent legislators from voting on Hascall's proclamation, Governor James barricaded the entrance to their meeting hall. A few Senators and even fewer Representatives broke through the barrier. When they set a fire to warm the room, the acting governor cut off their coal supply.

A few days later, the Nebraska Supreme Court ruled that the legislature had not been in legal session. So Hascall's bill, noted the *Tecumseh Chieftain*, "died to slow music."

Despite Hascall's gerrymandering attempt and other assorted trickery of that winter, Governor James didn't notice any deception in the Harlan County voters' request for a new election.

However, the pro–Alma City *Harlan County Standard* did. The paper noted that Melrose and Republican City backers, by claiming that votes had been illegally cast in 1871, had "induced" Governor James to call an election.

Induced or not, on May 20, 1872, he did order an election, this one for June 29, a Saturday.

As in the 1871 election, voters would choose a variety of county officers and "designate upon their ballots the Place of their choice for the County Seat." Four townsites vied for that county seat—Alma City, Melrose, Republican City, and Napoleon.

Napoleon? Oh, yes, few settlers lifted eyebrows when that tricky Maine lawyer, Gaslin, had weaseled Gen. Vifquain out of Napoleon by homesteading on the general's townsite. They took it in stride when Gaslin mocked Napoleon as "that ethereil [sic] burg" with "the high sounding name." But when the lawyer put his half of the old Napoleon in the running for county seat, folks noticed. How curious! Out of the blue, that "ethereil [sic] burg" had assumed a worldly form.

Of the contenders for county seat, only Gaslin's Napoleon remained a paper town. Melrose, Republican City, and even Alma City had flourished into communities. Melrose and Republican City rivaled each other. Republican City now sported two hotels, two mills, a general store, and a drugstore. Melrose, close to the center of the county, seemed positioned to excel as a business center. Indeed, historian Andreas considered the town, "One of the most important points ... in the Republican valley."

This 1872 election differed from the first election in several significant ways.

First, it had only two polling places rather than three as in 1871.

Its eastern Precinct 1 included Alma City, Prairie Dog settlers, and Republican City. All would vote in Republican City. Note how the center of power has shifted. Prairie Dog settlers, generally Alma City supporters, no longer had a separate precinct south of the river. To vote, they must cross the river and travel 15 miles. Alma City settlers, who once voted in their home town, now had to trek 10 miles to vote.

The western Precinct 2, like Precinct 3 in the 1871 election, contained most of the western area's legal voters. More modern now, they would vote in Melrose instead of in Squire Guillet's dugout.

The two elections also differed in the officers that Governor James appointed to oversee the election. The ten officials in 1872 came from Republican City, Melrose, and a variety of rural homesteads. Only one supported Harlan's group: James O. Phillips, also an officer in 1871 when every official supported Alma City.

Settlers in Alma City, lamented the *Harlan County Standard*, now stand "in a distinct minority" against the combined Melrose and Republican City citizens. Even worse, Alma City voters will cast their ballots on an issue already decided in their favor.

Last, in the 1872 election, 110 more men voted than in 1871, or 152 compared to 42. Waves of immigration into the county accounted for the increase. All 152 men cast legal ballots, according to the county clerk's recorded list of eligible voters. No one claimed that anyone imported votes or stuffed ballot boxes.

When clerks counted votes for the 1872 election, Alma City scored better than expected. Five of ten elected officials supported Alma City. What a surprise, although not such a victory compared with 1871 when Alma City won all county offices. (I can almost hear settlers smirking: "She got her comeuppance.")

Worse than that loss, only one county commissioner, James O. Phillips, an Alma City director, supported Alma City. The other two, Thomas "Tom" Sheffrey and John

Bartelt, sided with Melrose. Sheffrey's western claim lay near today's Oxford, but Bartelt, although he never boosted Alma City, homesteaded in the eastern part of the county.

Unlike the 1871 officers, these newly elected officials did serve. Governing of the county began. The first official county commissioners' journal, a bound volume, dates from this election.

Yet none of the four townsites vying for county seat— Alma City, Melrose, Napoleon, and Republican City— had enough votes to win. Republican City got 57 votes; Melrose, 36; Alma City, 31; and Gaslin's Napoleon, 24.

Republican City voters became jubilant when they heard the election results. Since their town received the most votes they believed they had won the election. However, Nebraska election law required a majority vote to determine the county seat. No Harlan County town won more than 50 percent of the votes cast. That would have been 75 of the 148 county seat votes, not 57.

Far from settling the question of the county seat, this election only served to muddy matters.

27

COUNTY SEAT ON WHEELS

The 1872 election muddied plans for meeting places. Since voters elected officials but had chosen no county seat, where would those officers meet?

Some state that they met in one another's sod houses, but the Harlan County commissioners' journal records that they met in stores. When commissioners met in Alma City, they met in George Moore's store; when they met in Republican City, they met in Dr. John McPherson's store; and when they met in Melrose, they met in Franklin A. Bieyon's store.

No matter where the Harlan County officers met, citizens of that town lorded it over less fortunate towns, flaunting their supposed superiority. "Flimsy circumstances often controlled public affairs," the *Harlan County Standard* wrote, noting that "the county seat was 'upon wheels.'"

However, Harlan County officials, who moved from store to store, had it easy compared to Rush County, Kansas, officers. Those men dragged a 16-foot-square wooden courthouse for five miles from La Crosse to Rush Center or back each time courts changed locations.

The 1872 election not only put the county on wheels, it also propelled county records, the key to the county seat, on several unexpected excursions.

At the board's election day meeting, Alexander Burke of Alma City, elected clerk in 1871, still held the county records, which he had recorded on loose sheets of paper. The just-elected clerk, John Whiting, a Free Methodist minister who supported Alma City, had a new bound volume to record his minutes.

When the board met in Republican City the next day, all the county records had vanished—into Harlan's hands. Clerks Burke and the Reverend Whiting, both loyal to Alma City, no doubt gave their records to Harlan. He refused to return the county stationery, seal, and county records, both the loose sheets Burke used in 1871 as well as the Reverend Whiting's new bound volume. What possessed him to hold them?

It's comforting to believe that the county's future concerned Harlan. Or to hope that his "theft" wasn't just a power move. Or to wonder if he had legal reservations: did county officials, chosen in an illegal election, merit the records? But no. Harlan, namesake of the county, had a crasser motive in mind. Money.

The board sent Commissioner James Phillips as a committee of one to find out how much Harlan wanted to return the "retained" items.

Why Phillips? Perhaps the commissioners thought that Harlan would feel cordial toward Phillips, the only Alma City commissioner. Or perhaps they sent Phillips because they had just named him president of the county board.

Harlan's price to release the county records must have been steep, for Phillips met with him a second time in order to negotiate. The new board president bargained Harlan down to $75 for the return of the records, stationery, and seal. Thus $75, or almost $1,500 in today's currency, settled Harlan County's first theft of its records.

~

The county commissioners, eager to hold a runoff election for county seat, scheduled one on August 8. They dropped the Napoleon/Gaslin homestead site from the ballot, since that site had the fewest votes in the previous election. Now the race was among Alma City, Melrose, and Republican City.

Settlers voted eagerly. The election totaled 215 votes, or 63 more than on June 29. Curiously, no returns exist for this election. The commissioners justified this by arguing that they had no time to wait for election judges to examine results, as required by law. Besides, the officers reasoned, judges needn't report returns for just one more runoff election. The only thing known about this election is that Alma City came in last.

The commissioners then called a third election, this one for August 27. They dropped Alma City from the new ballot; that's how we know she lost. Melrose and Republican City remained the only contenders.

Scanty records remain for this final election, too, but we know Melrose won by 2 votes, 118 to Republican City's 116. This time, election judges examined results as required by law and gave these returns to the county clerk. The board expected the Reverend Whiting to record the results in his bound volume and then prepare them to be forwarded to Nebraska's secretary of state. That, they believed, would make Melrose the legal county seat.

But the Reverend Whiting did not bring the election returns to the board. Instead, he hid them.

~

After the August 27 election, county commissioners decided to switch their meeting place from Alma City to the expected county seat: Melrose. First they gathered that Tuesday in Republican City to discuss where in Melrose to get together.

Before they could decide, Nathan Cook, that New York lawyer and Harlan's buddy, rose to protest. "You can't declare the county seat anywhere but Alma City," he said. "It was legally chosen in that first election."

But the commissioners—Sheffrey, Bartelt, and Phillips—disagreed.

Of course Tom Sheffrey and John Bartelt would clash with Cook. True, Harlan had brought both to the county, but they'd broken away from him to become active Melrose supporters. And what about the president, James Phillips? He'd been tight with Harlan every step of the way. Why didn't Phillips support Cook?

Maybe he knew he'd be outvoted. Or maybe he planned to fight on another front. For whatever reason, he agreed with Sheffrey and Bartelt to meet next time in Melrose in old-timer Frank Bieyon's "storehouse."

(But this is not the last we'll see of Phillips. Keep an eye on him. He's a major player.

As for Bieyon's "storehouse," why meet there if a court-house could be built in the meantime?)

Later on Thursday, August 29, three men asked L. J. Gronquist to build a courthouse. A newcomer, Gronquist had lived in the county since May. After the terrible Great Chicago Fire burned him out, he rode a train to Lincoln and jounced over open prairie to Harlan County in a wagon pulled by oxen.

Gronquist agreed to build the Melrose "courthouse"; it would be the first "courthouse" in the county. Within two days, he had enclosed the new house, located just east of Melrose.

On Tuesday, September 3, the board met at Bieyon's "storehouse" in Melrose only to adjourn and move to the new Melrose "courthouse." *Notice this: Phillips agreed.*

Whiting, the county clerk, never called the new Melrose house a "courthouse" in his journal. Instead, he wrote, "Bieyon's new house." Bieyon, who had supervised the construction of the Melrose Stockade and had built his log "storehouse," must have owned the new building.

(Who ordered Gronquist to build a courthouse? Was it Bieyon and a couple of pals? Or the commissioners?

My guess is Bieyon, Sheffrey, and Bartelt, but the record is silent on this subject.)

~

Whiting, the county clerk, sure knew how to make waves. Remember how he hid the August 27 election tallies so the commissioners couldn't forward them to the state? Well, now, about a week later, he's examining the ballots after all, assisted by George Moore, an Alma City merchant, and Charles Sealy, a newcomer allied with Alma City.

However, when the commissioners, at their September 5 meeting, called for the Reverend Whiting's report, he handed them a piece of paper. On it he'd written:

"I hereby submit the results of the canvas of the election returns of an election held in Harlan County, State of Nebraska, August 27 AD 1872 to wit: No legal election."

His action must have stunned the commissioners.

An ordained Free Methodist minister and the county's only pastor, the Reverend Whiting had tended to all the settlers' ministerial needs since he'd arrived in the spring of 1871. However, although the Reverend Whiting relished being everyone's minister, he also delighted in his homestead on Methodist Creek (named for him) located near the Alma City he now promoted for county seat.

Commissioners Sheffrey and Bartelt protested, of course. The Reverend Whiting's report is "not proper," they argued.

New York lawyer Cook popped up, as he had before, blasting the location of the county seat any place but Alma City.

Sheffrey ignored Cook and insisted that the Reverend Whiting make a full report of the election held August 27.

The clerk refused. "I have no authority to do so."

(Look at this: at last Phillips revealed his Alma City allegiance.)

As board president, he accepted the Reverend Whiting's report, turning this meeting into a major victory for Alma City.

Of course Sheffrey and Bartelt sounded off, but Phillips just moved that the Reverend Whiting post notices that the county seat had not been located.

Did that cause conniptions! Sheffrey and Bartelt, sitting in the new "courthouse," couldn't concede that the county seat was not there. Phillips's motion lost, 2 to 1.

(Consider this: Because the Reverend Whiting refused to call the August 27 election legal and because President Phillips accepted the Reverend Whiting's report, no one ever filed the results of that 1872 election with the state government in Lincoln.

This meant that the only election that fulfilled all legal obligations in locating the county seat continued to be the initial one, the one held in 1871, the one that Alma City won.)

THE HARLAN COUNTY SHUFFLE

The absence of the board president and the clerk puzzled commissioners Sheffrey and Bartelt. Why had Phillips and the Reverend Whiting skipped meetings for more than a month?

The two remaining officers could manage without Phillips's vote, but they needed the Reverend Whiting's records in order to perform their duties. The clerk held the county seal, all the minutes since the first election, plus the recent election results, still not filed in Lincoln. Those records, Sheffrey and Bartelt knew, had never left the hands of an Alma City supporter: first, clerk Burke, then Harlan, and now the Reverend Whiting. Had he hijacked county records again?

On October 7, 1872, Sheffrey and Bartelt stopped waiting for the Reverend Whiting to show up. Instead, they swore in Frank Bieyon, a staunch Melrose supporter, as temporary clerk and went ahead with their long-overdue meeting.

When the Reverend Whiting failed to show up the following week, Sheffrey and Bartelt, fuming, swore to retrieve everything that sneak had snitched. But how? Last July when records disappeared, the commissioners had sent the board president to negotiate with Harlan, but President Phillips remained absent. So the commissioners sent Sheriff Martin Fitch, armed with an official summons.

Whiting appeared at his door as Fitch knocked.

"You're free to find them," the clerk said, "if you can."

The sheriff ransacked the Reverend Whiting's possessions, hunting for the missing seal, ballots, and minutes, but he ferreted out nothing.

Where were those records? Perhaps Harlan knew.

Then a Jacob "Jack" Young burst on the scene. An Alma City supporter, he had arrived in the county early and served as a member of Alma City's townsite committee, distributing free lots to boost the town. Then, sometime during the following year or two, Young evolved into a turncoat. Now a Melrose supporter, he accepted the task that Sheffrey and Bartelt begged of him: "Help us snare Whiting."

On November 6, Young came to the Harlan County board meeting and set the ball rolling by charging the Reverend Whiting with malfeasance in office and willful neglect of duty. *Malfeasance* is a curious word that applies primarily to public officials. Basically, it means misconduct or wrongdoing.

Sheffrey and Bartelt, maintaining that the Reverend Whiting had treated them with "contempt and defiance," summoned the clerk for a November 9 trial.

Sheriff Fitch, an Alma City supporter, nevertheless prepared to haul the Reverend Whiting to the board's court, but the clerk amazed everyone by arriving and turning over the county seal, the journal, election reports, etc. Then he pleaded "not guilty" to all charges.

The trial began at 10 a.m. and dragged on into evening. Five men testified against the Reverend Whiting, and he cross-examined each. The five included Young, of course, and other Melrose supporters, namely old-timer Franklin A. Bieyon who helped Gen. Vifquain christen "Napoleon," the county's bad boy John Carrothers so often in some kind of nasty trouble, and perhaps a Joseph Weaver. Plus the sheriff, Fitch, an Alma supporter who seemed willing to swap allegiances when convenient.

After the lengthy testimony, Sheffrey and Bartelt deliberated. I suppose their rapid verdict of guilty shocked no one. The commissioners removed the Reverend Whiting from office and charged him court costs for his trial, $15.95, an amount that they calculated in petty detail.

～

For the first time ever, Alma City supporters no longer controlled the Harlan County records. Instead, the positions of clerk and temporary clerk went to staunch Melrose boosters.

At the November 26 meeting, to complete the Reverend Whiting's term as clerk, Sheffrey and Bartelt swore in Joseph Painter, now a Melrose supporter. He then held the county records, including the August 27 election returns, still not filed with the secretary of state. Painter, however, never attended meetings. Instead, another strong Melrose supporter, Bieyon, the temporary clerk, continued to function as clerk.

Power began to shuffle west. With the Painter and Bieyon appointments, Melrose's representation on the ten-officer board climbed from four to six county officials. Alma City, no longer in the lead, once claimed five officials, but now had only four.

On November 28, the tempo of the shuffle picked up. Bartelt resigned as commissioner, and Melrose's John W. Carrothers, that rough character, took his place. Little Squire Guillet from Melrose was sworn in as sheriff, replacing Martin Fitch from Alma City.

But what to do about Phillips? Still president, he hadn't attended a meeting for thirteen weeks, not since August 27 when he accepted the Reverend Whiting's "no legal election" report. On December 2, the commissioners replaced Phillips, naming Fitch as the third commissioner. Next—are you following this?—Melrose's Jacob C. Young replaced Alma City's Gilbert Parish as county treasurer. And the board swore in Bieyon, the temporary clerk, as deputy county clerk, a new position.

As a result of all this fancy dancing, six of the now eleven county officers had been appointed, not elected. Five of these six new officers were loyal to Melrose. Alma City now had two positions. Instead of four, Melrose held eight. Republican City remained constant at one.

In less than two months, the makeup of the county offices shifted from an elected group split between the interests of the east and the west sections of the county to a predominantly appointed board controlled by the interests of the west.

The plot thickened. A new town sprang up.

Warren M. Fletcher, hailed as an exceptionally worthy young man, had arrived in Harlan County in December 1871. He bought property near the center of the county; its land sloped to the river.

On November 2, 1872, Fletcher sold that tract for $800 to D. N. Smith, a noted townsite locator. Smith selected townsites along the southern route of the Burlington and Missouri River Railroad Company.

He founded a town on the tract he'd bought and named it "Orleans," probably after Orléans in France, an important rail junction.

"Orleans will win the county seat," Smith predicted, "thanks to its central location and its ties with Burlington." The new railroad would connect with the transcontinental Union Pacific, only 60 miles away.

Smith, also an ordained Methodist minister, expected to preach the first sermon in the town he founded, but the Reverend Whiting beat him to it. The white tents of the Reverend Whiting's revival meetings fluttered in Orleans long before Smith erected the town's first building.

The new town grew rapidly. Smith constructed four buildings, one on each side of the public square. In January 1873, the town's first resident built a small hotel. Then—notice this—Bieyon, the Melrose "courthouse" owner and deputy county clerk, moved from Melrose into a building on Orleans's north side. And Frank Shaffer—remember him? He built Alma's first house—got so wound up by Orleans's potential that he relocated. He rolled that same log house seven miles to the flourishing new town. That go-getter must have opened a tavern, for he would be fined $30 for selling liquor without a license.

Jealousy cropped up between Orleans, with its railroad connections, and Melrose, with its presumed county seat. Residents of each town surged with pride, scholar Everett Dick wrote, "Until their citizens felt the air was purer, the soil more fertile, and natural advantages in every way more desirable, than in the neighboring vicinity."

No one could predict which town would survive. They lay two miles apart "too close together for both to succeed," Andreas wrote, "and yet too far apart to consolidate." Melrose, the older community with established business interests, seemed to have the advantage, but then Orleans had Smith.

Smith "fought the town of Melrose every way that was possible by law and every other way," Ada B. Kolb noted. In these battles, Smith "incurred the animosity of many," Gaslin observes. The locator had "an iron will."

Competition between Melrose and Orleans divided citizens and threatened personal violence such as broke out in seven other Midwestern county seat fights, including Nebraska's Washington County where a zealous opponent killed a man.

The townsite locator deliberately had placed his new town of Orleans near an old town, Melrose. A smart move. When the old town died, its former residents would boost the nearby population of his new one. Smith had achieved just that in Gen. Vifquain's home county of Saline by placing his "Crete" near the older Blue River City, a village now extinct.

Poor Melrose! It had just wrested the county seat from Alma City and Republican City, and now it was locked in a death struggle with Orleans.

~

Alma City, the clear loser in the 1872 election, began to break up. Frank Shaffer had rolled his house to Orleans, and Painter, long displeased with Harlan, had left. As postmaster, he moved Alma City's post office to his homestead. Soon people called both Painter's post office and the original townsite "Alma City."

In January and February 1873, the county board continued to meet in the Melrose "courthouse." Painter, the clerk, attended no meetings so Bieyon recorded the minutes. The board paid forty-seven hunters a couple dollars each for every wolf or wild cat killed. Commissioners okayed a dirt road—the county's first—that would link Alma City, Melrose, Orleans, and Republican City.

In Republican City, the more voters thought about the elections that had placed the county seat in Melrose, the less they liked it. Hadn't they "won" the first of the three 1872 elections? In 1873, Dr. McPherson, town founder, addressed the matter in district court, which now met regularly in Republican City, because, as court records noted, no place had yet been fixed as county seat. In court, Dr. McPherson demanded that the county board, now headed by former Sheriff Fitch, the vacillator, explain why Republican City, winner of the 1872 election, shouldn't be the legal county seat.

That spring, Harlan County experienced a terrible blizzard, the Easter blizzard of April 13, when two storms crashed together. A cold rain, which started that afternoon, turned into driving sleet that felt like stings of bird shot until it turned to fine snow.

Then a tempest roared. The "wind howled like a banshee," author Wayne C. Lee wrote. It "sucked the breath right out of a man's lungs." Long gusts of wind slammed doors open, lifted roofs off houses, blasted them to smithereens, collapsed them into kindling. The wind rocked homes until it moved them from their foundations, sending clothes, chairs, bedsteads on long journeys.

The blizzard lasted three days. Temperatures dropped well below zero. Snow drifted eighteen to twenty feet high. Twenty people died, smothered or frozen. So did thousands of head of livestock, even though many settlers took horses, cows, pigs, and chickens into their dugouts or cabins until the storm stopped.

After the storm, later in April, the board appointed Thomas D. Murrin as sheriff to replace Melrose's Little Squire Guillet who had "removed from the County." Had Murrin, like Painter, left the Alma City group? Or had the commissioners added a third Alma City official?

That summer, Orleans continued to flourish. The town's optimistic citizens, sure now of winning the county seat, added nine new buildings, and Carl Boehl started a flour mill on nearby Sappa Creek. The county commissioners selected Orleans's *Republican Valley Sentinel* to be Harlan County's official organ.

County business continued. The board licensed a ferry to run across the Republican River where Alma City and Orleans townships met. It also laid plans to build a river bridge at Republican City, a plan that voters later would approve. The commissioners also decided to pay the Reverend Whiting's bill for his services as clerk—minus what they considered he owed them.

THE FLOATING COURTHOUSE

As of March 1873, the Harlan County "courthouse" exhibited signs of wanderlust.

The county board had met in the Melrose "courthouse" since September 3, 1872, but at its March 4 meeting, Commissioners Sheffrey and Fitch (without absent Commissioner Carrothers) decided to move to Orleans.

Why?

The Melrose "courthouse" lacked "conveniences," they said. This makes the building sound primitive, which no doubt it was. But up-and-coming Orleans had offered a place presumably with "conveniences" and certainly "free of expense."

Meetings at this Orleans location lasted about a month until L. S. Dickenson, who had come to the county with Gen. Vifquain, offered to let the county use two Melrose rooms for $20 a quarter. All three commissioners agreed and planned to meet in Dickenson's expensive building after April 25, which they did.

Then, on June 14, an M. Willsie offered a free building— in Orleans. So off the board went to Orleans where they stayed for months.

Consider how curious this is. The board no longer meets in Alma City, the town that won the July 3, 1871, county seat election. Nor does it meet in Melrose, the town that "won" the August 27, 1872, runoff election. It doesn't even meet in Republican City, the town that claimed it won the June 29, 1872, election by racking up so many votes. No, now the board meets, and will continue to meet, in Orleans, the only town in the county not on any ballot for county seat because it hadn't existed until November 1872.

No wonder Orleans citizens were optimistic about gaining the county seat!

On September 18, a vital Wall Street investment firm failed. That closed the stock market's doors for nearly two weeks and set off the biggest panic yet known, the Panic of 1873. A six-year period of depression and distress followed. In Nebraska, farmers watched prices for produce and stock dip too low to sell even staples.

This widespread disturbance, however, did not stop William Parker Carr from getting married. He chose, as his Jeanee with the light brown hair, Miss Harriet Lucinda Ellenberger, a native of Iowa. They produced two children who, like their parents, lived in Harlan County. Carr's family satisfied his dream of settling down, the dream he'd had in Wyoming while working for the railroad. Now forty-two, his life hadn't ended at the predicted age of thirty-five, either. Maybe after all he'd live to a ripe old fifty.

Harlan County's ballot that October 1873 featured the election of eight of the county's eleven officers. Only two appointed officers now remained, Commissioners Fitch and Bieyon, the deputy clerk. The settlers' vote shifted governmental power. Now, instead of eight Melrose officers to two Alma City, the total was five to five.

The three new Alma City supporters included Sheriff Thomas Murrin, who ran for commissioner and won. James E. Ryder, once an Alma City director, became sheriff. And the board had a new clerk: John M. Roberts, who supported Alma City. (Keep an eye on these three.)

Since June 14, 1873, when the board moved to Orleans, the county records had been kept there in Willsie's free building where the commissioners met. One of the clerks held them there, either the official clerk, Painter, who had replaced the Reverend Whiting but attended no meetings, or more likely the deputy clerk, Bieyon, who substituted for Painter. But now, with the election of Roberts as the new official clerk, those records roved again.

At the January 6, 1874, board meeting, Commissioner Fitch, whose loyalty to Alma City had waffled, moved that county records be taken to, of all places, Alma City. Commissioners Sheffrey and the just-elected Murrin overruled Fitch; they moved to keep the records at Orleans. When that motion carried, the matter seemed settled.

(Note this: When Murrin, one of Alma City's most prominent members, voted with Sheffrey, he seemed to shift his allegiance to the west. This despite his homestead southwest of Alma City.)

Then, on January 28, under the leadership of Sheffrey, now senior commissioner, the board met at Orleans only to adjourn and meet again in Melrose. Why? Because that's where the county seat had been located. Commissioner Fitch protested, but that did no good.

Then Commissioners Sheffrey and Murrin ordered John M. Roberts, clerk, and James E. Ryder, sheriff, both newly elected, to move all records, books, and other county property, including the stove, from Orleans to the Melrose building.

Commissioner Fitch again protested: "We should take those records to Alma City and meet there the moment that residents could provide a building for us." But the two other commissioners overruled his motion.

The next day, the board met in Melrose and decided— with Fitch protesting—to rent the Melrose building for three months.

In the meantime, Fitch—or someone—brought Murrin to his senses. On March 21, when the board met in Melrose, Fitch, as usual, moved to adjourn and meet in Alma City. Then, in an astonishing twist, Murrin agreed. Together they voted to meet in Alma City, and where? At Nathan Cook's cabin. That cabin, where county records had been hidden again and again. That cabin, where the very first commissioners met and readied papers to take to Lincoln to register Alma City as the county seat. That cabin radiated Harlan County history.

Fitch might have thought that Murrin, in voting to meet in Alma City, had decided to return to his Alma City ties. He had been a fireball in the county's early days. A member of Harlan's scouting party, then Alma City's secretary, Murrin helped choose Alma City's townsite. Governor James had appointed Murrin an election officer, and his dugout became a voting place in the 1871 election. He even took election results to

Lincoln to be filed with the secretary of state. After that, however, he kept a low profile.

But now he turned active again. "We'd better have the sheriff take all our records and other county property out of the clerk's Melrose office and move them to Alma City."

Fitch agreed, and ordered Sheriff Ryder to make that move.

Commissioner Sheffrey, of course, protested their every decision, but he objected in vain. The board did move. They met in Alma City April 7, 1874, except for Sheffrey. He still protested.

(At this point, the records moved into the hand of the new clerk, John M. Roberts, and into Cook's log cabin. Roberts would keep county records in those places, as you'll see.)

~

Remember the heated arguments in Nebraska's territorial legislature? How the group split in two, meeting in Florence and in Omaha? Something of the same sort happened in Harlan County. The issue: whether to continue to meet in Alma City.

On Monday, April 20, the board split this way for the first time. In Alma City, when Commissioner Fitch and County Clerk Roberts showed up for the scheduled board meeting, they sat alone for some time.

"Where's Murrin?" Fitch said. "I didn't expect Sheffrey to show up, he's so dead set against meeting here, but what happened to Murrin?"

Since Fitch's meeting lacked a second commissioner, he couldn't transact business, so he adjourned the meeting.

Where was Murrin? Sheffrey, who refused to meet in Alma City, must have bent Murrin's ear, for those two commissioners ended up back in Melrose. Look at that! Murrin's great love of Alma City didn't last long.

Two commissioners, a majority, can act as a board, so they did, but they needed a clerk. Sheffrey corralled the sheriff. "Go tell Roberts to bring us the county records."

"This is urgent," Murrin told Sheriff Ryder. "We need them to do county business."

"That's right. Make sure you get it all, the county seal, the journal, everything."

Ryder rode off to Alma City. "They want it all," he told Roberts. But the clerk refused to give Ryder anything, not even the journal.

On Tuesday, April 21, the board split again between Alma City and Melrose. Both adjourned. But on Wednesday, Murrin and Sheffrey in Melrose didn't adjourn. Instead, they took a recess to buy books so they could conduct business. Then on Thursday, the two commissioners named John R. King, who ran a hotel in Orleans, temporary clerk.

In the meantime, on Tuesday and Wednesday, Fitch and Roberts had met in Alma, only to adjourn.

As soon as they swore in their new clerk, Murrin and Sheffrey could conduct Harlan County business in earnest. They promptly sat as the Board of Equalizations and made a wide variety of changes in assessments of personal property, all in Precinct 1, which included Alma City and Republican City. Then the pair voted to send the temporary clerk, John R. King, to notify Roberts of their actions.

Sheffrey grinned. "And be sure you tell him you're our new clerk. See if that flusters him."

Evidently that news did fluster Roberts, for on May 11, he attended the Melrose board meeting. Fitch did not, but the other two commissioners did.

"Look what the wind blew in!" Sheffrey muttered to Murrin as Roberts entered the room.

As soon as the clerk settled in his chair, Sheffrey said, "Now enter all those April meetings in your bound commissioners' journal."

Roberts nodded.

"Yes," Murrin added, "enter all the meetings we held in Melrose. And those with you and Fitch in Alma City."

Roberts seemed pliable enough, and by the end of the board meeting, he had penned the minutes for all those meetings. However, instead of leaving his journal with Sheffrey in Melrose, as expected, he took it with him.

That did not sit well with Sheffrey.

The next day, everyone met in Melrose: clerk Roberts, the sheriff, and all three commissioners, including Fitch, no longer meeting by himself in Alma City.

After Roberts read the minutes of the last meeting, Sheffrey turned to Sheriff Ryder, "We need you to remove our records from Cook's cabin in Alma City."

"And we want everything," Murrin said, "books, papers, journals, seals. Everything."

Sheffrey cleared his throat. "Bring it all here. We'll hold those records here in Melrose until the county seat question's is settled by law."

Roberts lifted his pen and looked up. "And when might that be?"

"Summer," Sheffrey said. "We expect to know by summer."

Commissioner Fitch, of course, protested the action, but the air went out of his balloon when Roberts let the sheriff bring the county records to Melrose. By this time, Roberts had hung on to the records in Cook's Alma City log cabin for almost two months. That made him more successful in retaining the records than either of his predecessors, the Reverend Whiting or Harlan.

Sheffrey had expected the county seat question to be settled by summer, but Judge Daniel Gantt surprised the commissioner. The judge presided over that dispute not in July or August but in June.

Folks called the legal action "the McPherson case" because Dr. John McPherson, founder of Republican City, had initiated it the previous year. He'd gone to court then to ask for a ruling to declare Republican City, not Melrose, the legal county seat. After all, his town had won that first 1872 election, hadn't it?

Before the June hearing started, almost-dead Alma City got into the act. Lawyer William Gaslin (remember him? he squatted on Gen. Vifquain's Napoleon) moved to include Alma City in the legal action. This complicated matters. If Alma City entered the controversy, then the judge would have to decide whether Melrose, already in the case, or Alma City had a rightful claim against Republican City.

The district court held the June 1874 hearing in Republican City in the only large room in the county. No doubt the place was packed. Harlan County citizens must have been eager to hear whether the county seat would be located at Republican City, as Dr. McPherson argued, or at Melrose, as the defending commissioners (Sheffrey, Murrin, and Fitch) maintained, or at Alma City, as Gaslin declared.

Besides, settlers enjoyed attending courtroom proceedings, a popular activity in those pre-TV days. Whenever folks noticed a big crowd in town, they'd say, "Court must be in session." Watching legal proceedings provided not just entertainment but also information. In the courtroom, settlers could find out who sold liquor without a license, who divorced whom and why, who attempted to commit murder, who stole goods, who had been falsely imprisoned, and who had failed to take care of the cattle.

A hush must have descended on the packed room when Judge Daniel Gantt entered. His peers considered the judge, of Pennsylvania Dutch–English stock, honorable and honest. At the time he heard the Harlan County case, he had turned almost sixty and cut an imposing figure.

A busy man, Judge Gantt had the largest district in the state. After he presided over his various courts, he'd travel to Lincoln where he served as an associate justice for Nebraska's Supreme Court.

But that June day, the judge focused his attention on the case at hand.

One by one, each town's lawyer stepped forward to argue that his town should be the county seat. All but Dr. McPherson. Perhaps he could produce no argument to favor Republican City over Alma City. After all, his town had never won the state-required majority vote for county seat.

A little shudder went through the settlers as Judge Gantt dismissed the Republican City case. "I'll consider only Melrose and Alma City," he said.

The best argument on Alma City's side proved to be time. "No matter how many people dropped into the county on that July 3rd to vote," the judge said, "the legal time for contesting the 1871 election has run out."

Besides, county officers had duly recorded the 1871 election in the office of the Nebraska secretary of state. "I know this for a fact," Judge Gantt said. "I went to the secretary of state's office in Lincoln and saw for myself that the county seat had been legally located in Alma City in 1871."

Therefore, he reasoned, Alma City had the valid right to the county seat unless they set that right aside in one of two ways. He held up a finger. "Unless court decree sets it aside," he raised a second finger, "or county citizens hold a proper election for a new county seat."

However, Judge Gantt refused to decide, with no ifs, ands, or buts, whether citizens should locate the county seat in Melrose or in Alma City.

"I can't consider the validity of the Alma election in a suit between Melrose and Republican City," the judge said. "That question of the 1871 election is not before me for consideration."

So he left that matter open, although he did call Sheffrey, Murrin, and Fitch to his side to say, "Just a word in your ears. As matters stand now, you'd be wise to hold your offices at Alma City."

30

A BILLION HOPPERS & TWO THIEVES

That summer, Harlan County residents experienced a new terror, grasshoppers, to add to Indian scares, snowstorms, and prairie fires. These hoppers weren't the local homegrown variety but the awful Rocky Mountain locust, whose slender bodies failed to forecast their enormous appetites.

Natives of foothills and high plains of the Rockies, these grasshoppers massed in gigantic swarms and flew, often hundreds of miles, in search of food. One throng of billions stretched from Canada to Oklahoma, in a dense cloud that darkened day.

These hoppers invaded Nebraska eight times. They peaked during 1874 to 1876, "the starving years," Harlan County settlers called them.

When hoppers settled in tree tops, branches bent and sometimes broke. Once the critters dropped to the ground to eat, they looked like "a heavy crawling carpet." Stalks of corn turned black with their bodies. The hoppers could, in a day, devour all the corn where they'd landed, leaving nothing but stubs of stalks. Corn disappeared, one settler said, "like dew before the morning sun."

After they'd eaten their fill, the females pierced the earth and laid their eggs. Each female laid about a hundred, then died; hopper carcasses blanketed the ground.

Numerous homesteaders left Harlan County during this time. So did many Melrose citizens who fled both grasshoppers and Orleans.

~

In June 1874 after Judge Gantt told Sheffrey, Murrin, and Fitch that they'd be wise to meet in Alma City, the commissioners agreed. Just one problem: Alma City had no courthouse.

(For heaven's sake, the board couldn't be expected to convene in Nathan Cook's log cabin or George Moore's store in Alma City, places where county officers had met before.)

So the three commissioners chose to ignore Judge Gantt. They continued to gather that spring in their illegal Melrose "courthouse."

L. H. Jewell, an Alma City resident, provided a partial solution. He showed up at a board meeting and told commissioners, "I'll give you a quarter section of my land in Alma City if you use it for a courthouse." His lot lay near the center of town, about two blocks east of the current courthouse.

Jewell never said as much, but he might have hoped that his donation would amend the damage he'd done the town. Three years ago, when Alma City had just gotten on her feet, Jewell purchased a store there. Local settlers expected him to open a business in the town. But he did not. He bought that store for a single purpose: to move it to Melrose.

The board accepted Jewell's gift, then bickered about how to acquire a courthouse. "We don't have to build," Sheffrey said. "Let's rent a courthouse."

"From whom?" Fitch snapped.

"From anybody who will put up a suitable building."

Roberts, the clerk, jotted down everyone's ideas about what would be suitable. He came up with this: a substantial, well-furnished house 22 by 40 feet.

"Let's say we rent it for $100 a month," Murrin said. The others agreed.

They waited and waited and waited, but no one volunteered to build this substantial courthouse. Eventually, the board scratched that idea.

"Looks like we'll have to hire a builder," Murrin said. Fitch and Sheffrey agreed, so they sketched out the building they wanted, smaller now, 16 by 24 feet instead of 22 by 40.

"Pine," Sheffrey thought. That should keep costs down.

Fitch proposed grander ideas: "A shingle roof and a ceiling 12 feet high."

They quarreled about the ceiling height, but Fitch refused to budge.

Then the commissioners advertised to accept bids. On August 15, the deadline, they extended it to September 10. At last, on October 6, they opened bids from Nathan Cook and L. H. Jewell. The board rejected both bids, neither quite up to snuff. It set a new deadline for revised proposals. But those revisions never surfaced, because, in the meantime, Frank Shaffer solved the problem.

Remember Frank Shaffer? He built Alma City's first house, of logs, and later rolled it to more profitable Orleans. However, he still lived half a mile east of Alma City where he'd homesteaded. There 1,200 Indians, possibly Pawnee, had once lived. They staked down hundreds of buffalo skins to dry, so before Shaffer could plow, he had to "weed" countless stakes.

On this land, Shaffer had built a fine two-story home. He considered it.

Don't need the whole thing, he must have thought. *What if I took that top story off, moved it to Alma for a courthouse?*

That's what he did. Plopped the upper story on the county seat lot. Rented it to the commissioners for $14 a month. Voilà! Alma snagged her first courthouse.

~

The county commissioners no longer had any reason to procrastinate. So they did not. As soon as Alma City had her courthouse, they moved there from Melrose. However, their records did not arrive with them.

Sheffrey, the senior commissioner, sent Sheriff Ryder to Melrose to fetch them, a familiar assignment. Since January, the sheriff had moved county records from Orleans to Melrose, from Melrose to Alma, from Alma to Melrose. But this time he returned empty handed.

"I found the county records in Melrose, all right," he told Sheffrey, "but I found them under the gun of an armed guard. He refused to give them to anyone, not even to me."

"What a pickle we're in." Sheffrey sat down heavily in the new courthouse. "And where's that Fitch when we need him?"

Murrin's mouth opened and closed, "P-p-playin' hooky?"

"Wouldn't put it past him. But seriously, what are we goin' to do?"

"Maybe you should go buy the guard off," Murrin said, "you know, the way President Phillips bought off Mister Harlan."

Sheffrey narrowed his eyes. "I'm not too keen about that idea." He rubbed the back of his neck and stared at the table. "And there's no point sending the sheriff to arrest him. That worked to get the records back from Roberts, but we've already sent Ryder, and he came back empty handed."

Murrin shook his head. "And that gun-toting mongrel doesn't even work for the county, so we can't impeach him like you and Bartelt impeached Whiting."

What should they do?

After a while, Sheffrey looked up and a smile tiptoed across his face. "Let's fight fire with fire."

"Meaning?"

"Let's steal those stolen records."

Sheffrey and Murrin chose to use young, strong Joel Piper, a transplanted Canadian, as their thief.

No one would suspect him.

Folks knew Piper, twenty-three, as a polite, attentive, and honest teacher in the county's first school. For two years now, he'd lived on his homestead 6 miles up Methodist Creek from the Reverend Whiting.

Piper agreed. He drove several helpers, under cover of darkness, to "move" the records. Knowing about the armed guard, Piper edged his team, wagon, and helpers up to the building where the records lay. So far, so good. The guard hadn't paid them much mind.

The first helper who slid off the back of the wagon posed as an "innocent" bystander; he engaged the guard in conversation. One at a time other helpers slipped off the wagon, each with a gunny sack folded and tucked inside his shirt. They wandered into the building that held the records.

Piper strained to remain nonchalant as he sat in his wagon, but his eyes darted this way and that: one eye on the building and one on the guard chatting and laughing with Piper's helper. Piper watched his men bring out the files. Camouflaged, of course. In burlap. Could have been sacks of potatoes.

As the guard talked, Piper's men tucked the wrapped records in the wagon. Harlan County, like many new Great Plains counties, had few deed or tax books, so the disguised records fit easily into Piper's wagon.

The thieves piled in. The "innocent" bystander waived good-bye to the talkative guard, and hopped in last. Still undetected, Piper drove to Alma City. There he and his helpers unloaded the documents in Cook's log cabin, which had served so often as an unofficial courthouse.

Piper acquired ample notoriety for his deed, enough so that 168 voters picked him out as sheriff in the next election. In fact, stealing those records gained Piper more fame than any other action of his life, including his election to Nebraska's secretary of state in 1894.

When Melrose residents woke the next morning, they realized that the records they had snitched had been swiped in return. This put them into quite a dither. The ruse of that "nice young Mr. Piper" astonished them. However, nothing followed but chatter.

~

Alma City's new courthouse perked up the village. John Guyer built a log hotel where the stagecoach stopped. Will Downs, a Union veteran, erected a little house. Other buildings followed. Alma City, or Alma, as folks now called the town, felt secure enough to register its townsite, its third try.

The first effort, shortly after the town's founding, backfired. The man sent to the U.S. Land Office in Beatrice to enter the townsite tried to steal it for himself. (Shades of Gaslin, who stole Gen. Vifquain's Napoleon.) Alma citizens promptly dismissed that man and named Frank Shaffer instead.

This second shot didn't work either. Shaffer accepted the position but idleness overtook him. Months went by, then years, but still he dawdled. Nearly four years after the first attempt, some Alma citizens hoofed it to Beatrice and filed their townsite. By happy chance, no "Gaslin" had homesteaded on it in the meantime.

To the east, Republican City continued to grow. Methodists built the county's first church there, and Flavius Macmillan established a newspaper.

Melrose, however, dwindled and wasted away. Many of her citizens moved two miles to Orleans. They lugged their businesses: a tin smith shop, a hardware store, a drugstore, a medical practice. Mike Manning, who once served the "foinest" of food in Melrose, moved his hotel and a saloon.

By 1876, Melrose no longer existed.

William Gaslin, the Napoleon squatter, gloated over Melrose's death. "For a full history of the rise, development and fall of Melrose," Gaslin wrote, "I refer the reader to those who actively took part and delighted in county seat boils and townsite fights." (Unlike himself.)

The Honorable Judge Gaslin, now forty-nine, served Nebraska's large Fifth Judicial District. Local lawyers called him "excentric [sic] to a marked degree." They dubbed him "Terror to Evil Doers," because he held court with his six-shooter visible on his bench and because of his zeal in pronouncing "hanged by the neck" punishments for wrongdoers.

"I never had any desire for *county seat fights*," he lied, "and will not enter into recitals of the same." (The judge forgot how he added his Napoleon to the 1872 ballot. Selective amnesia.)

And of course, Orleans, buoyed by Melrose's demise, prospered.

~

After that "nice young Mr. Piper" stole the Harlan County records and deposited them in Cook's log cabin, they remained in Alma for at least four months. The question of ownership seemed settled.

Then on April 12, 1875, the board received a request to remove the county records from Alma.

"What's this all about?" Commissioner Hugh J. McKee asked Murrin, now senior commissioner.

Murrin shrugged. "An odd proposal. Why would we want to move the records from Alma?"

"I suppose we should act on it."

"Not right away. We can lay it over to the next meeting." That's what Murrin did.

Maybe politics drove him. More likely the rush of other business. Floating bonds for a river bridge south of Republican City concerned the commissioners as did investigating charges of the Harlan County board's insolvency.

Then Murrin and McKee had to deal with Commissioner Martin Fitch. As usual, he hadn't shown up for the meeting. His office had been vacant now for five months.

"Looks like Marty ran for commissioner just to help land the courthouse in Alma," Murrin said. "After it opened, he never set foot in a meeting again."

"Can we replace him?"

"Sure." Murrin had arranged for a successor; a Dr. T. C. Hance waited in the wings. Murrin appointed him, and the third commissioner took a seat with the other two.

Roberts, as clerk, noted this activity in his regular minutes without comment. But that night, he went to his Alma office and removed the records, all of them.

(What a strange action! It defies explanation.)

Roberts must have acted in cahoots with someone, but who? Likely an Orleans representative. County historical records don't say, but consider how bizarre Roberts's action was.

Only a year ago, when the board split into two groups, Murrin commanded Roberts to bring the county records from Alma to Melrose. And Roberts stashed those records away from the Melrose commissioners for some two months—longer than any clerk before him.

During that time, Roberts seemed an Alma supporter. He met regularly with Commissioner Fitch in Alma and appeared to want the records in Alma. But now he had stolen the county records from his own office. How weird! What caused his about-face?

We'll never know, nor will we ever know where he put the records, but, logically, Roberts must have placed them with residents who supported a western courthouse. Perhaps this is the time, referred to in county histories, when settlers secreted the records north of Orleans.

The commissioners, shocked to discover missing records, ordered Roberts, the thief, to "put those records back where they belong."

"And do it within six days," Murrin growled. "That's by April 27."

When the county still lacked its records on April 27, the commissioners didn't bother to negotiate with Roberts. Instead, they charged their clerk with misdemeanors in office and prepared to try him.

The trial, which began Monday, May 24, ran the rest of the week. Murrin, McKee, and Dr. Hance acted as a court of impeachment. On Friday, the commissioners found Roberts guilty of neglect of duty.

Two and a half weeks later, Roberts resigned, and the commissioners named Will Downs temporary clerk. Surely Downs, a Union veteran, would be a straight shooter.

He was. Downs won the regular clerk position in the next election. He remained county clerk for more than six years, until Joel Piper became clerk in 1881.

Roberts must have turned the county records over to Downs, for no mention of missing records appears in the commissioners' journal again. Roberts's peculiar "theft" was the last one.

KNOCKING ALMA OFF HER COUNTY SEAT

By 1876, Alma's county seat seemed permanent. For more than six months, the Harlan County board and officers had met there in Shaffer's half-a-house courthouse, the county records had been stored there, and the courts had held their sessions there. All opposition seemed quiet.

The commissioners—Thomas Murrin, Hugh J. McKee, and Samuel Bowles—felt so secure they decided to build a more substantial courthouse to replace their little half-a-house. And so they did.

Mrs. Margaret Jewell donated land that the current courthouse stands on today. The contractors built an 18-by-36-foot structure from pine for $575. It had but one door. Inside, workers plastered, painted, and applied three-foot-high wainscoting. After they'd finished, the commissioners hired Levi J. Schrack to build a water closet—a structure "to be made of cottonwood at the cheapest possible rate."

That June, the commissioners—who knows why—decided to appoint "Honorable Thomas Harlan of Republican City" to write the history of Harlan County "from its first settlement and organization."

Odd enough on its face, this action seems even more preposterous because of Harlan's antagonistic relationship with the board. Only the previous fall, commissioners had attached Harlan's property to collect money he owed them. Harlan also had breached a contract with them to grade the approaches to a Republican River bridge, and he failed to repay the commissioners the money they'd shelled out to the state for Mrs. Harlan's treatment as an inmate of the insane asylum in Lincoln.

Nine months later Harlan finished writing his history, but alas, he faced a stern bunch of critics. The commissioners rejected his opus. Not a "true" history, they said. They must have explained why, for they offered him the opportunity to correct his mistakes. To date, I've found no record that Harlan ever did.

~

Alma, perched on her county seat, looked secure, but that newcomer, Orleans, burned to topple her. Reality demanded it. Orleans's central location, her soon-to-arrive Burlington Railroad, and her developed business district all indicated the town's importance. Who could dispute her right to rule?

Certainly Republican City couldn't. True, she could rival Orleans as a county seat contender, but not since Judge Gantt dismissed her claim. These days she backed up Orleans's effort to snag the seat. Together they scoured Judge Gantt's ruling until they found not one but two possible ways to knock Alma off her county seat: by an election or by court decree.

They chose election.

On October 3, 1876, the commissioners—Murrin, McKee, and Bowles—met as scheduled in their new courthouse with the fancy wainscoting. Calvin Bowman showed up for the meeting. The commissioners knew him as that Orleans guy who had teamed up with Mike Manning, the tavern owner famed for his thick Irish brogue. The two planned to build plows and wagons.

But Bowman hadn't come to the meeting to discuss implements. When the commissioners allowed him to speak, he stood solidly. "You know that the county seat has never been established by law," he spoke in a low-pitched but steady voice, "but it could be. All you have to do is put the question of locating the county seat to voters at the next general election."

He waited. The commissioners turned toward one another. "What's he talking about?" McKee muttered. "The county seat's right here."

Bowles shook his head, and the three commissioners hemmed and hawed for the better part of fifteen minutes.

Then Murrin, the board president, said, "Yours is not the sort of petition that the law requires," and the commissioners rejected Bowman's request.

Bowman left, but eight months later, the commissioners saw him again, this time standing solidly in district court. He had brought a case against them. As he had requested earlier, Bowman wanted the board to put the question of locating the county seat on the next ballot.

The presiding judge, George W. Riosk, heard the case on June 12, 1877.

Bowman argued, via his attorney, that earlier attempts to locate the Harlan County seat in 1871 and 1872 were illegal.

He detailed his reasons.

In the July 3, 1871, election, commissioners illegally divided the county into precincts, gave short notice of the election, and failed to post notices as required. They also didn't register voters or swear in judges and clerks.

After that election, the commissioners failed to notify the public of the seat location and their elected officers didn't serve, so the county remained unorganized until the 1872 election.

That election failed to locate the county seat so elected commissioners had no official place to meet. They conducted business and kept county records at a variety of places.

"County officers moved records by 'caprice,'" Bowman's attorney argued. "Sometimes commissioners held sessions in one spot, the clerk transacted business in another, and the county treasurer in still another place. Not knowing where anyone would meet next caused great uncertainty."

Then the lawyer described how Bowman attended the October 3, 1876, session of the county commissioners and requested that they put the question of the location of the county seat on the ballot. The commissioners "utterly refused," the attorney said. "They claimed the 1871 election located the county seat in Alma." He faced the judge. "But as you see, the 1871 election was void and no election since has given any place the legal majority of votes."

The lawyer asked the court to order the commissioners to place the question of locating the county seat on the October 2, 1877 ballot or show cause why they haven't done so.

Judge Riosk granted Bowman's request.

The judge's decision rattled the commissioners.

By July 14, they found themselves in double trouble. John Guyer, an Alma hotel owner, served an injunction on the board to stop the October 2 election. The county judge who heard the case granted Guyer's request.

So the board didn't place the seat location on the ballot. Instead the three commissioners, now Samuel Bowles, Hugh J. McKee, and John H. Olson, had to justify to Judge Riosk their failure to act.

They chose a powerful lawyer to represent them: Nebraska's Attorney General George H. Roberts. He used a simple strategy to defend the commissioners: he took exception to practically every point that Bowman's lawyer had made, for a total of twenty-four denials. He rejected every negative thing said about that 1871 election. He maintained that the June 29, 1872, election did not first organize the county, and he disagreed that county records were moved from place to place at the "caprice" of county officers.

Flying in the face of fact, Attorney General Roberts declared that Governor William H. James did not order the 1872 election. The attorney even—(how amazing!)—denied that Bowman had ever shown up at the commissioners' meeting. Had the commissioners forgotten? Or did they neglect to consult their own minutes, which recorded Bowman's appearance? Perhaps, in deference to their prestigious attorney, they chose to dog his footsteps.

Then Roberts introduced a previous court case, the one that Republican City's Dr. McPherson had brought against the commissioners in June 1873. At that time, Judge Gantt ruled that the July 3, 1871, election, the first one, had located the Harlan County seat in Alma. Roberts noted more than four years had elapsed since that decision, and no one had appealed it. Therefore, he argued, Judge Gantt's decision should remain final.

Final, hah! Granted, the commissioners pussyfooted for four more years, but eventually they would ignore their own lawyer's arguments and reconsider Bowman's request themselves.

Only two houses stood in Alma when Wells Willits, fifty-one, came to the town in the summer of 1878. Wells Willits had run a general store and a pork packing business in Illinois for twenty years. But way out there in Illinois he could hear that Burlington and Missouri Railroad a-comin' down the Republican River valley—clickety click, clickety clack. He knew it would pass through Alma, so he sold both businesses and headed west.

Once he arrived in Alma, he homesteaded near town and started to invest in property. He traded fast as he could for every vacant lot not already given away. He bagged 275. Not enough. He bought up forty acres north of Alma and laid out plots.

Wells Willits proved right about the railroad. During the winter of 1879–1880, Burlington and Missouri built its line through Alma.

Soon people rushed there, buying lots from Wells Willits, buying, buying until he'd sold every lot he owned. By September, more than fifty Alma businesses and homes had been built; soon they'd total 100. The little town's population jumped from 20 to 300.

Clickety click, clickety clack.

By the summer of 1879, Orleans contained enough people and resources to incorporate, which it did in August. But incorporation alone failed to satisfy. Orleans citizens clung to their belief that their "right" to the county town would be "undisputed" since they had located so near the center of Harlan County.

Orleans had an additional reason to be optimistic. Since 1879, Nebraska law no longer required 60 percent of the votes to win a county seat election. Now the highest number of votes could win such an election. By that new measuring stick, Republican City, as it had long maintained, would have won the 1872 election, not Melrose.

Bathed in these certainties, Orleans citizens decided not to wait to become the big smoke in the county. Instead, in the center of their town square, they built a substantial courthouse. When Orleans became the capital of the county—surely only a matter of time!—the town would present the building to Harlan County.

"If we build a courthouse, a county seat will come" seemed a common fallacy on the plains. Logan, Nebraska, promoters, for instance, built a spacious two-story frame hall. Certain that "prepared was half the battle," they believed the new building would help them win the seat, but they lost the election.

However, Holdrege, Nebraska, used this game plan and succeeded. First citizens stole the county records at gunpoint, then they built a frame courthouse to hold the records, and then they won the election.

Alma citizens eyed the new Orleans courthouse with suspicion. Alma's courthouse set back citizens $575, but the Orleans mansion cost the tidy sum of $2,000. Even that proved a mere drop in the bucket alongside Gibbon's huge, handsome brick castle. That courthouse had a price tag of $22,000. The Gibbon citizens hoped—futilely, as matters turned out—that their ample investment would guarantee that the Buffalo County seat would stay in their town.

Afraid that Orleans's splendor would make her look like a country cousin, Alma formed a courthouse building committee. The committee, including Frank Shaffer and Wells Willits, offered to build a two-story frame

The Alma courthouse

courthouse every bit as sumptuous as the Orleans plum. The square white structure featured a 12-foot ceiling. Inside, contractors painted two coats on two coats of plaster and installed plain baseboards.

The commissioners dedicated the courthouse April 14, 1880. After they paid Wells Willits $355 for furnishings and $20 for moving their safes, the commissioners owned the new courthouse. Alma could stop gnashing her teeth about Orleans's villa.

32

THE IMPULSIVE ELECTION

The Harlan County board simply ignored that 1877 district court order to hold a county seat election. Then in 1881, it unexpectedly reversed its decision.

"We have no desire," the commissioners said, "to defer action."

What brought that on? No one had challenged the board's previous choice to do nothing. But for some reason, the commissioners experienced "a mandate to call a new election," even though citizens had not petitioned them to relocate the county seat, as required by law.

Some folks said their "mandate" took the form of promises of money or other goodies.

Others maintained that the mandate came from the three commissioners, themselves—Samuel M. Bowles, Nicholas B. Vincent, Abraham Banta—all rabid Orleans supporters. In 1877, the board's allegiances had been mixed.

Trying to justify their sudden action, the commissioners argued, as Calvin Bowman had, "The county seat never has been located 'by law.'" They ignored the fact that the seat had been in Alma by Nebraska law for ten years. It had, in fact, been in Alma and nowhere else for six years, ever since commissioners met in the half-a-house courthouse that Frank Shaffer knocked together.

Here's the funny part.

Where, indeed, did the commissioners sit as they pronounced this new decision?

In Alma. In the courthouse. The third Alma courthouse that the Harlan County commissioners had occupied, the expensive one built to trump the Orleans building.

On this October 6, 1881, day of their reversal, the commissioners even ordered the clerk to record that they'd gathered "at a regular meeting of the board at the Alma courthouse."

Their primary business? They ordered that the question of a "permanent" location of the county seat be placed on the November 8 general election ballot.

Then they rushed to get ready. By law, they had to post notices in three most public places in every voting precinct. These notices needed go up at least thirty days before the election. This deadline fell only two days away, but that didn't deter the commissioners. They churned out forty-five notices and delivered them to the sheriff to post. They also published notices in the Orleans *Sentinel* and the Alma *Herald*.

On November 8, 1881, more than a thousand men streamed to their various polling places in the county. They rushed from Alma and from Orleans, they also hustled from other precincts and dashed from Oxford, Nebraska; Columbus, Ohio; Iowa, Texas, or the Black Hills. Some whizzed by train and left the next day, some once lived in Harlan County but didn't anymore, some were too young or, in the case of immigrants, too new to vote. Still others voted more than once.

When county officers examined the ballots, they saw that the Alma precinct had polled twice as many votes as they had registered voters, the whole county registered 30 percent higher than normal.

The officers added up 608 votes for Alma, listed as the People's Ticket, and 566 for Orleans, listed as Republican, for a total of 1,174 votes.

So Alma won by a margin of 42 votes. Or, as Supreme Court Judge Manoah Reese would later say, the "apparent majority" was in Alma's favor.

Of course Orleans contested this election.

First her case went to county court June 24, 1882, where nearly everybody and his brother testified before County Judge L. H. Kent.

Wells Willits said that Alma's precinct officers hid in a schoolhouse. If a man wanted to cast a vote, he had to pass his paper through an open window. Despite the open window, voters couldn't see the officers inside.

"The ballot box was blinded from view," Silas Segars, twenty-five, a painter, said. "The way the sun shone on the window I could not see in the room plain."

Inside, the officers accepted every vote, legal or illegal.

"I was just having fun," William Campbell maintained. "I didn't see anything out of order." He had carried a little boy up to the window and said, "Here's another voter." That raised a laugh "all round outside and in."

"He called it 'fun,'" Segars said, "but the boy held a piece of paper and handed it through the window, just as Mr. Campbell called the boy's name: 'J. A. C. Dawson.'"

Frank Shaffer got in quite a toot because his hired man, W. L. Cook, a horse doctor caring for Shaffer's stable and horses, didn't vote for Alma. "I thought he ought to have done so."

"He showed me a list of names he wanted me to swear to," Cook said. "Names of eighteen men he says work for him in his livery. I refused. It made me mad when he wanted me to swear to a lie. Shaffer said they'd jug me if I didn't take part and help them out."

Cook's wife, Annie, had a run-in with Frank Shaffer, too.

"He asked me if we'd come from Columbus, Nebraska, to Harlan County on September 12, so my husband would be eligible to vote. And I said, 'No, we came October 12.' And he said, 'You better keep that to yourself or your husband will be an illegal voter. He's already deep in mire. If he works against the Alma ring, they'll send him over the road surer than hell.'

"So I says to him, 'You told me my husband was a legal voter.' He just laughed."

George Hightsman of Alma said he knew Cook well, so the court inquired about Cook's reputation for truth. "I would not trust him for anything," Hightsman said, "though he does know a good deal about horses."

"I did not make any threats," Shaffer swore, "as to fatal consequences if Cook did not testify in a certain way."

The line of testifying shifted to another Willits.

"Ed Willits encouraged me to vote twice," Silas Segars said. "He told me I could get some other clothes so no one would recognize me, which I did. I went to Willits's store and got a new suit of clothes. Changed, shaved my mustache—and shaved off my eyebrows, too. Then I went to the polls and voted a second time. Voted first in my real name and then as Silas Eliaser."

"Segars is a deadbeat principally," Ed Willits said. "I don't know whether or not he voted more than once. I didn't tell him to vote twice. He's the one who broke the law. He gave me six names to use, all registered voters who weren't in Alma on Election Day."

"Blazes!" an Orleans supporter said, "Ed Willits didn't just add six names. He added sixty-four fake names to the Alma poll books, and I can prove it."

(What? Only sixty-four phony names? And not nearly as fanciful as those in the town of Virginia, Illinois. When those folks added hundreds of names to their poll book, they included Civil War heroes, the signers of the Declaration of Independence, and ancient philosophers.)

Orleans supporters went wild with hope when they realized that erasing Willits's sixty-four fake names from Alma's total would hand the election to Orleans by 22 votes.

But County Judge Kent urged restraint. He ordered the commissioners to refrain from giving notice of the county seat placement until the district court had time to act.

In the meantime, on December 5, young Willits, Ed Willits's son, appeared in court on the matter. His lawyer, John Dawson, moved for dismissal. "No one even mentioned which names were false," Dawson said. The court did dismiss young Willits's case, but the charge of adding names to the Alma poll book lingered.

~

By this time, Thomas Harlan, the county's namesake, had left the area for good.

Chester A. Arthur, U.S. vice president and loyal Republican, tumbled into the presidency in 1881 after an assassin shot James A. Garfield. The gunman nailed Garfield in his back but didn't kill him. That, his ignorant doctors did.

In 1882, Arthur appointed Harlan special timber agent in the Dakotas. Harlan, then forty-eight, accepted that position. He never again lived in Harlan County.

Instead, he established himself in the Northwest, taking up a homestead in Oregon and becoming a pioneer newspaper owner, establishing four newspapers.

"A brilliant man in his younger days," according to his 1918 obituary, "Thomas Harlan became rather erratic and peculiar as old age crept upon him."

("Rather peculiar?" The commissioners might have agreed, after Harlan's theft of the county records, his avoiding payment for his wife's stay in Lincoln's mental hospital, and his dismal failure as a historian of his own county.)

But Harlan set his name "in stone" on our county, and his legal skills surely benefited Alma's rise to the county seat in that first election in 1871.

~

In February 1883, Harlan County's district court heard the case of the bloated 1881 election to locate the county seat.

Part of the dispute revolved around the illegal votes cast, but that provided only one topic. The secrecy of Alma precinct officers furnished another.

The lawyer who represented Alma didn't argue that she'd won the election. He maintained that the entire election was void.

His evidence is familiar. He noted that Harlan County's boundaries had been set June 3, 1871, when the acting governor appointed commissioners to call an election for county seat. At that election, Alma won, beating Napoleon.

Then, with no petition presented to the commissioners, the lawyer noted, they held an election August 27, 1872, which named Melrose as the county seat. The next year, the district court declared the 1872 election void because the county seat had been located in 1871.

Since then, the lawyer said, Alma has been the recognized county seat. District and county court sessions are held there; the county board meets there. A courthouse was built there and used as a courthouse. (*Used*—unlike the Orleans courthouse.)

Then, in 1881, without petition from citizens, the commissioners, all strong partisans of Orleans, called an illegal election in an attempt to move the county seat from Alma to Orleans.

The judge, who listened to both sides, found it difficult to settle the issues. Even after the court had taken 3,000 pages of evidence, the place of the county seat seemed uncertain.

Eventually the matter would go to the Nebraska Supreme Court.

In the meantime, the fight over the courthouse location lingered in Harlan County citizens' minds. In 1883, *Leading Industries of the West* noted that Orleans citizens "believe today that the majority of voters of Harlan County want the seat in Orleans, and though the judicial decision has said otherwise, some future election may yet find the county business being transacted in that court building erected in Orleans."

33

THE SUPREME COURT RULES

On July 16, 1884, the Nebraska Supreme Court heard the Harlan County courthouse case. Judge Manoah B. Reese, an attentive, patient listener, reviewed the dispute. His hair cascaded over his broad forehead; keen piercing eyes looked out under bushy eyebrows. He would examine all three county elections, the first one in 1871, the second in 1872, and the last in 1881.

Leaning in to listen sat Gilbert L. Laws, the plaintiff, a forty-two-year-old newspaper man who represented Orleans. From Wisconsin, Laws had called Harlan County home for five years.

In many ways a typical journalist, Laws tended to be nosy and too often certain he was faultless. But in this case, he knew he was right because he had canvassed the Alma precinct a few weeks before the 1881 election. Just as he suspected, the precinct had few voters, only 138 by his count. Alma never could have racked up the 608 votes she claimed if she'd played fair! Indignant, he had brought this suit, which contested the results of that unfair 1881 election.

Those who opposed Laws sat across the aisle, among them, Frank Shaffer, the half-a-house Alma courthouse donor, and Wells Willits, who made a mint selling lots in Alma. Relaxed, as certain of victory as Laws, the men sat with their legs flung apart. They lounged alongside the challenged county commissioners: Nicholas B. Vincent, Abraham Banta, and Samuel M. Bowles, who sat stiffly and stared at Judge Reese.

Although interest in this case among Harlan County citizens must have been keen, few would have ridden by horseback or wagon the 200 miles to Lincoln to observe it. However, two journalists had their notebooks at the ready, one Guy Brown, official reporter for the *Lincoln State Journal*, and the other Robertson Howard, editor of the *North Western Reporter*, which published summaries of court cases.

Judge Reese initially addressed the last election: "The 1881 county commissioners had no authority to call an election to locate the county seat." This must have dashed Laws's hopes. The reporter stopped drumming on his leg. This wasn't what he wanted to hear.

Here's how Judge Reese reasoned. "County commissioners can call an election to locate a county seat in one of two ways: (1) They can receive a petition from citizens requesting an election, or (2) They can act without a petition if a previous election fails to locate a county seat."

So, since the commissioners had received no petition from citizens, the question was this: Had a county seat ever been located in Harlan County "as provided by law"?

Judge Reese noted that the county had held two previous elections, one in 1871 and one in 1872, both "under the forms of law." Both times, voters made a decision.

"One of those elections evidently settled the question," he noted. "If the first, then the second election was void. If not at the first then at the second."

The judge hadn't specified yet which election had located the Harlan County seat. Those seated in the courtroom must have wondered why Judge Reese considered the 1872 election at all, since voters in that election had chosen the now defunct Melrose.

However, the judge looked at the original election first. The 1871 election, he noted, had been held under an act of the legislature. A majority of voters elected Alma. Its election returns were "duly certified to and filed by the secretary of state."

By contrast, in 1872, no one had ever "officially declared" that election.

Of course not! Remember how the county clerk, the Reverend John Whiting, refused to report his count of votes, writing instead, "to wit: No legal election."

As a result, Judge Reese said, the 1872 election, with its "apparent" victory for Melrose, had never been properly certified and filed by the secretary of state.

By this time, the cluster of people from Alma must have been congratulating themselves. When the judge, like the district court, focused on the "irregularities" in the 1881 election, Laws took a deep breath and clasped his fingers into a steeple. But the judge hadn't finished. He, like the district court, considered the "irregularities" in the 1881 election, and decided that citizens in the Alma precinct practiced "fraud and malconduct [sic]." This misconduct caused Judge Reese to rule that the Alma precinct vote in that election should be tossed.

That meant Orleans had the clear majority of votes. Laws must have swollen with that feeling one gets when they know they've been right all along.

But before Laws could crow, Judge Reese ruled that the illegal 1881 election had no authority.

"The 1871 election legally located the county seat at Alma," Judge Reese noted. "Alma has been and still is the county seat."

He pointed out that Harlan County citizens thought the matter settled, since the county offices and the district court sessions had been held at Alma without "serious question" for six years before 1881.

Laws must have slumped in his seat. If only those county commissioners hadn't been so hasty! If only they'd taken the time to arrange for some citizens to circulate a petition. That petition! Nothing else stood between Orleans and success.

But Judge Reese hadn't finished. Therefore, he concluded, the only way county commissioners could legally submit this question to the voters would be by receipt of a petition to relocate the county seat. Then the commissioners would have the authority to act.

This ruling left an opening for friends of Orleans, but they never attempted to distribute a petition.

However, they did ask for a rehearing. The court refused to grant them a new trial.

Perhaps it felt, after sifting through voluminous pages of testimony, that all the generalizations and particularizations about locating the Harlan County seat, all the arguments, pro and con, had been made many times, that litigants added little new logic to dispute.

Nothing seemed left to ventilate, although of course that didn't stop Harlan County residents from continuing to squabble and bicker as they have done down to this day.

~

Six years later, Alma Township built a brick courthouse for Harlan County. Still later, the county would seed the old alfalfa yard to bluegrass, stucco the building and remove its steeple. The spruced-up courthouse even contained a furnace, lights, and water.

The new brick Harlan County courthouse

This building, which stood where the present courthouse stands, served the county for seventy-six years until the county built the current courthouse.

In Orleans, folks enlarged the square courthouse they'd built and added a stage. It became known as the Opera House. It held two lavish Tom Thumb weddings, based on the wedding of midget General Tom Thumb, a P. T. Barnum circus performer, with little person Lavinia Warren.

The Opera House also held innumerable plays, acted sometimes by local residents and sometimes by stock companies. Carrie Nation, William Jennings Bryan, and other notables spoke there.

Eventually, needing room to build a library, Orleans moved the old Opera House. In 1946, it became a movie theater. Much later, it housed a local museum.

Folks still identify the building as the "old courthouse" even though it never was.

~ CHAPTER ~
34

PICKING AT OLD BONES

Orleans never forgave Alma. More than 125 years later, some descendants of these early settlers still harbor hard feelings. They see Alma as greedy: Alma wants everything to come to Alma, some said. She doesn't want to give anything, she just wants to take.

The most remarkable expression of Orleans's grudge surfaced in 1993. Then residents in Orleans, Oxford, and Beaver City had to decide whether to combine into a single school district. The merger, plus a new school building, would cost about $12 million. Orleans's share would be $4 million.

Two local citizens, hoping to avoid such a hefty financial commitment, suggested that the town's students attend nearby Alma's school, instead. That school could take in Orleans's students—seventh through twelfth graders—at little or no additional cost.

But sending students to Alma failed to appeal to many Orleans citizens. Why? Because of the way Alma "stole the courthouse." This conviction made some Orleans citizens willing to spend millions in construction costs and teachers' salaries.

On April 6, 1993, many Orleans citizens—68 percent of
the eligible voters—turned out for the merger election. Of
those, 75 percent voted for consolidation and for issuing a
$4 million bond.

"Alma-Orleans feuding over the years probably had
something to do with the outcome of the vote," the *Harlan
County Journal* noted, "and it's probably not just coincidence
that mention of merging with Alma at public meetings last
spring coincided with the rejuvenation of a 120-year-old
argument about how Alma 'stole' the county courthouse."

Just what does stealing the courthouse mean?

That Alma City settlers stuffed the ballot box and
perhaps set a prairie fire to get its way in the first election?
But Orleans didn't exist then, or Republican City or Melrose,
for that matter.

The second election in 1872 didn't list Orleans either. Its
four competitors were Alma City, Melrose, Napoleon, and
Republican City.

So Orleans citizens must be thinking about the
third election, in 1881, the one that the Harlan County
commissioners illegally called. That election did list Alma
and Orleans as contenders.

Is that when Alma "stole" the courthouse?

True, this 1881 election had many "irregularities," the
Supreme Court said, including Alma election officers'
practice of "fraud and malconduct [sic]." But even when
the court threw Alma's votes out, leaving Orleans to win,
she lost, for the judge ruled the entire election invalid; the
three commissioners, all of them Orleans's supporters, had
illegally called it.

Perhaps, to Orleans citizens, Alma seemed to have stolen the county seat because Orleans wanted it so badly. The central location Orleans settlers chose, the connection with the Burlington Railroad they had, the $2,000 courthouse they built as a gift to the county made them feel as though they deserved the county seat. By their logic, perhaps, they did. But logic didn't locate county seats. People did.

And people in Nebraska's early days were notorious for their irregular and dishonest dealings.

In the seventeen-year period from 1854 when Nebraska Territory opened for settlement to 1871 when Harlan County became a county, dirty deals surfaced so often they seemed customary. Men were quick to reach for firearms to settle arguments.

On a national level, John Wilkes Booth killed Abraham Lincoln. A U.S. Representative beat a Congressman senseless with a cane; angry citizens burned another Congressman in effigy.

Next door to Nebraska, Border Ruffians riddled Kansas with guerrilla warfare (looting, kidnapping, tar and feathering, killing) plus colossal fraud in voting.

On the plains, the U.S. government and Indians battled. Brig. Gen. Mitchell fired the plains to kill the Sioux; whites took Cheyenne and Arapaho genitalia as trophies at the Sand Creek Massacre. Wild tribes terrorized stagecoach stations and ranches along the Platte. The national government lied and cheated to force Indians off their land. Both Sioux and the army spilled blood in the Republican River valley before white settlement.

Nebraska territorial government set off a long, intense haggle for power between South Platters (Democrats) and North Platters (Republicans). The acting territorial governor flouted math to create "politically correct" counties. Young legislators fought over the right to drink in their legislative seats; meanwhile, they accidentally eliminated all existing territorial laws. They defied national law to create an illegal constitution that, fortunately, did result in Nebraska's statehood.

State officials acted as unethically as the territorial officers had. After all, when legislators organized Harlan County, the Nebraska governor himself had been impeached for lining his pockets with state money.

So in the early days of Harlan County, a settler could safely assume that his rivals would resort to skullduggery, especially in county seat contests.

Take, for instance, the tricky behavior of these South Dakota land agents, greedy to create a state legislature through the ballots of their many paper towns. On election day, the agents split into parties of three and four and traveled the nearby countryside. Every few miles they'd stop, take a nip or two of whiskey, and establish a "polling place" in one of their invisible towns. There each agent voted many times, using their friends' and relatives' names. In this way, they managed to dominate South Dakota's first legislature.

Or take the shrewd fight about county records in Sherman County, Kansas. Goodland convinced the county sheriff, a Goodland partisan, to arrest every able-bodied Eustis man—on trumped-up charges. When the sheriff brought those men to Goodland for their court hearings, an army of Goodland men sped to Eustis, threatened to burn the town, and carried off the county records.

Given this level of double dealing, it's not surprising that, as historian Andreas noted, "Much personal abuse, calumny and vituperation was indulged in by both parties" in county seat fights. Such behavior must have been the norm.

Actually, nothing that happened in Harlan County's county seat conflict was the least bit unusual. Everything that happened in Harlan County happened elsewhere, too. In Nebraska, nineteen counties (including Harlan) were organized in 1871, 1872, or 1873. Nearly every one, historian James C. Olson noted, had a county seat fight.

All over the Midwest in the 1800s, men fought to determine where county seats should be located. They clashed in Illinois, Indiana, Iowa, Kansas, Michigan, Minnesota, Missouri, Nebraska, North Dakota, Ohio, South Dakota, and Wisconsin. They stuffed ballot boxes, they imported voters, they stole county records, they impeached county officers, they built courthouses that were never used, they went to court, they even set prairie fires to discourage opposition.

We in Harlan County (including myself, as a native) might consider ourselves fortunate. We squabbled about the placement of our county seat, but we didn't get violent, as men did in forty-nine Midwestern counties, including five in Nebraska, eleven in Kansas. But Alma and Orleans fought no actual battles. No one was wounded; no one was killed. We stole county records, but we didn't forcibly remove them at gunpoint; we snitched them.

Mobs never arrived on the scene. No one had to face 96 two-horse wagons, 82 mounted horsemen, and 478 armed infantry coming to get the county records, as citizens in Crawford County, Indiana, did. No one burned down any of their many courthouses.

No one had to call the state militia to quiet things down, as happened in eight Midwestern counties, six of them in Kansas. Their county seat fight was polite, compared to many Midwestern scraps, although they weren't as polite as folks in Stanton County, Nebraska, who let election officers take the ballot box to dinner with them. Harlan County never, like them, served whiskey at the polls, thanks, perhaps, to the influence of their tee-totaling Methodists.

Because county seat fights were so universal in the Great Plains in the 1870s and the 1880s, it's hard to understand why such a residue of animosity should attend the Harlan County fight. But it did. Andreas, writing in 1881 about the Alma-Orleans fight, noted that "much bitterness of feeling has been generated." The contest has "seriously retarded public improvements in the county," he noted, and "prevented that harmony among the citizens that should exist in any new county in order that it be prosperous."

That animosity likely started, according to historian Addison Sheldon, with the first groups in Harlan County. Sheldon believed that these initial groups fix, largely, the future population and its institutions. So the rivalry between Alma and Orleans, so active even today, seems to have started the moment two distinct groups of men colonized the county—one group choosing to settle in western Harlan County, the other in the eastern portion.

Why did Harlan and his boys pick the Alma site instead of joining the already partially settled group at Melrose? Why did Harlan's men, and not the Melrose settlers, ask the state legislature to organize a county? Is it true, as oral history claims, that Harlan's men set fire to the prairie in order to control that first election? That they imported voters? That the greed they presumably displayed has been passed down to their descendants, a legacy as solid as coin or land?

Precise answers to those questions are, of course, lost to us, looking back through time. But let's suppose those claims about Alma are true. Then what are we to say of the Melrose-Orleans settlers, the time, money, energy, and sometimes chicanery they spent trying to reverse what already had happened. Were they, like Alma citizens, motivated by greed? Or were they in the grip of revenge?

One thing is clear: none of the active participants in this conflict came out looking, from this vantage point, admirable. Rather, they look all too human: grasping, squabbling creatures, sore losers. On both sides.

Their attitudes seem to mirror those described by historian Patricia Nelson Limerick. The first arrivals in an area, she wrote, feel their courage and their "nerve" should be rewarded. Adventurers like General Victor Vifquain tend to view the land as theirs because they saw it first. Gen. Vifquain, for instance, might have felt that Napoleon deserved to win the county seat because he had had the "instinct" and the "enterprise" to found that town.

Second comers, like Harlan and his followers, display what Limerick calls a "curious moral attitude, a combination of self-righteousness and a propensity for cunning deceit."

Clearly such a "curious moral attitude" defeated Gen. Vifquain's "deserving" Napoleon. Later, those in Republican City and Orleans seemed to believe they had been at an "unfair advantage."

Any settler who failed to get his way, noted Limerick, tended to assume the role of "innocent victim." Settlers with the "victim" attitude felt that "selfish individuals took advantage of the innocent and hard-working, whose labors constituted the real improvement of the county."

"Neither loser nor winner," Limerick wrote, "wasted much time in wondering how the other party felt." However, we, at this point, can wonder. Perhaps we can even begin to understand the forces that combined to make our legacy, although clearly we cannot remake those forces. Our heritage is ours, as it is, like it or not. And perhaps it's idealistic to suggest that, out of our understanding, we might create a new tradition for our descendants, an inheritance that would break the endless cycle of finger pointing, of blame, of assumed superiority, of desire to get even. Perhaps we could forgive, if not forget.

To forgive a county seat war is not impossible, as some histories of county seat fights show. Take Saline County, Nebraska, the county that Gen. Vifquain returned to after he walked away in disgust from the Harlan County fight. The Saline County fight lasted much longer than ours—sixty years compared to our thirteen. Like our five contestants, many different Saline County towns, some real, some on paper, initially contested for the prize. Pleasant Hill won it in 1871, but Wilber claimed it in 1877 after a bitter campaign against its major rival, Crete.

When Crete challenged the election in the courts, Wilber champions, expecting the judge to rule in its favor, showed up at the Pleasant Hill courthouse with at least 300 men and 160 wagons to take the county records, safe, and furniture. Three days later, when the judge ruled in Wilber's favor, Wilber citizens already owned the county property.

Conflict between Crete and Wilber simmered. Crete believed it should be the county seat because it was the county's largest town. In 1920, it tried to win the seat in an election. Crete won, but not by the required majority.

Wilber citizens, ecstatic, held a celebratory feast for 5,000 people.

Angry, Crete supporters again took the matter to court. They also refused to vote a bond to build a new, badly needed courthouse at Wilber. The animosity between the two towns grew so keen that friends felt unable to visit each other if one lived in Wilber and the other in Crete.

When the court again ruled in Wilber's favor, people in Crete began to talk about calling off the fight. "It's beneath our dignity as a city to continue to try to win the courthouse," they said and named a committee to bring about a permanent truce.

Wilber citizens, naturally, felt suspicious when they heard this news, but on June 17, 1927, the two towns signed a formal treaty. The settlement was an "unbelievable spectacle," wrote one historian. This resolution included the recognition that the strife had been a "detriment" to the county as a whole. The former rivals agreed to a special fund to construct a new courthouse and a special election to vote on bonds for that purpose. Bonds for building a new courthouse were voted in 2,736 to 813 that July.

In August, nearly 2,000 people came to Crete's city park to celebrate the truce by hearing the Wilber town band play music composed by a Crete musician. The animosity between the two towns had been replaced with a feeling of "sincere cordiality." At last friends felt free to visit each other without fear of being called disloyal.

Hamilton County, Nebraska, provides another example of healing. The fight for the county seat was long and bitter there, including five hotly contested elections, forceful removals of the county records, and charges of fraud, corruption, and ballot-box stuffing. Then voters chose Aurora by 81 out of 881 ballots cast.

"A great deal of ill-will and bad blood resulted from it," the Hamilton County Historical Society wrote, "causing a bitter sectional feeling to prevail." This bitterness lasted for many years and affected county politics, but "time gradually healed the wounds and smoothed away the scars."

Not all county seat fights are resolved. "Hard feelings" between Ingalls and Cimarron, Kansas, continue to this day. Citizens of Ingalls, who lost the county seat fight, never forgave Cimarron for winning despite Ingalls's raids at gunpoint. Some Ingalls residents still drive right through Cimarron and go to Dodge City to shop for groceries. A few years ago, when unification of the school districts was proposed, folks just wouldn't hear of that. Ingalls sounds a bit like Orleans.

Alma and Orleans could, if residents wish, emulate the Saline County and the Hamilton County citizens and forget the animosity that has lasted so long between the two towns. We could. But more than likely, we'll continue to prove true historian Sheldon's contention: that what happens when a county is first settled determines the population and the institutions in that place.

Indeed, in our case, Harlan County's first groups of settlers still determine the tone of our current life. Depending on where we're from in the county, from east or west, from Alma or Orleans, we'll no doubt continue to view the history of Harlan County through the eyes of our own ancestors.

This, in turn, will set our attitudes and determine much of what we "choose" to do. Orleans residents will persist in donning the mantle of resentment and injury worn so dashingly by Gen. Vifquain when he left our county. They'll continue to claim that Alma "stole" the courthouse. And Alma residents will maintain their wide-eyed innocence, insisting, like Harlan, that they did nothing but follow the letter of the law. That way, each group can rest on its particular righteousness and craft its tales to pass on to generations yet unborn.

What an odd lot we Harlan County residents are!

EARLY SETTLERS IN HARLAN COUNTY

Appendix A: General Vifquain's 1870 Settlement*				
Last Name	**First Name**	**Date of Arrival**		**Comment**
Andrews	Dr. A. A.	1870	c. August 20	
Beiyon	Franklin A.	1870	c. August 20	
Carmon		1870	c. August 20	
Christenson	Henry	1870	c. August 20	s. of Sappa
Dickenson	L. S.	1870	c. August 20	Melrose/ rented 2 rooms to county
Ekberg	Hans J.	1870	c. August 20	
Ericson	Lou	1870	c. August 20	
Fisher		1870	c. August 01	
Fly	Thomas	1870	c. August 20	lived in Melrose stockade
Foster	Joseph W.	1870	c. August 20	claim: Cook Cr. s. of Alma City site
Guillet	Squire	1870	c. August 20	first claim was in Elm Swamp
Hanson	Gustay/ Gustave	1870	c. August 20	
Hewett	Ellis	1870	c. August 20	
Hofnagle	Frank	1870	c. August 20	on what became Hofnagle Creek
Hubner/ Hubnor	Joseph (bro of L)	1870	c. August 20	
Hubner/ Hubnor	Lewis (bro of J)	1870	c. August 20	

Appendix A: General Vifquain's 1870 Settlement*				
Last Name	**First Name**	**Date of Arrival**		**Comment**
James	Galen	1870	c. August 20	moved to Furnas County
Johnson	Charlie	1870	c. August 20	permanent settler
Johnson	Magnus "Little"	1870	c. August 20	Sappa, south of
Jones/Jonas	George F.	1870	c. August 20	
Lideen	Eric	1870	c. August 20	
Liesinger	Herman	1870	c. August 20	
Lorson	Lewis	1870	c. August 20	
Melchert	Henry	1870	c. August 20	
Mitchell	John B.	1870	c. August 20	
Olson	John B. "Big"	1870	c. August 20	
Peterson	Truls (Nels' bro)	1870	c. August 20	lived in Melrose stockade
Peterson	Nelson "Nels"	1870	c. August 20	stockade builder
Ruben/Rubin	Andrew	1869	11-Feb	settled in now Reuben township
Schottle		1870	c. August 20	
Sullivan	Frank	1870	c. August 20	first claim was in Elm Swamp
Toeppfer/ Toephfar	M. V. or H. V.	1870	c. August 20	located on Sappa/soon left county
Vifquain	Jean B. V. "Victor"	1869	11-Feb	colony leader
Watton	S.	1870	c. August 20	
Wolf		1870	c. August 20	
*Gen. Vifquain and thirty-four of his forty men are listed here.				

Appendix B: Thomas Harlan's 30 Alma City Settlers, March 1871				
Last Name	First Name	Date	of Arrival	Comment
Arlington/ Arrington	Nansel A.	1871	in March	Alma colony
Ballou	John W. or E.	1871	in March	Scottish laborer/ Alma colony
Broadball/ more		1871	13-Feb	owned blacksmith shop
Burgess	John	1871	in March	Alma colony
Burke/Burk	Alexander	1871	in March	Alma colony
Burke/Burk	John	1871	in March	Kansas soldier/ Alma colony
Carr	Wm. Parker	1863	in March	teamster/hunter
Coad/Code	Mark/Marcus	1871	Feb & March*	Treasurer, Alma colony/Irish retail grocer
Cook	Nathan P.	1871	in March	Director, Alma colony/New York lawyer
Downs	Will	1872	14-Feb	built house/ co. clerk/NE of Alma
Harlan	Thomas	1871	Feb & March*	President, Alma colony
Londeville	Peter	1871	13-Feb	Alma townsite committee member
Mitchell	John C.	1872	in March	homesteaded near Alma
Moore	George	1871	13-Feb	owned store
Mullally/ Mullaley	Thomas	1871	Feb & March*	Director, Alma colony
Murray	Captain	1871	13-Feb	Alma townsite committee member
Murrin	Thomas	1871	Feb & March*	Secretary, Alma colony/lived sw of Alma
O'Donell/ O'Donale	Richard	1871	in March	Alma colony

Appendix B: Thomas Harlan's 30 Alma City Settlers, March 1871				
Painter	Jos. H.	1871	Feb & March*	V. P., Alma colony/ postmaster/ rebel
Phillips	James O.	1871	in March	Director, Alma/ Penn. shoe maker
Richmond		1871	13-Feb	Alma townsite committee member
Ryder	James E.	1871	in March	Director, Alma colony
Sappington		1871	13-Feb	owned store
Shaffer	Franklin "Frank"	1871	13-Feb	head of Alma townsite committee
Sheffrey	Thomas "Tom"	1871	in March	Director, Alma colony/near now Oxford
Talbot/Talbott	John	1871	Feb & March*	Alma colony/ Irish saloon keeper
VanNess		1871	13-Feb	Alma townsite committee member
Wise	Henry	1871	in March	Austrian soldier/ Alma colony
Young	Denton	1871	in March	Alma colony
Young	Jacob "Jack"	1871	13-Feb	Alma townsite committee member
*Member of Harlan's scouting party, February 1871				

Appendix C: 205 Harlan County Settlers, 1871						
Last Name	First Name	MFK*	Date	of Arrival	Allegiance	Comment
Anderson	Christine	f	1870	c.	western county	lived with brother, Andrew Ruben
Andrews	A. A.	m	1870	c. Aug 20	Vifquain	
Arl(or Arr)ington	Nansel A.	m	1871	on Feb 17	Alma City	added to Alma colony
Askey	Samuel	m	1871		Oxford	
Ballou	John W. or E.	m	1871	on Feb 17	Alma City	Scottish laborer/Alma colony
Bartelt/Bartell	John	m	1870	or '71 Feb 17	not loyal to Alma	
Bartelt/Bartell	Mary, daughter	k	1870	or '71 Feb 17	East county	Alma (came with)
Bartelt/Bartell	Mrs. John	f	1870	or '71 Feb 17	East county	Alma (came with)
Bartlett	father	m	1871	spring	East county	added to Alma colony
Bartlett	mother	f	1871	spring	East county	
Bartlett	son	k	1871	spring	East county	
Beiyon/Bieyon	Franklin A.	m	1870	c. Aug 20	Vifquain	
Bennett	Clark (husband)	m	1871	13-Feb	Orleans	
Bennett	Emily (wife)	f	1871	13-Feb	Orleans	
Bird		m	1871	spring/summer	unknown	
Blum/Bloom	Anna Bartelt (wife)	f	1871	on Feb 17	Alma City	1 mi. west of Alma
Blum/Bloom	Carl (husband)	m	1871	on Feb 17	Alma City	1 mi. west of Alma
Bowman	Calvin	m	1870	or '71 or '72	Orleans	makes plows & wagons
Brady	John	m	1871	by June	East county	on Metholdist Creek

Appendix C: 205 Harlan County Settlers, 1871						
Broadball/ more		m	1871	13-Feb	Alma City	owned blacksmith shop
Brown	Mrs.	f	1871	by Nov	unknown	lost cattle in snow
Burgess	John	m	1871	on Feb 17	Alma City	added to Alma colony
Burke/Burk	Alexander	m	1871	on Feb 17	Alma City	added to Alma colony
Burke/Burk	John	m	1871	Feb / April	Alma City	Kansas soldier/ Alma colony
Burtchet	John	m	1871	22-Apr	unknown	
Cady	Lafayette	m	1871	in Dec	Republican City	general merchant/ active in town
Carmon		m	1870	01-Aug	Vifquain	
Carr	Wm. Parker	m	1863	/17 Feb '71	Alma City	teamster/ hunter
Carrothers	John W.	m	1871	spring/ summer	Orleans	testified against Whiting/real estate
Casey	John	m	1871		western county	in court for embezzlement
Chapman	William	m	1871	c.	Republican City	first white boy born in Rep. City
Chrisler	Byron H.	m	1871	13-Feb	Prairie Dog	
Christenson	Henry	m	1870	c. Aug 20	Vifquain	lived south of Sappa
Clark	Ellis	m	1871	spring/ summer	unknown	
Coad/ Code	Mark/Marcus	m	1871	early Feb	Alma City	Irish retail grocer/Alma colony
Coble(or el)dick	Jabez (father)	m	1871	Feb 13 or 28	Prairie Dog	
Coble(or el)dick	Jabez S. (son)	k	1871	13-Feb	Prairie Dog	
Connelly	Thomas	m	1871		Melrose	owned store

Appendix C: 205 Harlan County Settlers, 1871						
Cook	Nathan P.	m	1871	on Feb 17	Alma City	New York lawyer/Alma colony
Coon	Lewis	m	1871	early July	S. of Rep. City	
Coon	W . H.	m	1871	early July	S. of Rep. City	
Coppons		m	1871		western county	
Costello		m	1871	by July	Melrose?	stationed in Melrose
Cress	Eliza (wife)	f	1871	or 1872	Oxford	mothered nine children
Cress	Madison J.	m	1871	or 1872	western county	from VA/claim near Spring Creek
Crockford	Joseph	m	1871	or sooner	Alma City	posted election notices
Danforth	C. A.	m	1869		Vifquain	explorer, settled in Furnas Co.
Delimont	Antoine	m	1871		western county	Fairfield Township
Delimont	Augusta (Mrs.)	f	1871		western county	Fairfield Township
Delimont	Gregoire	m	1871		Fairfield Township	Free Methodist church preacher
Delimont	Mary J. D.	f	1871		Fairfield Township	Antoine Delimont's grandmother
Dickenson	L. S.	m	1870	c. Aug 20	Vifquain/ Melrose	rented 2 rooms to county
Donaldson		m	1870	summer	unknown	
Drew	Jason J. (boy)	k	1870	spring	Prairie Dog	came later than dad
Drew	Mr. (father)	m	1870	fall	Prairie Dog	homesteaded
Duncan	James	m	1870	70-71 winter	western county	

Appendix C: 205 Harlan County Settlers, 1871						
Duncan	Mrs. James	f	1870	70-71 winter	western county	
Ekberg	Hans J. (father)	m	1870	c. Aug 20	Vifquain	
Ekberg	Martin (son)	m	1871	13-Feb	Vifquain	
Ericson	Lou	m	1870	c. Aug 20	Vifquain	
Essicks	Mrs. Elizabeth	f	1871	?	Melrose	did mail n. of Melrose
Fergi (or u) son	H. T.	m	1871	spring/ summer	Sappa/ Orleans	place to vote/ helped build Orleans
Fergi (or u) son	W.	m	1871	by June	Sappa	
Fisher		m	1870	01-Aug	Vifquain	
Fletcher	Warren M.	m	1871	by Dec	Orleans/ Alma	founded it/ Gaslin/lawyer
Fly	Thomas	m	1870	c. Aug 20	Vifquain	lived in Melrose stockade
Foster	Hannah (Mrs.)	f	1871	spring/ summer	East county	In court '74, divorce from Pat
Foster	Joseph W.	m	1870	c. Aug 20	Vifquain/ Alma	claim Cook Ck. at RepR junction
Foster	Patrick "Pat"	m	1871	spring/ summer	East county	In court 1874 for divorce
Friday	Jacob	m	1871	by July	Alma City?	bond for Charles McPherson
Friday	Miss Susie	f	1871	by July	Alma City?	down Methodist Creek
Gaslin	William	m	1871	by fall	Napoleon	
Gehley/ Gahley	Anna (Mrs. G)	f	1871	13-Feb	Melrose	
Gehley/ Gahley	Anna (Mrs. J)	f	1871	13-Feb	Melrose	childbirth death after prairie fire fight

Appendix C: 205 Harlan County Settlers, 1871						
Gehley/ Gahley	Christina (J's girl)	k	1871	b. 7/18	Melrose	born in 1871
Gehley/ Gahley	Francisea "Frank"	m	1871	13-Feb	Melrose	born in 1800
Gehley/ Gahley	George F. (F's son)	m	1871	13-Feb	Melrose	carried mail, Orleans township
Gehley/ Gahley	John A. (F's son)	m	1871	13-Feb	Melrose	
Gehley/ Gahley	Mary (Mrs. F)	f	1871	13-Feb	Melrose	born in 1810
Gipe	George W.	m	1871	11-Jun	Prairie Dog	became prosperous farmer
Gould	Albert H. (son)	m	1871	13-Feb	W of Rep. City	lived on Tipover
Gould	Hattie	f	1871	13-Feb	W of Rep. City	lived on Tipover
Gould	John/Joseph (dad)	m	1871	13-Feb	W of Rep. City	lived on Tipover
Gould	Mary E.(Mrs.?)	f	1871	13-Feb	W of Rep. City	lived on Tipover/early woman
Guillet	Squire	m	1870	c. Aug 20	Vifquain	
Guston		m	1871		western county	
Hanson	Gustay/ Gustave	m	1870	c. Aug 20	Vifquain	
Harlan	Elizabeth	f	1871	?	Alma City	Harlan's wife
Harlan	Thomas	m	1871	early Feb	Alma City	leader of Alma colony
Harvey	Hon. Andrew E.	m	1871	early	East county	Cheyenne colony, lawyer
Heth	R. E.	m	1870	early 1870	Prairie Dog	Prairie Dog
Hewett	Ellis	m	1870	c. Aug 20	Vifquain	
Hinze (brothers)	Fred	m	1867	before	Oxford	German/lived N. of Oxford

Appendix C: 205 Harlan County Settlers, 1871						
Hofnagle	Frank	m	1870	c. Aug 20	Vifquain	
Holden	William C.	m	1871		unknown	charged Roberts/ newsman
Holly		m	1871	spring/ summer	unknown	
Houk	John	m	1871	April/ May	Prairie Dog	independent?
Hubner/ Hubnor	Joseph	m	1870	c. Aug 20	Vifquain	
Hubner/ Hubnor	Lewis	m	1870	c. Aug 20	Vifquain	
Irwin	Milt	m	1870	early 1870	Prairie Dog	Prairie Dog
James	Galen	m	1870	c. Aug 20	Vifquain	moved to Furnas County
Jenkins		m	1871	spring/ summer	unknown	
Johnson	Charlie	m	1870	c. Aug 20	Vifquain	permanent settler
Johnson	John Manuel	m	1871	spring	Sappa, south of	Swedish
Johnson	Magnus "Little"	m	1870	c. Aug 20	Vifquain	Sappa, south of
Jones	J. J.	m	1871	fall	western county	on Sappa
Jones/ Jonas	George F.	m	1870	c. Aug 20	Vifquain	
Joyce	George W.	m	1870	early 1870	Prairie Dog	Prairie Dog
Kammerer	John Theobold	m	1870	c.	Oxford	
Kammerer	Magdalena (Mrs)	f	1870	c.	Oxford	
Kauk	Mrs. Barney	f	1871	13-Feb	East county	Blums daughter, b. in wagon

Appendix C: 205 Harlan County Settlers, 1871						
Kellogg	T. G./Gordon	m	1871	spring/ summer	western county	on Sappa
Kennedy	John R (John K)	m	1870	or 1871	Melrose/ Orleans	owned drug store
Kiser	E. H.	m	1870	early 1870	Prairie Dog	Prairie Dog
Laughton		m	1871	spring/ summer	unknown	
Lawton	C. D.	m	1871	summer	Orleans	1 mi SE of now Orleans
Lawton	Mrs. C. D.	f	1871	summer	Orleans	1 mi SE of now Orleans
Lideen	Eric	m	1870	c. Aug 20	Vifquain	
Liesinger	Herman	m	1870	c. Aug 20	Vifquain	
Londeville	Peter	m	1871	13-Feb	Alma City	townsite comm. member
Lorson	Lewis	m	1870	c. Aug 20	Vifquain	
Luce	Hiram M. (uncle)	m	1871	early July	E. of Rep. City	found Eureka!/ Rep C drug store
Main	Alice (L's girl)	k	1871	in July	Melrose/ Orleans	N. of Orleans on Rope Creek
Main	Arthur (L's boy)	k	1871	in July	Melrose/ Orleans	N. of Orleans on Rope Creek
Main	Elisha	m	1871	in July	S. of Rep. City	
Main	Julia (L's wife)	f	1871	in July	Melrose/ Orleans	N. of Orleans on Rope Creek
Main	Lorenzo Juddson	m	1870	12-Feb	Melrose/ Orleans	stockade; brought back brothers
Main	Mrs. Elisha	f	1871	in July	S. of Rep. City	

Appendix C: 205 Harlan County Settlers, 1871						
Main	Mrs. Stillman	f	1871	in July	S. of Rep. City	
Main	Stillman D. "Still"	m	1871	in July	S. of Rep. City	
Manning	Mary (Mrs. Mike)	f	1870	or Aug 1872	Melrose/ Orleans	
Manning	Michael "Mike"	m	1870	or Aug 1872	Melrose/ Orleans	ran a tavern/ general merchant
Manning	Thomas H.	m	1870	or 1871	Melrose/ Orleans	owned tin shop/helped build Orleans
Manson		m	1871		western county	
Martin	Jerry?	m	1871		western county	
McBride	John/William	m	1871	by July	East county	
McPherson	Charles E. (J's son)	m	1871	in July	Republican City	
McPherson	Dr. John	m	1871	in July	Republican City	general merchant
McPherson	Elizabeth (J's wife)	f	1871	in July	Republican City	
McPherson	John (J's son)	k	1871	c.	Republican City	
McPherson	Pearl	k	1871	c.	Republican City	first white girl born in Rep City
McPherson	Sarah (C's wife)	f	1871	July?	Republican City	C. McPherson's wife
McPherson	William (J's son)	k	1871	c.	Republican City	
Melchert	Henry	m	1870	c. Aug 20	Vifquain	
Mitchell	John B.	m	1870	c. Aug 20	Vifquain	
Moore	George	m	1871	13-Feb	Alma City	owned store
Moss	J. H.	m	1871	spring	Orleans	boots, shoes, groceries

Appendix C: 205 Harlan County Settlers, 1871							
Muir	James	m	1869	& 1871	East county	S of riv. near Rep. City
Mullally or aley	Margaret (wife)	f	1871	early Feb	Alma City	
Mullally or aley	Thomas (husband)	m	1871	early Feb	Alma City	Alma colony
Mullally or aley	William (son)	k	1871	early Feb	Alma City	
Murray	Captain	m	1871	13-Feb	Alma City	townsite comm. member
Murrin	Thomas	m	1871	early Feb	Alma City	Lived sw of Alma/Alma colony
Newell	L. T.	m	1871	spring/ summer	western county	on Sappa
O'Donell or nale	Richard	m	1871	on Feb 17	Alma City	added to Alma colony
Olson	John B. "Big"	m	1870	c. Aug 20	Vifquain	
Olson	John H.	m	1871	13-Feb	western county	co. comm./ claim N of Orleans
Painter	Jos. H.	m	1871	early Feb	Alma City	postmaster/ Alma colony rebel
Palmer	Homer (son)	k	1871	c.	Sappa township	
Palmer	Joshway (father)	m	1871	13-Feb	Sappa township	sheriff write-in
Palmer	Judson A.	m	1871	13-Feb	unknown	
Parish	Gilbert R.	m	1871	11-Jun	Prairie Dog	independent?
Parish	Margaret	f	1871	11-Jun	Prairie Dog	independent?
Peterson	Nelson "Nels"	m	1870	c. Aug 20	Vifquain	stockade builder
Peterson	Truls (N's bro)	m	1870	c. Aug 20	Vifquain	lived in Melrose stockade

Appendix C: 205 Harlan County Settlers, 1871						
Phillips	James O.	m	1871	on Feb 17	Alma City	Penn. shoe maker/Alma colony
Pond	Lewis J.	m	1871	or 1872	Prairie Dog	
Pond	Print	m	1870	early 1870	Prairie Dog	Prairie Dog
Rebman	Christian	m	1871	by fall	unknown	
Reynolds	Mrs. Kate	f	1871	by July	unknown	among first women
Richardson		m	1871		western county	
Richmond		m	1871	13-Feb	Alma City	townsite comm. member
Robbins	Albert C.	m	1871	in June	Orleans	S of Sappa/ postmaster/ co. judge
Robbins	son of Albert C.	k	1871	in June	Orleans	Sappa, south of/postmaster
Ruben/ Rubin	Andrew	m	1869	11-Feb	Vifquain	Swedish, Lutheran, 5 kids
Ryder	James E.	m	1871	on Feb 17	Alma City	added to Alma colony
Sadin/ Sandine	Eric (father)	m	1871	by fall	unknown	ferry
Sappington		m	1871	13-Feb	Alma City	owned store
Schottle		m	1870	c. Aug	Vifquain	
Shaffer	Franklin "Frank"	m	1871	13-Feb	Alma City	head of townsite comm.
Sheffrey	Thomas "Tom"	m	1871	on Feb 17	Alma/west	claim near now Oxford
Shoemaker		m	1871	spring/ summer	unknown	
Simon		m	1869	11-Feb	unknown	Hunter
Skinner	John	m	1871	spring/ summer	Orleans?	on Sappa
Starry	Alexander	m	1870	in July	Republican City	helped found town

Appendix C: 205 Harlan County Settlers, 1871						
Stewart	Linus's bro.	m	1871	by Nov	Prairie Dog	oxen with bloody feet
Sullivan	Frank	m	1870	c. Aug 20	Vifquain	
Talbot/ Talbott	John	m	1870	summer	Alma City	Irish saloon keeper/Alma colony
Thompson	Judge J.	m	1871	spring/ summer	western county	county judge/ on Sappa
Thompson	Judge's son	k	1871	spring/ summer	western county	on Sappa
Toeppfer or far	M. V. or H. V.	m	1870	c. Aug 20	Vifquain	located on Sappa/soon left
Trimble	Hugh "Huey"	m	1871	c. July	unknown	probably Alma City
Van Beem		m	1871		western county	
VanNess		m	1871	13-Feb	Alma City	townsite comm. member
Vifquain	Jean B. V. "Victor"	m	1869	11-Feb	Vifquain	colony leader
Watton	S.	m	1870	c. Aug 20	Vifquain	
Whitford	Algernon L.	m	1871	summer	Orleans	
Whitford	Vernette	f	1871	summer	Orleans	
Whiting	Rev. John E.	m	1871	by July	Alma City	Methodist minister
Wise	Henry	m	1871	on Feb 17	Alma City	Austrian soldier/Alma colony
Wolf		m	1870	c. Aug 20	Vifquain	
Woolworth	Charles (L's son)	k	1870	12-Feb	Melrose/ Orleans	on Rope Creek
Woolworth	Leonard	m	1870	12-Feb	Melrose/ Orleans	stockade; brought back brothers

Appendix C: 205 Harlan County Settlers, 1871						
Young	Denton	m	1871	on Feb 17	Alma City	added to Alma colony
Young	Jacob "Jack"	m	1871	13-Feb	Alma City	townsite comm. member
Ziegler	John F.	m	1871	April or '72	Prairie Dog	hunter/JP
*M=male, F=female, K=son or daughter						

Appendix D: Harlan County Men in 1871					
Last Name	**First Name**	**Date**	**of Arrival**	**Allegiance**	**Comment**
in eastern Harlan County*					
Arl (or Arr) ington	Nansel A.	1871	on Feb 17	Alma City	Cheyenne colony
Ballou	John W. or E.	1871	on Feb 17	Alma City	Scottish laborer/ Cheyenne colony
Blum/Bloom	Carl	1871	on Feb 17	Alma City? claim 1 mi w	traveled with Harlan from Kearney
Brady	John	1871	by June		on Methodist Creek
Broadball/ more		1871	13-Feb	Alma City	owned blacksmith shop
Burgess	John	1871	on Feb 17	Alma City	Cheyenne colony
Burke/Burk	Alexander	1871	on Feb 17	Alma City	Cheyenne colony
Burke/Burk	John	1871	on Feb / April	Alma City	Kansas soldier/ Cheyenne colony
Carr	Wm. Parker	1863	& 17 Feb '71	Alma City	teamster/ hunter
Coad/Code	Mark/ Marcus	1871	Feb early	Alma City	Irish retail grocer/ Cheyenne colony
Cook	Nathan P.	1871	on Feb 17	Alma City	New York lawyer/ Cheyenne colony
Foster	Joseph W.	1870	c. August 20	Vifquain/ Alma	claim: Cook Ck. at RepR junction
Friday	Jacob	1871	by July	Alma City?	
Gould	Albert (J's son)	1871	13-Feb	Rep City, west of	lived on Tipover

Appendix D: Harlan County Men in 1871					
Gould	John/ Joseph	1871	13-Feb	Rep City, west of	lived on Tipover
Harlan	Thomas	1871	Feb early	Alma City	leader of Cheyenne colony
Harvey	Hon. Andrew	1871	early		Cheyenne colony, lawyer
Londeville	Peter	1871	13-Feb	Alma City	townsite comm. member
Luce	Hiram M.	1871	early in July	Republican City, east	found Eureka!/ Rep C drug store
McBride	John/ William	1871	by July	Alma City	killed July 4, 1871
Moore	George	1871	13-Feb	Alma City	owned store
Mullally or aley	Thomas	1871	Feb early	Alma City	Cheyenne colony
Murray	Captain	1871	13-Feb	Alma City	townsite comm. member
Murrin	Thomas	1871	Feb early	Alma City	Lived sw of Alma/ Cheyenne colony
O'Donell or nale	Richard	1871	on Feb 17	Alma City	Cheyenne colony
Painter	Jos. H.	1871	Feb early	Alma City	postmaster/ Cheyenne colony rebel
Phillips	James O.	1871	on Feb 17	Alma City	Penn. shoe maker/ Cheyenne colony
Richmond		1871	13-Feb	Alma City	townsite comm. member
Ryder	James E.	1871	on Feb 17	Alma City	added to Cheyenne colony
Sappington		1871	13-Feb	Alma City	owned store

Appendix D: Harlan County Men in 1871					
Shaffer	Frank	1871	13-Feb	Alma City	head of townsite comm.
Sheffrey	Tom	1871	on Feb 17	Alma City/ west	claim near now Oxford
Starry	Alexander	1870	in July	Republican City	helped found town
Talbot/ Talbott	John	1870	summer	Alma City	Irish saloon keeper/ Cheyenne colony
VanNess		1871	13-Feb	Alma City	townsite comm. member
Whiting	Rev. John E.	1871	by July	Alma City	Methodist minister
Wise	Henry	1871	on Feb 17	Alma City	Austrian soldier/ Cheyenne colony
Young	Denton	1871	on Feb 17	Alma City	Cheyenne colony
Young	Jacob "Jack"	1871	13-Feb	Alma City	townsite comm. member
south of the Republican River*					
Chrisler	Byron H.	1871	13-Feb	Prairie Dog	
Coble(or el) dick	Jabez (father)	1871	on Feb 13 or 28	Prairie Dog	
Coon	Lewis	1871	early July	Republican City	below Republican City
Coon	W . H.	1871	early July	Republican City	below Republican City
Drew	Mr. (father)	1870	fall	Prairie Dog	
Gipe	George W.	1871	11-Jun	Prairie Dog	
Heth	R. E.	1870	1870's early	Prairie Dog	
Houk	John	1871	in April/May	Prairie Dog	

Appendix D: Harlan County Men in 1871					
Irwin	Milt	1870	1870's early	Prairie Dog	
Joyce	George W.	1870	1870's early	Prairie Dog	
Kiser	E. H.	1870	1870's early	Prairie Dog	
Muir	James	1869	& 1871		S of riv. near Republican City
Parish	Gilbert R.	1871	11-Jun	Prairie Dog	
Pond	Print	1870	1870's early	Prairie Dog	
Pond	Lewis J.	1871	or 1872	Prairie Dog	
Ziegler	John F.	1871	April or 1872	Prairie Dog	hunter/JP
in western Harlan County*					
Andrews	A. A.	1870	c. August 20	Vifquain	
Askey	Samuel	1871		Oxford	
Bartelt/Bartell	John	1871	17-Feb	not loyal to Alma	traveled with Harlan from Kearney
Beiyon/ Bieyon	Franklin A.	1870	c. August 20	Vif/Melrose/ Orleans	
Bennett	Clark (husband)	1871	13-Feb	Orleans	
Carmon		1870	01-Aug	Vifquain	
Carrothers	John W.	1871	spring/ summer	Orleans	testified against Whiting/real estate
Casey	John	1871		west county	in court for embezzlement
Christenson	Henry	1870	c. August 20	Vifquain/s. of Sappa	
Connelly	Thomas	1871		Melrose	owned store
Coppons		1871		west county	
Cress	Madison J.	1871	or 1872	west county	
Delimont	Gregoire	1871		Fairfield Township	preacher at Free Methodist church
Delimont	Antoine	1871		Fairfield Township	

Appendix D: Harlan County Men in 1871					
Dickenson	L. S.	1870	c. August 20	Vifquain/ Melrose	rented 2 rooms to county
Duncan	James	1870	1870-71 winter		
Ekberg	Hans J. (father)	1870	c. August 20	Vifquain	
Ekberg	Martin (son)	1871	13-Feb	west county	
Ericson	Lou	1870	c. August 20	Vifquain	
Fergi (or u) son	W.	1871	by June	Sappa	
Fergi (or u) son	H. T.	1871	spring/ summer	Sappa/ Orleans	place to vote/ helped build Orleans
Fisher		1870	c. August 01	Vifquain	
Fletcher	Warren M.	1871	by Dec	Orleans/ Alma	founded it/ Gaslin/lawyer
Fly	Thomas	1870	c. August 20	Vifquain	lived in Melrose stockade
Gehley/ Gahley	Francisea "Frank"	1871		Melrose	born in 1800
Gehley/ Gahley	George F. (Frank's son)	1871		Melrose	carried mail, Orleans township
Gehley/ Gahley	John A. (Frank's son)	1871		Melrose	
Guillet	Squire	1870	c. August 20	Vifquain	
Guston		1871		west county	
Hanson	Gustay/ Gustave	1870	c. August 20	Vifquain	
Hewett	Ellis	1870	c. August 20	Vifquain	
Hinze (brothers)	Fred	1867	before	Oxford	German/lived N. of Oxford
Hofnagle	Frank	1870	c. August 20	Vifquain	
Hubner/ Hubnor	Joseph	1870	c. August 20	Vifquain	
Hubner/ Hubnor	Lewis	1870	c. August 20	Vifquain	
James	Galen	1870	c. August 20	Vifquain	would move to Furnas County

			Appendix D: Harlan County Men in 1871			
Johnson	John Manuel	1871	spring	Sappa, south of	Swede
Johnson	Charlie	1870	c. August 20	Vifquain	permanent settler
Johnson	Magnus "Little"	1870	c. August 20	Vifquain	Sappa, south of
Johnson	John M.	1871		Sappa	Swedish
Jones/Jonas	George F.	1870	c. August 20	Vifquain	
Kammerer	John Theobold	1870	c.	Oxford	
Kellogg	T. G./ Gordon	1871	spring/ summer		on Sappa
Kennedy	John R. or John K.	1870	or 1871	Melrose/ Orleans	owned drug store
Lideen	Eric	1870	c. August 20	Vifquain	
Liesinger	Herman	1870	c. August 20	Vifquain	
Lorson	Lewis	1870	c. August 20	Vifquain	
Main	Lorenzo Juddson	1870	12-Feb	Melrose/ Orleans	stockade; brought back brothers
Manning	Thomas H.	1870	or 1871	Melrose/ Orleans	owned tin shop/helped build Orleans
Manson		1871		west county	
Martin	Jerry?	1871		west county	
Melchert	Henry	1870	c. August 20	Vifquain	
Mitchell	John B.	1870	c. August 20	Vifquain	
Moss	J. H.	1871	spring	Orleans	boots, shoes, groceries
Newell	L. T.	1871	spring/ summer		on Sappa
Olson	John B. "Big"	1870	c. August 20	Vifquain	
Olson	John H.	1871	13-Feb	west county	claim a mile N of Orleans
Palmer	Joshway (father)	1871	13-Feb	Sappa township	sheriff write-in
Peterson	Truls (Nels' brother)	1870	c. August 20	Vifquain	lived in Melrose stockade

Appendix D: Harlan County Men in 1871					
Peterson	Nelson "Nels"	1870	c. August 20	Vifquain	stockade builder
Richardson		1871		west county	
Robbins	Albert C.	1871	in June	Orleans	Sappa, S of/ postmaster/co. judge
Ruben/Rubin	Andrew	1869	11-Feb	Vifquain	
Schottle		1870	c. August	Vifquain	
Skinner	John	1871	spring/ summer	Orleans?	on Sappa
Sullivan	Frank	1870	c. August 20	Vifquain	
Thompson	Judge J.	1871	spring/ summer		county judge/ on Sappa
Van Beem		1871		west county	
Vifquain	Jean B. V. "Victor"	1869	11-Feb	Vifquain	colony leader
Watton	S.	1870	c. August 20	Vifquain	
Wolf		1870	c. August 20	Vifquain	
Woolworth	Leonard	1870	12-Feb	Melrose/ Orleans	stockade; brought back brothers
*The east, south, west designations show which precinct each man probably lived in,					
Precinct 1 in the south, Precinct 2 in the east, or Precinct 3 in the west.					

Acknowledgments

I wish to thank the Nebraska Humanities Council's call for local history articles, Harlan County commissioners' journals and court records, Hoesch Memorial Public Library in Alma, Cornelia Preston Library in Orleans, Nebraska Historical Society in Lincoln, Ernie Kuhl of Orleans for his *Orleans Centennial* and interviews, and Verdeen Leopold of Alma for sharing invaluable oral history.

Among those who helped me fashion this manuscript are Annie Moncayo, Jack Loscutoff, Dan Reynolds's Omaha NightWriters, editor Sandra Wendel, and Lisa Pelto of Concierge Marketing. A slew of thanks.

I'm also deeply indebted to numerous Nebraska writers—journalists, historians, memoirists—who recorded such massive amounts of information and misinformation about Harlan County's early days. From their records I wove this history, grateful for their help but acknowledging all mistakes to be mine.

SELECTED BIBLIOGRAPHY

I list here the writings most useful to me when I researched "Part V—Harlan County's Bitter Birth." This bibliography is not a complete record of all the works I consulted, but only those I think would be useful to anyone wishing to read further about early Harlan County.

Andreas, A.T. *History of the State of Nebraska; Containing ... Cities and Towns,* 2 vols. Chicago: Western Historical, 1882.

Brown, Guy. *Reports of Cases in the Supreme Court of Nebraska, 1881,* vol. 16. Lincoln, Nebr.: State Journal, 1884.

Federal Writers' Project, WPA, Nebraska. *Origin of Nebraska Place Names.* Lincoln, Nebr.: Stephenson School Supply, 1938.

Fitzpatrick, Lilian Linder. *Nebraska Place Names.* Lincoln, Nebr.: University of Nebraska, 1925, 1933, 1960.

"Gen. Vifquain Dead: Pioneer Nebraskan, Soldier and Statesman." *Lincoln State Journal,* January 8, 1904, p. 1.

Grimes, Mary Cochran. "Chief Justice Daniel Gantt of the Nebraska Supreme Court: Letters and Excerpts from his Journal, 1835–1878." *Nebraska History* 61.3 (fall 1980): 280–309.

Harlan County Commissioners. *Abstract of Elections,* vol. 1. (Oct. 12, 1875–May 1, 1885). Harlan County Courthouse, Alma, Nebr.

——. *Commissioner's Journal A* (May 20, 1872–Oct. 2, 1882).

——. *Commissioner's Journal 2* (Nov. 20, 1882–Dec. 11, 1884).

——. *Harlan County Census,* 1880.

Harlan County District Court. *Foster vs. Foster,* Nebraska 71, *Complete Record A: Harlan County,* 1873.

——. *Bowman vs. Harlan County Commissioners,* Nebraska 1, 1882.

——. *Laws vs. Bowles et al.,* Oral Evidence. Nebraska 1, 1883.

Harlan County Journal. "History of Alma, Nebraska, Harlan County, from 1870 to 1906," c. 1906.

——. J.A. Russell, "Pioneer History of Harlan County, Nebraska," reprint, Feb. 23, 1978, p. 2.

Haskell, John. *Judge William Gaslin: Nebraska Jurist.* Omaha, Nebr.: John Haskell, 1983.

"J.A. Piper Gives Early Day Experiences in Harlan County." *Orleans (Nebr.) Chronicle,* June 13–Aug. 8, 1940.

Johnson, Harrison. *Johnson's History of Nebraska.* Omaha, Nebr.: Henry Gibson, 1880.

Kuhl, Ernest E. & William J. Dunlay. *Orleans Centennial: 1872–1972.*

Laws, Joint Resolutions and Memorials Passed at the Eighth Session of the Legislative Assembly of the State of Nebraska Begun and Held at the City of Lincoln January 5, 1871. Des Moines, Iowa: Mills, 1871.

Laws of Nebraska. Des Moines, Iowa: Mills, 1871.

Laws vs. Vincent et al. Nebraska Supreme Court. Assignment of Errors, Nebr. 1 (1883).

——. Transcript of District Court Case, Nebr. 7 (1883).

——. Motion for a Rehearing, Nebr. 1 (1884).

Lemonds, Leo L. "Nelson Buck Massacre 1869 Nebraska," Harlan County, NEGenWeb, http://www.rootsweb.com/~neharlan/buck.html.

Limerick, Patricia Nelson. *The Legacy of Conquest.* New York: W.W. Norton, 1988.

Link, John T. *Nebraska Placenames.* Copy, research notes. Nebraska Historical Society, Lincoln, Nebr.

——. *The Origin of the Place Names of Nebraska (The Toponymy of Nebraska).* Nebraska Geological Survey, University of Nebraska, Bulletin 7, Series 2, 1933.

McGregor, H.B. "H.B. McGregor Letter." *Publications of the Nebraska State Historical Society,* 18 (1917) 106–109.

Nebraska and Bowman vs. the County Commissioners of Harlan County. Harlan County Courthouse Records of Nebraska District Court, Kearney, Nebr., June 12, 1877.

——. Answer. Oct. 31, 1877.

——. Amended Answer. March 16, 1882.

Nebraska State Historical Society. *Nebraska Constitutional Convention of 1871,* vols. 12–13.

"Newspaper Clippings," Victor Vifquain's papers. Nebraska State Historical Society, Lincoln., Nebr.

Nelson, Ann. Senior Historian, Wyoming Department of Commerce, Letter to Author, Dec. 9, 1992.

Nimmo, Sylvia. *Maps Showing the County Boundaries of Nebraska: 1854–1925.* Papillion, Nebr.: Sylvia Nimmo, 1978.

Perkey, Elton A. "Perkey's Names of Nebraska Locations." *Nebraska History* 59.2 (summer 1978).

——. *Perkey's Nebraska Place Names.* Lincoln, Nebr.: Nebraska State Historical Society, 1982.

Reports of Cases in the Supreme Court of Nebraska, vol. 16, pp. 208–216. 1884.

Republican City. *Centennial Book (1867–1967): In & Around Republican City (Nebr.).*

The Republican Valley Sentinel, Jan. 1, 1876, pp. 1–2.

Rogers, Jean McKee *History of Harlan County, Nebraska: 1870–1967.* Alma, Nebr.: n.p., 1967.

Sheldon, Addison Erwin. *History and Stories of Nebraska.* Chicago: University Publishing, 1914, 1926.

———. *Nebraska: The Land and the People,* 3 vols. New York: Lewis, 1931.

———. ed. *Official Report of the Debates and Proceedings in the Nebraska Constitutional Convention Assembled in Lincoln June Thirteenth, 1871,* vols. 11–13. Lincoln, Nebr.: Nebraska State Historical Society Publication, n.d.

Smith, Jeffrey H. *A Frenchman Fights for the Union: Victor Vifquain and the 97th Illinois.* Bellevue, Nebr.: Patrick, 1992.

Vifquain, Russell M. *The Vifquain Genealogy: 1789–1957.* Ames, Iowa: Vifquain, 1959.

ABOUT THE AUTHOR

A national prize-winning and internationally published author, Marilyn June Coffey has composed roughly 7.5 pounds of poems, a gazillion prose pieces, and six books, often set in the Great Plains states of Kansas and Nebraska. She's a Pushcart Prize winner; her writing has appeared in Australia, Canada, Denmark, England, India, and Japan.

In 1959, Coffey won a prize and University of Nebraska publication for her fact-finding senior paper about the state legislature. Since then, she has researched many of her works.

Her sleuthing on Charlie Starkweather, Nebraska murderer, earned her a cover story in *Atlantic Monthly*. Fifteen other publishers, including Harper & Row, McGraw-Hill, Macmillan, and Harcourt Brace Jovanovich, also used excerpts from her *Great Plains Patchwork* about the wondrous strange Nebraska plains.

This book, *Thieves, Rascals and Sore Losers*, required a tour de force of researching. To discover what happened in the 1800s to make Alma and Orleans, Nebraska, lasting enemies, Coffey probed hundreds of handwritten pages of Harlan County commissioners' journals, read innumerable court proceedings and other legal documents, interviewed local historians, and spent days in the Nebraska State Historical Society reading newspaper clippings, convention reports, letters, and other histories.

The result is the definitive story of the Harlan County seat fight, 1871–1884, told here in its entirety for the first time.

A trained journalist (B.A., University of Nebraska, 1959) and creative writer (M.F.A., Brooklyn College, 1981), Coffey is known as a prose stylist.

In 1977, the University of Nebraska named her a Master Alumnus for distinction in writing, and Governor J. James Exon made her an Admiral in the Great Navy of Nebraska, one of the state's highest honors. However, the title is given tongue in cheek, since Admirals in landlocked Nebraska claim jurisdiction over little but tadpoles.

Now retired, Coffey taught writing at Boston University, Pratt Institute in Brooklyn, and Fort Hays State University in Kansas for a total of thirty-four years, twice earning tenure. Since 1987, the University of Nebraska Library Archives has collected her papers.

If you'd like to learn more about Coffey, visit her website at www.marilyncoffey.net or her blog at marilynjcoffey.blogspot.com or check her out on Facebook: www.facebook.com/marilyn.j.coffey.

Marilyn June Coffey's books:

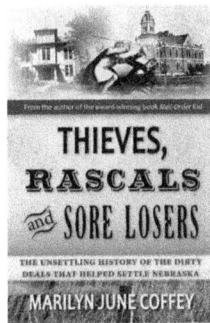

Great Plains Patchwork - A Memoir
A Cretan Cycle - Poetry

Available at MarilynCoffey.net
or order from your favorite bookseller.

INDEX

53rd Regiment, NY volunteers 67

97th Volunteer Infantry Regiment
(Illinois) 73-79

Alabama 67, 78

Albion 208

Alderdice, Alice 142, 148

Alderdice, Frank 142, 154

Alderdice, John 142

Alderdice, Susanna 142, 147-149

Alderdice, Willis 142

Alexander, George (Captain) 70

Alma 1-3, 166, 169-170, 179-303

Antrim 19

Antwerp 48

Aquia Creek 69

Arapaho 4, 31, 38, 77-78, 117-138,
295

Arkansas 73-74, 120, 134, 139

Arkeketah 13

Army of the North 23-24

Arthur, Chester A. (President) 284

Atlantic 57

Aurora 302

Banta, Abraham 279, 288

Bartelt, John 228, 232-261

Battle of Carrion Crow Bayou 75, 77

Battle of Carthage 28

Battle of Eylau 53

Battle of Fort Sumter 27

Beaver City 293

Beaver Creek 154-158

Belgian colony 46-47, 57-58, 166

Belgium 4, 48, 55-56, 62, 71, 166

Bellevue 11-12, 87-89

Bennett, Gideon 7, 9, 23

Bieyon, Franklin A. 169-170, 229, 232-249

Big Blue 14, 57-58, 75, 77, 163, 170

Big Talk 131, 133

Bitter Creek 39-41

Black Kettle (Cheyenne chief) 117, 120-122

Boehl, Carl 244

Boone 208

Boone County 184, 208

Booth, John Wilkes 103, 295

Bowles, Samuel 269, 271, 273, 279, 288

Bowman, Calvin 271-279

Broadmore (Mr.) 220

Brooks, Preston (Representative) 21-22

Brown, Guy (Reporter) 288

Brownville 96, 225

Brussels 48-49

Buchanan (President) 26

Buck, Nelson (Surveyor) 152-159

Burbridge, Stephen G. (Brigadier General) 75-76

Burke, Alexander (clerk) 210-211, 230, 237

Burt, Francis (Governor) 87-88

Butler, David C. (Governor) 109, 152-153, 184-191, 197-198

Butler, Andrew (Senator) 21

Cady, Lafayette 218

California 7, 35

Camp Rankin 126-129, 148

Campbell, Lewis D. (Representative from Ohio) 85-86

Campbell, William 281-282

Canby, Edward (Major General) 78

Carey, Charles H. 218

Carr, Eugene A. (Maj. Gen. "The Black-Bearded Cossack") 142-151, 156

Carr, William Parker 7-41, 83, 86-87, 99, 117, 131, 142, 151, 163, 173, 176-179, 202, 215, 248

Carrothers, John W. 239-240, 247

Cass County 109, 185

Central Pacific 40

Champion Hill 75

Cherry Creek 125-128, 137

Cheyenne 4, 31, 38, 77-78, 117-130, 134-138, 141-151, 178, 295

Chicago 23, 86, 100, 102, 153, 180, 197, 233

Chivington, John Milton (Fighting Parson), 119-124

Chiwere 11, 14

Cimarron 302

Cipriani, Alfred 68

Civil War 4, 27-28, 35, 40, 80, 86, 102, 119, 131, 136, 143, 173, 176, 179-180, 207, 283

Clark, C. M. (Dr.) 215

Coad, Mark 173-178, 181-188, 192-
194, 200-201

Cody, William (Buffalo Bill) 143-
147, 157, 159, 164, 218

Colorado 38, 77, 87, 93, 101, 119-
124, 138-139, 145-146

Comanche 59-65, 73, 136

Committee on the Territories 84

Comstocks 216

Confederate 28, 68-79, 143

Congress 3, 11, 13, 20, 83-84, 93, 96,
102-104, 110-112, 124, 173, 194

Constitution 20, 67, 102-112, 198,
206, 296

Constitutional Convention 102-104,
198, 206

Cook, Alma 181

Cook, Annie 282

Cook, Nathan 181, 232, 250, 258-259

Cook, W. L. 282

Cook Creek 170, 211

Costello (soldier) 207, 210

Council Bluffs 7, 88-89, 153

Crawford County 298

Crete 242, 300-302

Crockford, Joseph 202

Cumberland Gap 29

Cuming, Thomas B. (Acting
Governor) 88-92

Curtis, Samuel R. (General) 28

Dakota Territory 38-41, 87, 101, 284,
296-297

Davis, Jefferson (Confederate
President) 67-73

Dawson, John 282-283

de Beaumont, Maurice 68-71

de Vuyst, Marie 49-50

Democratic Party 84, 107, 197

Dennison, William Wallace
(Reservation Agent) 17

Denver 9, 119-125, 137

DeSoto 200

Dickenson, L. S. 247

Dobytown 215

Dodge City 302

Dog Soldiers 117-118, 123, 141-149,
151

Douglas, Stephen A. (Little Giant)
83-86, 90

Downs, Will 263, 266-267

Drew, Jason J. 214

Duncan, Thomas (General) 156-159,
163

Duvergnies, Eugene 62

E'lon 37

Edmundson, Henry Alonzo
(Representative from Virginia)
85-86

Ellenberger, Harriet Lucinda 248

Elon, Thomas 62,

Esquirol (Doctor) 52

Estabrook, Experience 106-107

Eureka Creek 215

Eustis 296

Fitch, Martin (Sheriff) 238-240, 243, 247-260, 265-266

Flag Creek 206

Fletcher, Warren 198, 241

Florence 95-96, 251

Florida 67

Fly, Thomas 177

Fort Blakeley 78-80

Fort Calhoun 200

Fort Cottonwood 132-138, 142

Fort Hindman 74

Fort Kearny 8-9, 109, 132, 138, 142, 153-156, 194

Fort Laramie 9

Fort Lyon 121

Fort McPherson 142-145, 156-159

Fort Melrose 166-170

Fort Saunders 23-24

Fort Titus 24

Foster, Joseph 166-170, 178, 181-184, 201-214

France 53-55, 241

Franco-Americans 67

Fredericksburg 69

Free Staters 19-20, 23, 26

French 4, 45-47, 51, 53, 55-56, 61, 67-71, 166, 169, 213-215

Frenchman Creek 145

Friday, Susie (Miss) 206

Gantt, Daniel (Judge) 254-274

Garfield, James A. (President) 284

Gaslin, William (Terror to Evil Doers) 218-219, 226, 228, 231, 242, 254-255, 263-264

Gatewood, James (Major) 11, 13-14

Georgia 23, 67

Gillespie, John (State Auditor) 186, 197

Golden Spike 40

Goodland 296-297

Gould, Albert 180

Gould, Garvin 180

Gould, Hattie 180

Gould, Joseph 180

Gould, Mary 180

Grand Island 35, 153, 174

Grant, Ulysses S. (General) 40, 74, 176, 206

Great Platte River Road 89, 118, 131, 134, 136

Green, Thomas (Brigadier General) 76

Green River 39

Gronquist, L. J. 233

Guillet, Squire 167-169, 201, 227, 240, 244

Guyer, John 263, 273

Hamilton City, Nevada 8

Hamilton County 302-303

Hance, T. C. (Dr.) 265-266

Harlan, Thomas 3-4, 40-41, 86, 163,
    173-185, 188-193, 261, 269, 270,
    284, 299

Hascall, Isaac S. 224-225

Healy, Michael 142

Hell on Wheels 38-39

Hightsman, George 282

Hofnagle, Frank 168, 216-217

Hofnagle Creek 168

Holdrege 200, 276

Holladay, Benjamin (Ben) 29-32,
    36-37

Homestead Law 167

House of Bollandistes 56

Howard, Robertson (Editor) 288

Illinois 20, 41, 73, 75, 78, 83-84, 152,
    155, 176, 221, 274, 283, 297

Impeachment 111, 113, 189-191, 266

Independence Day 205-206, 210

Indian 3, 11, 13-17, 31-38, 41, 46,
    59-65, 77-78, 86, 119-122, 125,
    127-133, 136-159, 164-165, 170-
    171, 174-180, 207, 213-217, 257,
    260, 295

Ingalls 302

Internal Revenue Collector 40, 176

Iowa 7, 11, 38, 88-92, 101, 153, 179,
    192-193, 220, 248, 280, 297

Jackson, Claiborne Fox (Missouri
    Governor) 27-28

James, William H. (Acting
    Governor) 189, 190-193, 224-
    227, 250, 273

Jewell, L. H. 258-259

Jewell, Margaret (Mrs.) 269

Jim Lane Trail 23

John Deere 15

Johnson, Andrew (President) 110-
    113

Johnson, Orion 62

Jones, Sarah 62,

Julesburg 38, 77, 125-129, 132, 136-
    142, 148

Kanesville 7, 153

Kansas 14, 19-29, 37-38, 57, 84, 86,
    90, 93, 96-99, 107, 113, 123-125,
    136, 139, 141, 143, 145, 147,
    151-152, 154, 165, 200, 208, 229,
    295-298, 302

Kansas-Nebraska Act 83, 85-86, 107,
    118

Kennard, Thomas P. (Secretary of
    State) 186-188, 197-198

Kent, L. H. (County Judge) 281, 283

Keokuk 88

Kine, Bridget 142

King, John R. 252

Kiowa 59-65

Kolb, Ada B. 242

[La Marseillaise] 69

Lancaster 186-189

Lane, Wild Jim 19-26

Laramie 40

Laws, Gilbert L. 287-290

Lee, Fitzhugh (Colonel) 69

Lee, Robert E. (General) 80

Legion of Honor 54, 169

Lewis and Clark 205

Lincoln, Abraham (President) 27, 35, 40, 80, 102-103, 110, 121, 153, 167, 176, 186, 192, 295

Lincoln County 194

Little Blue River 32, 77

Little Bluestem 138

Louisiana 47-48, 67, 74-75, 78, 87

Loup River 31

Luce, Hiram M. 214-215

Majors, Alexander (Russell, Majors and Waddell) 99-100

Manning, Mary 219

Manning, Mike 219, 263, 271

Manypenny, George (Colonel) 11-13

Massacre 3, 124-125, 129, 295

Mayhew, Allen 100-101

McBride, William (or John) 207

McGregor, H.B. (Youngest surveyor) 154

McKee, Hugh J. 264-266, 269, 271, 273

McPherson, John (Dr) 213-214, 229, 243, 254-255, 273

Medal of Honor 80, 143

Meigheroff, Fred 141

Melrose 170-171, 177, 181-182, 197-203, 206-212, 218-233, 237-244, 247-265, 275, 285, 289, 294, 299

[Merrimack] 70

Methodist Creek 234, 261

Minnesota River valley 73

Mississippi 47, 67, 73-74

Missouri 7, 9, 19, 27, 29, 47, 57, 75, 95, 99, 119, 134, 151, 208, 274, 297

Missouria 11

Mitchell, Robert B. (Brigadier General) 131-139, 295

Mobile 78, 80

Moore, George 220-221, 229, 234, 258

Morton, J. Sterling 93, 96, 107-109

Mullally, Thomas 173

Murrin, Thomas 173, 181, 183-185, 188, 193-194, 200, 202, 206, 244, 249-261, 264-271

Musketeers 67-72

Napoleon 46-47, 53-56, 67, 76, 119, 121, 169-170, 181-182, 199, 201-203, 208, 210, 215, 218-221, 225-228, 231, 239, 254, 263-264, 285, 294, 299-300

Natchitoches 47

Neapolis 95

Nebraska Supreme Court 1, 225, 255, 285, 287

Nebraska-Kansas border 154

Nelson, John Y. (Scout) 157-158

Nettleton, John (Surveyor) 154

New York City 45

Niobrara River 13, 90, 132, 134

Norfolk Navy Yard 70-71

North, Frank (Pawnee Agency clerk) 134-135, 143, 146-147, 157

North, Luther 146-147

Nuckolls, Stephen Friel 9, 89, 99, 100

Occoquan, Virginia 68

Olson, John (Big) 202

Olson, John H. 273

Omaha 11, 35, 103, 106, 119, 132, 185, 186, 187, 197, 198, 251

Omaha City 89-96, 182

Omahas 12-13

Opelousas 75

Oregon Trail 9, 57, 77, 142

Otoe-Missourians 7, 13, 15-17

Overland Stage Company 29, 36

Oxford 228, 280, 293

Pacific Railroad Bill 35

Painter, Joseph 173-175, 183-185, 221-223, 239-244, 249

Parish, Gilbert 240

Parker, James 215

Pawnee 8, 31, 36, 60-62, 64-65, 73, 134-135, 145-147, 153, 214, 260

Pawnee Killer (Sioux chief) 125, 151, 154, 156, 158-159, 163

Pawnee Killer's mother 158-159

Pawnee scouts 134-135, 143, 145-146, 157, 159

Peter-nash-arrow (Pawnee chief) 61

Peterson, Nels 171, 177

Peterson, Truls 177

Phelps Center 200

Phelps County 200

Phillips, James O. 183-188, 192-194, 200-201, 227, 230-240, 261

Pierce, Franklin (President) 17, 19, 83, 86-87, 106

Piper, Joel 4, 261, 262, 264, 266

Platte River 9, 35, 84, 90, 93, 96, 126, 128, 131, 138, 174-175

Pleasant Hill 200, 300, 301

Plum Pit 16

Pony Express 99, 119

Population 11, 59, 90, 101, 118, 185, 189, 242, 275, 298, 303

Port Gibson 74

Prairie Dog Creek 145, 200

Radical Republican 102, 110, 112, 113

Red Willow County 154

Redoubt #4 78-79

Reed, Joseph 37

Reese, Manoah (Supreme Court Judge) 281, 287-290

Republican 90, 101-104, 106-113, 183, 185-187, 197-198, 214, 219, 281, 284, 296

Republican City 213-218, 221-232, 240-248, 252-256, 263-275, 294, 300

Reuben Township 167-168

Reynolds, Kate (Mrs.) 206

Richardson, William A. (Governor) 96

Richmond 68, 70-72

Riosk, George W. 271, 273

Roberts, George H. (Attorney General) 273-274

Roberts, John M. 249-254, 259-267

Rock Springs 39

Rocky Mountains 9, 35, 47, 60, 257

Round Hill 47

Ruben, Andrew 166-171, 206

Ruffians 19-25, 295

Rulo 8

Rush County 200, 229

Russia 53

Ryder, James E. 201, 249-253, 260-261

Saline County 58-62, 198, 200, 220, 242, 300, 303

Saline River 141-142

Salt Creek 57

Sand Creek 121-125, 129-130, 295

Sand Hills 13

Sappa Creek 155, 244

Sappington (Mr.) 220-221

Saunders, Alvin (Governor) 102-112

Schellenberg, James A. 199

Schrack, Levi J. 269

Seal 187, 212, 224, 230-231, 237-239, 252-253

Sealy, Charles 234

Second Kansas Cavalry 27

Segars, Silas 281-283

Shaffer, Frank 220, 241, 243, 259-260, 263, 269, 276, 280, 282, 288

Sheffrey, Thomas (Tom) 210-211, 227-228, 232-239, 247, 249-261

Sherman County 184, 296

Sigel, Franz (Colonel) 27

Sioux 4, 11, 31, 38, 73, 77-78, 117-118, 125, 131-138, 146, 151, 154-159, 163, 170-171, 177, 295

Slave 19-21, 26, 47, 84, 86, 99-102, 110-111, 119

Smith, D. N. 69, 241-242

Smoky Hill 37-38, 123, 125

Snyder, Joseph 215

South Carolina 21, 67, 87

South Dakota 87, 296-297

South Platters 92-97, 107, 183-185, 296

Spillman Creek 141

Springfield 24, 73, 154

St. Cyr 55-56

St. Louis 47

Stanton County 298

Summit Springs 146, 151, 159

Sumner, Charles 21-22

Swede Stockade 181

Sydenham, Richard (Guide) 174-178

Table Creek 8-9

Talbot, John 173

Tall Bull (Cheyenne leader) 117-125, 141-148, 151

Texas 67, 139, 280

Thayer County 184

Thompson, J. (Judge) 198

Tipover Creek 181

Tipton 75

Titus, Henry (Colonel) 24

Topeka 20, 97

Trimble, Hugh 210-211

U.S. 5th Cavalry 143

U.S. Army 31, 35, 151

U.S. Commissioner of Indian Affairs 11

U.S. House of Representatives 84

U.S. Land Office 175, 203, 263

U.S. Mail 32

U.S. Senate 20-21, 26, 84

Underground Railroad 100-101

Union 26-28, 67, 70-71, 74-80, 110, 180, 218, 263, 266

Union Pacific 31, 35-40, 173-176, 241

Union troops 28, 71, 75, 78

United States 3, 35, 60, 107, 109, 134, 194, 205

Unorganized Territory 7, 11, 83

Veuleman, Caroline 47-48, 57-80, 163

Veuleman, Joannes 48

Veuleman, John 47, 57

Vicksburg 74-75

Vifquain, Anne 52, 56

Vifquain, Françoise 50-51, 56

Vifquain, Jean-Baptiste 46, 50-57

Vifquain, Louise 50, 52, 56

Vifquain, Pierre 50, 52, 56

Vifquain, Victor 3, 4, 43-80, 83, 86-87, 117, 131, 151, 163, 165-170, 181-182, 197-200, 206, 209, 218, 220, 26, 239, 242, 247, 254, 263, 299-303

Vincent, Nicholas B. 279, 288

[Virginia] (the ship) 70-72

Walnut City 200

Ware, Eugene F. 138

Warriors 63, 73, 77, 117, 126-130, 141-142, 154, 157-158

Washington, D. C. 11, 20, 86, 96, 109, 194

Washington County 242

Weaver, Joseph 239

Weichel, George 141

Weichel, Maria 141, 147-148

Wells Fargo 36

West, Isabella 62

West Fork 58

West Point 142

White Antelope (Cheyenne chief) 120-122

Whiting, John (Reverend) 4, 202, 206-207, 230, 232-261, 289

Wiebe, Fred 175

Wilber 300-302

Wild Tribes 4, 115, 117-118, 124, 127-128, 131, 134, 136-139, 152, 295

Willits, Ed 282, 283

Willits, Wells 274, 276-277, 281-283, 288

Winder, John H. (General) 70

Wyoming 3, 38, 40-41, 163, 173, 176, 179, 193, 199, 248

Yankeeland 68

Yankees 68-69

Yellow Buffalo (Kiowa chief) 64

Young, Jacob (Jack) 238-240

www.ingramcontent.com/pod-product-compliance
Lightning Source LLC
Chambersburg PA
CBHW031232090426
42742CB00007B/170